ROAD KILL

Cross-country killers on a high-speed rampage, homicidal truckers, roadside hustlers turned psycho-sex criminals, lust-murderers protected by the anonymity of the open highway—these are just some of the nightmarish figures who turn our nation's roadways into horrendous crime scenes.

Now, *TRUE DETECTIVE'S* ace crime writers expose the chilling truth about the depraved killers who ply the roads. And they capture all the pity, fear, and horror of the innocent victims who took a nonstop ride straight to hell.

—BERNARDINE PARRISH & BOBBIE JEAN HARTWIG: these two pretty moms hitched a ride near a Grifton, North Carolina, military base and were raped and slain by three mean marines!

—JESSICA GUZMAN: the 10-year-old schoolgirl unwittingly entered the cab of the taxi-driving "Beat of the Bronx" who'd committed five previous child-sex kills!

—TINA JO SUTTON: a teen hooker in Portland, Oregon, whose last roadside trick turned out to be her killer!

AND MANY MORE!

BOOK YOUR PLACE ON OUR WEBSITE AND MAKE THE READING CONNECTION!

We've created a customized website just for our very special readers, where you can get the inside scoop on everything that's going on with Zebra, Pinnacle and Kensington books.

When you come online, you'll have the exciting opportunity to:

- View covers of upcoming books
- Read sample chapters
- Learn about our future publishing schedule (listed by publication month *and author*)
- Find out when your favorite authors will be visiting a city near you
- Search for and order backlist books from our online catalog
- Check out author bios and background information
- Send e-mail to your favorite authors
- Meet the Kensington staff online
- Join us in weekly chats with authors, readers and other guests
- Get writing guidelines
- AND MUCH MORE!

**Visit our website at
http://www.pinnaclebooks.com**

FROM THE FILES OF
TRUE DETECTIVE **MAGAZINE:**

ROAD KILL

Edited by
David Jacobs

Pinnacle Books
Kensington Publishing Corp.
ht t p:/ / www.pinnacl ebooks.com

Some names have been changed to protect the privacy of individuals connected to these stories.

PINNACLE BOOKS are published by

Kensington Publishing Corp.
850 Third Avenue
New York, NY 10022

Pinnacle and the P logo Reg. U.S. Pat. & TM Off.

First Pinnacle Printing: October, 2000
10 9 8 7 6 5 4 3 2 1

Printed in the United States of America

CONTENTS

"SEX-CRAZED CABBIE CRUSHED KATHY WITH HIS WHEELS!"

by John Griggs

It didn't take a pathologist to see that a car had run over this woman. The tire tracks were there in the dirt, the dirt that the tires had carried right over the nude woman's chest and right arm.

Who was this woman, and why did somebody do this to her?

Her naked state suggested some type of sexual assault.

Detective-Sergeant Steve Shaver pondered those questions on Tuesday, November 6, 1990, as he worked the rural crime scene. Shaver serves on the Guilford County Sheriff's Department in central North Carolina.

A squirrel hunter had found the woman's body that Tuesday morning. The agitated hunter hotfooted it to the home of the man who owned the land, and the sheriff's department was called from there.

Notified of the call, Shaver left his office at headquarters in Greensboro and drove his unmarked car out to the crime scene, off Mount Hope Church Road in southeastern Guilford. The woman lay on a dirt path, just a few feet from an old barn. The body was in full rigor mortis, cold to the touch. She had obviously been here a few days.

Shaver studied the tire tracks around the corpse. They were about seven inches wide, with a moderately deep tread. There were no bald spots; the tires were in good condition, so they had to be fairly new.

Lab specialists made plaster casts of the tracks. They also shot photos of the body, the tracks, and the surrounding area. Officers worked outward from the body and soon turned up a black-and-white flowered dress lying nearby.

Otherwise, it was slow going.

Meanwhile, that morning, a clerical worker at the Greensboro Police Department heard about the found body through the law enforcement grapevine. The worker had recently talked to a relative in nearby Burlington, and that relative told her about a woman who was missing from that city.

The worker told Greensboro police what she knew, and they in turn told Guilford deputies. Soon, county detectives were on the horn with Burlington police investigators.

By late that Tuesday morning, Detective Donna Baker of the Burlington Police Department was at Shaver's crime scene with a photo of her missing woman, 28-year-old Kathy Clark Fogleman of Burlington. Officers looked at the photo and the body, and realized this was the same woman. In fact, the dress she wore in the photo matched the one found at the crime scene.

So, Baker's missing-person case had now turned into a homicide. She briefed Shaver on what she'd uncovered in the course of probing it as a missing-person case.

A relative had reported Fogleman missing the previous day. Witnesses said Fogleman disappeared after she called a cab to pick her up at her home the previous Saturday night and drive her to a local motel lounge.

Baker checked the log at Red Bird Cab in Burlington. A cabbie had picked up Fogleman at 11:14 P.M. on Saturday, November 3rd. The cabbie, Keith Allen Brown, said he dropped Fogleman at the lounge and left.

Baker talked to the people at the lounge, who said they didn't see Fogleman, either late Saturday or early Sunday.

Sergeant Shaver saw that he had his work cut out for him in Burlington. On Tuesday afternoon, after ordering that the body be sent for an autopsy in Chapel Hill, Shaver and Detective-Sergeant Jonathan Jacobs drove the 30 minutes from Greensboro to Burlington, and set up a command post at the Burlington Police Department.

Jacobs, Shaver, and Baker decided to check out the cabbie, Keith Brown. The log showed that, after dropping off Fogleman, an unidentified fare approached Brown outside the lounge. Brown drove that man to the Rock Creek Road area in Guilford County, according to the log.

Sergeant Jacobs talked to the dispatcher, who said that Brown, after reporting the unidentified fare, radioed in to say he was lost. He remained missing for an hour, the dispatcher said.

There was another reason why Brown, who was a former factory worker and a cabbie since the previous August, was worth checking out. A record check showed that he had been charged with rape twice. The first time he had faced the charge, in 1977, a jury acquitted him. He was charged with rape again in 1981, but pleaded guilty to a reduced charge of assault.

The investigators spoke with the cab company manager. He said Brown drove cab Number Two exclusively. As the detectives visited the cab company that Tuesday, Brown was off and Number Two was parked at the company.

Jacobs checked out the car, finding the right headlight frame broken and hair in the front grill. The detectives decided to impound the car. They laid out a plan: Jacobs would supervise the handling of the taxi, and Shaver would concentrate on Keith Brown.

While they waited for a wrecker to move the car to the Burlington Police Department (BPD), Brown, on foot, stopped by his workplace.

By now, the detectives knew that Brown usually drove a motorcycle. At 33, he was a biker kind of guy: he wore his long brown hair in a ponytail, and there was plenty of muscle in the 175 pounds on his 5-foot-9-inch build.

Sergeant Shaver, a big man himself, approached Brown. The investigator introduced himself, and told the cabbie about his suspicions.

Brown denied any involvement in Fogleman's death. He repeatedly asked, "Do you really think I could do something like that?"

Shaver observed that the cabbie didn't—maybe couldn't—hold eye contact with him. The sergeant didn't have anything to hold Brown on, so Brown was free to go when he ended the conversation. Shaver offered to give him a ride, but Brown chose to walk.

The wrecker came and towed the cab. Members of the identification section of the BPD, Guilford deputies, and agents with the State Bureau of Investigation (SBI) processed the vehicle. SBI Agent David Hodgecock, a serologist who had recently left the lab to become a field agent, found what appeared to be blood smeared underneath the cab, on its frame.

The lab specialists put the car on a lift and pumped it up in the air, so that they could study the vehicle's underside more closely. They found apparent blood in two more spots.

SBI lab tech Mark Nelson, who held a master's degree in biochemistry and who had over a decade of experience as a forensic serologist and lab technician, took samples of the blood. The next day, Wednesday, November 7th, Nelson did a special test on samples found on the right front undercarriage of the cab. He found that those samples were in fact blood.

Lab specialists studied the cab's tires. They found that the right front tire was about seven inches wide, was fairly new, was in good condition, and had no bald spots. In other words, it was consistent in every respect with the tire tracks from the crime scene.

Shaver concluded that the marks he saw on Fogleman's body were consistent with the cab's tire-tread width and pattern. Studying the areas where the blood was found on the undercarriage, Shaver believed that injuries to the victim's head could have been caused by the undercarriage.

Also that Wednesday, Sergeant Roy Lindell of the Guilford County Sheriff's Department identification section attended Fogleman's autopsy. Pathologists found that crushing injuries to Fogleman's chest had killed her. Her identification had been confirmed by relatives.

Lindell and the pathologists also noted marks on the victim's right arm and chest, marks that pathologists found were impressions and bruising left by a car tire. Pathologists made it official: Kathy Fogleman had been run over by a car.

Pathologists also found tearing and trauma to her vaginal area, marks consistent with forced sex. They collected sperm samples found in her. The pathologists determined that the sex took place on or about the time of Fogleman's death.

The case got more complicated that Wednesday afternoon when another body was found in the same wooded area where the Fogleman crime scene was. The new crime scene was about a half-mile north of the Fogleman crime scene.

The new crime scene had been stumbled upon by a mother and daughter who read about the Fogleman case in Tuesday morning's newspaper and had decided to check it out themselves. They went for a walk in the area where Fogleman's body was found. They spotted what looked like material on the ground, several yards off the McPherson-Clay dirt road. They walked closer.

"This looks like somebody," the mother said. Seconds later, she said, "It is someone," and started screaming.

The mother called authorities, and Guilford County deputies were soon on the scene. They found a set of skeletal remains, covered by a quilt and bound at the feet and arms by rope.

As lab specialists processed the scene, other officers with dogs searched through the woods, just to make sure they didn't have any more bodies waiting for them.

The mother who found the body told a reporter that she heard what she believed was a woman screaming in the woods about five months earlier. She went out to investigate, she said, but couldn't find anything.

Deputies combed area missing-person reports, trying to determine whose skeleton they had. Lab specialists did determine it was a woman's.

As the other officers worked on the new body late Wednesday, Sergeant Shaver decided to proceed against Keith Brown in the Fogleman case. He secured a warrant charging Brown with first-degree murder.

But the suspect was nowhere to be found. He was not at his house, his workplace, or anywhere else the edgy detectives could think of to try. They broadcast a computer lookout on him, describing Brown as armed and dangerous.

The next day, a man identifying himself as Brown called the cab company to arrange to come pick up his last paycheck. Officers waited at the business, but Brown never showed up.

Meanwhile, deputies working the other case developed two possibilities on whom the body belonged to. It was either an elderly woman with Alzheimer's disease who had walked away from her nursing home the previous July, or a 42-year-old woman missing since the previous July 25th.

Working with the victims' families, the deputies secured dental records for each woman, and sent those records and the bones to Chapel Hill for autopsy. Pathologists found the bones were those of the younger woman, Pamela Hoy. They could not determine the cause of her death. Her skull was intact, and the bones showed no gun or knife wounds. Analysis of her organs might have revealed the cause, but the organs had disintegrated.

Pathologists did determine that Hoy had died soon after she vanished. Deputies termed it a homicide of undetermined origin.

Hoy lived outside Burlington in the small town of Alamance. Four days after her disappearance, her van had been found behind a motel on Randleman Road in Greensboro.

Investigators looked for connections between the Fogleman and Hoy cases. But aside from the closeness of the crime scenes, there were none.

Guilford deputies weren't the only investigators who wanted to talk to Keith Brown. Detectives in nearby Orange County, aware of Brown through the computer alert, wondered if he knew anything about a female body found the previous September 19th within their own district's jurisdiction.

The badly decomposed body, still unidentified, was found near the intersection of Interstate 40 and New Hope Church Road. The woman stood 5 feet, 3 inches tall, weighed about 100 pounds, and had strawberry-blond hair.

"We are interested in him in the investigation for several reasons," Detective-Lieutenant Bobby Collins of the Orange County Sheriff's Department told a reporter. "Because of the condition of her body, we are interested in Keith Allen Brown."

The corpse was clothed only in a bra, socks, and a long-sleeve pink sweatshirt. The victim wore a gold-wire ring and a bracelet. The cause of death in her case was uncertain as well.

On the night of Monday, November 12th, a tipster told detectives that Brown was at his home on Seymour Street in Graham. By 6:00 P.M., officers from six law enforcement agencies surrounded the two-bedroom rental house.

Brown had holed up in a ceiling crawl space, and indicated that he was armed and would kill himself if the law officers rushed him. Officers used a bullhorn to try to coax Brown out, but it wasn't working.

Detective-Lieutenant Alan Cates, of the Alamance County Sheriff's Department, knew Brown from Brown's 1981 arrest. Using a mobile phone, Cates called Brown's phone number. Brown answered, and the men began talking.

The suspect repeatedly said he wanted a relative to come to the house and talk with him. The officers couldn't allow that because Brown might take the relative hostage.

Cates told Brown that the standoff had already caused Brown's family enough embarrassment. The lieutenant used that logic and general conversation to build a rapport with the suspect. Cates stressed that they didn't want anyone—including Brown himself—to get hurt.

About 10:45 P.M., Brown came out of the house with his hands over his head.

"I guess he didn't want to run anymore," Lieutenant Grady Bryant of the Guilford County Sheriff's Department told a reporter. "It's hard for a person to run. Sooner or later, they are going to come back."

Sergeants Shaver and Jacobs served the murder warrant on Brown, and put him in their car for the trip to headquarters.

"Y'all got me wrong," Brown told the investigators as they placed him in the car. "I didn't kill all them women."

Serving a search warrant in the yellow, wood-frame house, officers found a metal bar with hairs sticking in the end. They confiscated the bar for testing.

At headquarters, Shaver and Jacobs settled down with Brown in a small interview room. By then, it was early Tuesday morning, November 13th, though far from light outside. Brown waived his rights and agreed to talk.

The sleuths showed him photos of the tire tracks at the scene. Brown refused to look at the pictures. Visibly upset, Brown said that no one deserved to die like that. But he wouldn't get specific. Brown did say that he was doing cocaine on November 3rd, the night Fogleman died. Shaver asked the suspect whether coke made him kill Fogleman.

Brown, crying at times, said nothing.

The investigators offered Brown food and sodas. He just took water.

Shaver told Brown that the question wasn't *if* he killed Fogleman. Rather, it was *why* did he kill Fogleman.

Brown replied that he couldn't tell him that. He said the state was going to execute him, and that he was going to save them some money: he would ask the state to kill him.

During the interview, Brown never confessed to killing Kathy Fogleman. Nor did he deny that he killed her.

The detectives, however, were sure they had the right man. The motive: depravity; Brown killed the woman after he raped her.

Authorities from other jurisdictions questioned Brown

to no avail about the unidentified body and about Pamela Hoy.

"Sometimes, when you talk to a guy like this, you find out things about other cases—if their conscience gets to them or something," said Alamance County Sheriff Richard Frye.

Pamela Hoy had lived in his county.

Days later, investigators ruled Brown out as a suspect in Hoy's death. The only reason to suspect him had been the proximity of the Hoy crime scene to that of Fogleman. There was no other evidence to link Brown to the crime. Besides, there were basic, but important, differences in the crime scenes. For example, Hoy was bound and blanketed; Fogleman was not.

The detectives, however, continued to suspect Brown in the death of the unidentified woman.

Brown was placed in the Greensboro jail. Three days later, the detectives secured a search warrant to take samples of blood from Brown. The investigators turned these samples over to forensic scientists for testing, in the hopes that DNA testing of the blood could prove that the semen in the victim was Brown's.

While he awaited the test results, Sergeant Shaver kept working. He traced Brown's movements in the days after Fogleman's death, finding out that Brown made indirect admissions of guilt to a friend who took him to the bus station. Apparently, Brown spent several days at a relative's house in Massachusetts before returning to his home.

Shaver tracked down the woman whom Brown had assaulted in 1981, and interviewed her. The woman was a teenager then. She said Brown had stabbed her, raped her, and left her for dead. She made it to help on her own.

It turned out that the assault had taken place not far from the Fogleman crime scene.

Shaver's theory was that Brown had made up the story about picking up another fare at the motel lounge where he supposedly took Fogleman. In fact, Brown never went to the lounge, as evidenced by interviews with lounge employees.

Instead, Shaver felt, Brown just picked Fogleman up and kept driving, returning to a spot near the scene of his 1981 crime.

FBI lab specialists found that the tire tracks at the crime scene were consistent with the cab's right front tire. They made the match when they found that both the tire and the tracks showed a pebble in one of the treads.

The best part was that the FBI scientists, through the DNA testing comparing samples of Brown's blood and the semen collected from the victim, found that the semen was Brown's.

Other tests weren't as promising. The hair found on the mental bar from Brown's home was not Fogleman's. So whose was it? The lab specialists compared it with samples of Brown's hair and found that it wasn't his. They found that the hairs caught in the cab grill were from a deer.

Lab specialists were unable to match the blood found underneath the cab with Fogleman's blood.

Still, the DNA and tire evidence was pretty damning.

Prosecutors were pursuing the death penalty against Brown. His trial was set to begin at the Guilford County Courthouse on Monday, March 23, 1992.

At 5:50 that morning, a jailer making routine rounds found Brown dead in his cell. He had apparently wrapped one end of his bedsheet around his neck, and wrapped the other end around an air vent. Then he sat down on his bed, hanging himself.

The jailer had been by just 10 minutes earlier, and Brown had been fine then. His trial was set to start that morning at nine o'clock.

Captain Roy Forrest, Sergeant Shaver's supervisor, told a reporter that there were no warning signs.

"Our investigation indicates he had contact with family members and a doctor the day before, and his behavior appeared to be normal," Forrest said.

Prosecutor Richard Panosh had been set to try the case.

"We were prepared to show the results of a DNA test proving that his [Brown's] semen was found in her [Fogleman's] body," Panosh told a reporter. "We had evidence matching the front passenger tire of his cab to the marks on her body. We had evidence matching that tire to the tracks of the car that caused her death."

Shaver said he hates to see anybody commit suicide. But he would have liked to have seen Brown get the death penalty. Now, Brown is gone—with all his secrets.

Sergeant Shaver does not think Brown killed Pamela Hoy. Her murder remains unsolved. The detectives continue to suspect Brown in the slaying of the unidentified woman.

Among other evidence supporting this is that Brown occasionally drove a cab route that took him from Burlington and passed the site where that woman's body was found. And, while the woman has never been identified, the sweatshirt she was found wearing had an unusual pattern on it. Witnesses reported seeing a woman wearing such a shirt at the Burlington truck stop in the days before the body was found.

No one has ever been charged in connection with that woman's death.

"THEY WHACKED WALTER FOR HIS WHEELS!"

by John Griggs

The woman pulled up alongside the brown van at the neighborhood grocery store, expecting to see a male member of her family inside. Instead, an unfamiliar face caught her stare. The man leaned out of the driver's-side window of the vehicle and told her, "You won't drive this damn van tonight!"

It was July 1, 1991, a balmy Monday night on east Garner Road in North Carolina's state capital—Raleigh. The time was about 9:30 P.M.

The late-model van lurched out of the parking lot at high speed. The woman followed in her own car, but quickly lost the van in the heavy traffic. She had heard scuffling noises and yelling coming from inside the van. But she didn't think the member of her family was in the van. She figured she would get an explanation from him later.

The fact was 21-year-old Walter Eugene Burnett had borrowed the van a few minutes earlier to drive to the neighborhood store for something to eat. He'd just finished his day job. Burnett worked 'round the clock, obsessed with saving money for college.

When Walter had still not returned by early the next morning, which was Tuesday, his family filed a missing-person report with the Raleigh police. The officers promised to do what they could. But Burnett hadn't been missing long, and the department had to cope with more than its share of missing-persons reports, balancing those cases against a heavy load of violent crime.

About 12:15 A.M. that same Tuesday, Sam Lee was pulling into a truck stop in Alamance County, about 50 miles west of Raleigh. The truck stop is at Interstate 85 and Trollingwood Road.

A brown, late-model van suddenly pulled up behind Lee's vehicle, flashing its lights. Lee stopped. A man got out of the driver's side of the van and walked up to Lee's rolled-down window.

"Hey, my man, do you know the way to Frog Hollow?" the man asked. Almost simultaneously, a second man appeared at Lee's rolled-up passenger-side window, tapping on the glass and pointing a revolver at him.

Let hit the gas. The man on the driver's side grabbed on to the door and hung on. Lee's vehicle dragged him a short way before he finally let go.

Lee sped through the darkness. As soon as he felt he'd gone a safe distance, he stopped at a pay phone and called the Alamance County Sheriff's Department with a description of the van and its dangerous occupants.

Within minutes, county deputies had an all-points bulletin out for the van over area law enforcement channels. In other counties, deputies, as well as state troopers with the North Carolina Highway Patrol and officers from other jurisdictions, began hunting the brown van.

A short time later, Officer N. F. Dickens of the tiny Haw River Police Department spotted a van matching the broadcast description on Interstate 85, near the Jimmy Kerr Road exit. Dickens hit his blue light and siren. The van pulled off the side of the interstate and began to slow down.

Then, suddenly, two men jumped from either side of the van and ran into the darkness. The driverless van rolled on, crashing into a tractor-trailer parked beside the road.

Dickens radioed for backup. Moments later, law enforcement cars descended on the scene, their headlights cutting wide yellow-and-white paths across the blackness of that summer night. Officers hopped out of their vehicles and quickly caught up to the two men who'd bolted from the van.

With the pair securely in tow, the officers searched the van and recovered a .38-caliber revolver. The Alamance deputies then transported the two men to headquarters, in Graham, the county seat. They soon got Sam Lee down to the station, and he identified the men as the guys who had tried to rob him.

The men identified themselves as 23-year-old Ellerek Dermot Vaughters, of Charlotte, North Carolina, and Gregory Sean Fray, a 25-year-old bricklayer from Raleigh.

The deputies charged them with one count each of attempted armed robbery.

The deputies soon realized that the van the men had been driving didn't belong to the pair. They ran its identification and registration numbers through the North Carolina Division of Motor Vehicles computer records.

According to the computer, the van belonged to the family of Walter Eugene Burnett. Deputies telephoned the family in Raleigh and got a quick briefing on the situation. Then the Alamance officers called the Raleigh police.

Within the next couple of hours, Raleigh detectives arrived at the Graham headquarters. There was a strong probability that Vaughters and Fray knew something about what happened to Burnett, unless they just came upon Burnett's van abandoned. The two men, however, weren't talking.

A preliminary search of the van yielded few clues. Burnett's family member had already told the officers that she didn't get a good enough look at the men driving the van to identify them.

The Raleigh sleuths and Alamance deputies continued to work the frustrating case through Tuesday night. They soon obtained hard copies of Vaughters's and Fray's rap sheets. Neither man had a serious record.

Vaughters's record included arrests for misdemeanor larceny and driving during revocation. The only blots on Fray's record were a couple of misdemeanor convictions.

Early on Wednesday morning, the Raleigh sleuths interviewed Vaughters and Fray again. This time, the men said that Burnett's body was back in Durham, about 30 minutes from Raleigh, near an exit ramp off Interstate 40.

The men did not elaborate on how the body got there, nor did they say they were involved in Burnett's death.

By now, it was shortly before 8:00 A.M. The Raleigh detectives contacted the Durham police, who issued a radio alert for all available officers to check the exit ramps off Interstate 40 in their city for the body. The Durham officers went to work.

About 20 minutes later, identification technician Eric Campen was searching a grassy knoll beside the westbound Fayetteville Road exit ramp when he found a body beside a stand of woods. The body was cold; rigor mortis had set in. Drivers on the westbound ramp would not have been able to spot it.

Durham officers cordoned off the scene. Detective Darrell Dowdy, assigned to the case, arrived minutes later.

The scene offered little evidence other than the body— a fully clothed man apparently shot in the forehead. The Raleigh sleuths got to the scene a few minutes after

Dowdy. They identified the dead man as Burnett from a photo his family had provided. The family would soon confirm the identification.

A preliminary autopsy soon showed that Burnett had died of a single .38-caliber bullet which entered his forehead at close range. The slug was the same caliber as the revolver recovered from the van. Within a short time, forensic scientists would check the fatal bullet recovered from the body to see if the handgun from the van matched it.

Since the body had been found in Durham, that city would have jurisdiction in the case, according to North Carolina law. The Raleigh detectives briefed Dowdy on the case. While Vaughters and Fray had led the police to the body, there was no evidence that they themselves had killed Burnett. Nonetheless, they were likely suspects.

Picking the truth out of their reluctant brains would now be Detective Dowdy's job.

Dowdy, a friendly fellow but a sharp investigator, was then 34 years old. He'd earned a graduate degree in criminal justice at North Carolina Central University in Durham, and had originally wanted to become a probation and parole officer. But when he couldn't find a job fast enough in that field, he accepted a position with the Durham Police Department.

He found that the work suited him. Then he won an assignment to the homicide division as a detective after being on the force just three years.

Dowdy had been in homicide for just a few months when he was assigned the Burnett case. But Dowdy's had been a baptism by fire, and he'd already probed a few slayings by the time fate—and his superiors—handed him the Burnett probe. His city would mark 33 murders in 1991, and the rookie sleuth would be the lead detective on 9 of those cases.

A fellow homicide detective with the Durham PD, Mar-

shall Thaxton, joined Dowdy on the Burnett case. On
Wednesday afternoon, the two sleuths picked up Ellerek
Vaughters and Gregory Fray and drove them to Durham
police headquarters.

At 6:30 P.M. on Wednesday, Dowdy read the suspects
their Miranda rights. Detectives Thaxton and Dowdy
placed the suspects in adjacent interview rooms. Both
men refused to make any statements.

Detectives Dowdy and Thaxton decided to leave
Vaughters alone in one room while they took a shot at
interviewing Fray. Fray finally began to talk, saying that
Vaughters had killed Burnett, whom the pair didn't know.
They simply spotted him at the Raleigh store where
Burnett's female relative saw the van drive away, Fray told
the sleuths.

Fray said that he himself was in the store buying beer,
and he was surprised when he came out to find that
Vaughters had pulled a gun on Burnett. Fray said he
thought that they were going to strand Burnett somewhere, alive. But, he told the sleuths, Vaughters shot the
man.

Now Detective Dowdy slipped out of the interview
room and into Vaughters's room. Again, the meek,
slightly built suspect refused to make any statement.
Dowdy and Vaughters could hear Fray talking through
the wall, although they couldn't hear what he was saying.

Fray was confessing and implicating Vaughters, Dowdy
told Vaughters. If Vaughters wanted the sleuths to accept
Fray's word as gospel, the sleuth said, that was fine. But
if Vaughters had anything to say, Dowdy told him, he'd
better say it now.

Vaughters still said nothing.

Detective Dowdy left the room, leaving Vaughters alone
inside and shutting the door. About 30 to 45 minutes
later, Vaughters knocked on his door from inside the

room. When Dowdy opened the door, Vaughters said he was ready to make a statement.

Vaughters began to talk as the sleuth started a tape recorder running. The suspect said that he and Fray consumed about 15 quarts of beer each, as well as some wine, in the hours before they met Burnett.

"We had been drinking all that day," Vaughters said. "And we was going to get more beer from the store."

They walked to the neighborhood grocery in Raleigh for more beer. In front of the store, Fray suggested that they go to Charlotte, which is about three hours south of Raleigh.

When Burnett pulled into the parking lot in his van, Vaughters whipped out his .38-caliber revolver. He said he wanted to take the van so that he and Fray could drive to Charlotte. They wanted to leave the driver, but Burnett crawled to the backseat.

Fray got in the driver's seat and after leaning out of the window to tell Burnett's relative that she wouldn't be driving the van, they sped away. Fray drove west on Interstate 40. Vaughters was in the back of the van with Burnett, beating him on the head with the revolver.

"We both was drunk," Vaughters told the detective. "We just got on the highway. We started riding and riding and riding. We stopped several times to get more beer. I was already drunk."

About 30 minutes later, Vaughters said, Fray pulled off at the Fayetteville Road exit in Durham and stopped the van. All three men got out. Vaughters marched Burnett up the grassy knoll at gunpoint.

Vaughters declared that Fray repeatedly urged him to kill Burnett. Burnett pleaded for his life. Fray knocked Burnett to the ground. Burnett reached for Vaughters's handgun, and Vaughters and Burnett scuffled.

"We started tussling," Vaughters said. "The guy was kind of big for me to mess with. He just reached up and

grabbed at me, grabbed the gun—and the gun went off.
It shocked me. I couldn't believe it had went off. I panicked. I was dead drunk."

Vaughters and Fray left the body, hopped in the van,
and took off, continuing to drink until their arrest. The
rest of the night, Vaughters said, was a daze.

Thus ended Vaughters's statement. Outside the interview rooms, Detectives Dowdy and Thaxton compared
that statement with the one Fray had made. Essentially,
both men had given the same version of events. The only
major difference was that Fray said taking the van and
killing Burnett had been Vaughters's idea, while
Vaughters said it was the other way around.

Both suspects, however, did say that Vaughters was the
shooter.

Investigators Dowdy and Thaxton charged the suspects
with one count each of first-degree murder, armed robbery, and kidnapping. The men were placed in the Durham jail without privilege of bond.

That night, Captain E. E. "Eddie" Sarvis of the Durham police explained the case to reporters. "The next
person who pulled into that store would have been a victim," the captain said. "It just happened it was Mr.
Burnett."

In the months before the trial, the sleuths wrapped up
the loose ends. The ballistics test scored a hit: the gun
recovered from the van had indeed fired the fatal bullet
into Burnett's head. Attempts to lift prints from the gun
were unsuccessful, however.

Vaughters's trial began in late October 1992 at the Durham County Courthouse in Durham. Mike Nifong, as assistant district attorney, was seeking the death penalty for
the defendant.

North Carolina death-penalty trials consist of two
phases. In the first phase, attorneys argue guilt or innocence. If prosecutors secure a first-degree murder convic-

tion, lawyers argue for and against the death penalty in the second phase.

As the first phase kicked off, the state's case went well. Gregory Fray chose not to testify against his codefendant, but the prosecutors played Ellerek Vaughters's tape-recorded confession for the jury.

The defense began its case on Friday, October 23rd. Vaughters, who had remained in jail since his arrest, took the witness stand on his own behalf.

The defendant shocked the courtroom when he broke down and tearfully admitted that he kidnapped, robbed, and fatally shot Burnett. He cried as he stared at Burnett's family and said he shot the victim during an alcoholic binge.

"I'm mostly thinking about his family," Vaughters told the nine-woman, three-man jury. "I'm asking God to help his family's broken hearts." He went on to say that he had "prayed every night" since the shooting.

Vaughters testified that he'd been drinking hard in the days preceding the slaying. "I would get up in the morning, drink, and then pass out," he said. He said hangovers made it impossible for him to work. He said he slept late, borrowed money from his family, and drank 15 quarts of beer a day.

In describing the events leading up to the killing, Vaughters said he'd pulled his gun on Burnett without thinking. He said he'd stolen the gun from his grandfather a few days before the slaying. He added that he needed the weapon "for protection. The gun made me feel really safe."

Once they had Burnett in the van, Vaughters said, "We rode. I don't remember much that happened in the van. Greg [Fray] kept saying, 'Kill the ——.' I remember striking Mr. Burnett several times on the head with the gun. I wasn't in control of the situation."

When they stopped the van at the Fayetteville Road

exit and got out, Vaughters said, Fray began beating Burnett. There was a struggle, and Vaughters's gun "went off" in the process.

Defense Attorney Bill Cotter asked his client exactly how the gun "went off."

Vaughters replied, "I can't remember. I'm not sure."

Cotter prodded him: Did Vaughters have his hand on the gun when it fired?

Again, Vaughters said he couldn't remember. He wasn't saying what he had told the sleuths in the statement: that the gun went off as he held it and after Burnett grabbed for it. But otherwise, his testimony was essentially the same as what he had said in the statement.

Vaughters admitted he lied to detectives at first when he minimized his involvement in the crime.

"I didn't tell them the truth because I didn't believe the things I was remembering," he said. "I didn't want to believe they were true."

Prosecutor Nifong kept his cross-examination brief and to the point.

"So you're guilty of armed robbery?" the prosecutor asked Vaughters.

Vaughters: "Yes, I am."

Nifong: "You're guilty of first-degree kidnapping?"

Vaughters: "Yes, I am."

Nifong: "You're guilty of first-degree murder?"

Vaughters: "Yes, I am."

After Vaughters left the witness stand, Defense Attorney Cotter and co-Counsel Craig Brown discussed their options. In a few minutes, they nailed down a plea agreement with the state: Vaughters would formalize his witness-stand confession by entering guilty pleas to first-degree murder, kidnapping, and armed robbery. In return for his guilty pleas, the state would agree to stipulate that the crimes were not premeditated.

Whether Vaughters lived or took a one-way ticket to

the gas chamber might hang on that tiny stipulation. It would make it tougher for the state to secure a death penalty without evidence of premeditation.

The attorneys would come back on Monday and argue for and against the death penalty.

After court recessed on Friday, the lawyers gave reporters their take on the trial's dramatic turn.

"I think the defendant did the right thing," Prosecutor Nifong said. He added that he was "satisfied the defendant has been convicted of what he did."

"The guilty pleas more accurately reflect what happened," Defense Attorney Cotter said. "In our opinion, Vaughters did not intend to kill the man. But he did while intoxicated. The plea accurately reflects this" by ruling out premeditation.

On Monday, Vaughters again took the witness stand— this time in an attempt to save his own life. Crying again, he looked squarely at Burnett's family and said, "I'm truly sorry for taking your child away from you, for causing you so much grief. I've repented for this tragedy. I pray you will forgive me in the name of Jesus."

A parade of character witnesses took the stand and described Vaughters as a humble and nonviolent youth from a tough background. He'd moved from Charlotte to Raleigh, the witnesses said, and had fallen in with the wrong crowd in Raleigh. That crowd, they said, included Fray.

A psychiatrist who specialized in addictions said the defendant's dependence on booze was "in full flower and pretty much dominating his life" at the time of the slaying.

In his closing argument, Defense Attorney Brown told the jury, "What has unfolded is not just one tragedy—the death of Walter Burnett . . . it is also the tragedy of Ellerek Vaughters and his family. Killing Ellerek Vaughters will not bring Walter Eugene Burnett back."

The defense asked that their clients be given life in prison instead of the death penalty.

In his closing, Prosecutor Nifong's voice cracked as he argued that Vaughters deserved the death penalty because he had killed Burnett for money during a string of other crimes.

"Your task is not forgiveness," the prosecutor told the jury. "Your task is justice."

The jury reached its decision on Tuesday, October 27, 1992. Ellerek Vaughters showed no emotion as a court clerk read their verdict on the sentencing: life in prison.

The trial judge gave Vaughters an additional 25 years in prison for the robbery and kidnapping convictions.

After court was recessed and the bailiffs led Vaughters away, Defense Attorney Cotter told reporters, "It's just an incredible relief that the jury did what I think it should have done. It just struck me, based on his [Vaughters's] sincere remorse, this was a case deserving life in prison and not death. I'm glad the jury came to that conclusion."

Prosecutor Nifong said the jury made the right decision. "I don't think there can be any serious argument with the jury's verdict," he declared.

On Monday, November 30, 1992, bailiffs brought Gregory Fray from the Durham jail over to the courthouse. In Durham County Superior Court, Fray entered into a plea agreement. He entered guilty pleas to kidnapping, armed robbery, and murder. In exchange for those guilty pleas, the prosecutors reduced the murder count against him to second degree.

Judge Orlando F. Hudson entertained arguments before setting Fray's sentence.

Defense Attorney James D. "Butch" Williams told the judge that Fray was an accomplished bricklayer and artist who'd had only a minor record before the killing. The lawyer said his client's actions represented an aberration rather than a pattern of conduct.

"The socially redeeming value of Greg Fray is overwhelming," the barrister argued. "He has agonized over the fact that this young man [Burnett] lost his life and he [Fray] is still alive. I would submit that at the end of the tunnel, there is some light to Greg Fray. . . . He was not a cold-blooded, cold-hearted, calculating murderer."

Judge Hudson sentenced Fray to life plus 40 years in prison. As he passed sentence, the judge had only one comment: "I don't understand. I've stopped trying to understand."

Gregory Fray and Ellerek Vaughters are now doing their time in North Carolina prisons.

"BEAST OF THE BRONX!"

by Don Unatin

The flickering of hundreds of candles held in trembling hands cast an eerie shadow over the streets of the middle-class neighborhood of Castle Hill in the Bronx, New York. There were muted whispers as the ever-swelling group of marchers passed between rows of trees which during the past week had been decorated by a series of yellow ribbons.

From the worry apparent on the faces of the somber group, one could tell that by the autumn evening of October 16, 1990, the hope which had kept volunteer searchers for 10-year-old honor student Jessica Guzman going since she had mysteriously disappeared in the early evening of Wednesday, October 10th, was giving way to a sense of dread. Each passing moment now made it less likely that the yellow ribbons signifying the missing youngster's safe return had failed to work their spell.

A day after the candlelight vigil, a grieving woman would recall, "Since this little girl disappeared, the tension has been terrible. We all have kids. I have a son and anyone could get into that terrace [of Castle Hills Homes] and do something."

The woman's statement came in the late afternoon of

Wednesday, October 17th, as crowds once again gathered in tight knots on Randall Avenue to sob out their grief and offer their multilanguage prayers for the soul of the child. Her body had just been discovered (at 4:00 P.M.) by a city parks department employee in a stand of trees along the Bronx River Parkway.

Adding to the shock felt by those who now knew that the worst had happened was the grim description of the condition of Jessica's body as given by New York Police Department Spokesman Lieutenant Raymond O'Donnell. He said that the little girl's corpse had been badly decomposed, indicating that she had been dead for several days. She had been identified by the T-shirt she had been wearing when she vanished a week earlier. The garment bore the imprint of the Tasmanian Devil, a cartoon character. She also was clad in the jeans and blue sneakers which she had on on October 10th.

Deputy Chief Michael Philbin, Chief of Bronx Detectives, reported that nothing visible showed how Jessica had died and that a cursory examination of her remains at the crime scene had revealed no apparent sign of sex abuse. However, he noted that further word on such matters awaited the findings of the medical examiner's office following a complete autopsy of the young girl's remains.

Philbin added that the body did not appear to have been tossed from a vehicle, but rather had been placed on the spot where it had been discovered approximately five miles from Jessica's home.

Veteran police officers felt the same overwhelming sense of grief experienced by the tightly knit Bronx community.

Lieutenant O'Donnell remembered how a mobile police command unit had remained parked before Jessica's home since October 12th, as cops had distributed fliers and photographs of her. The officers had moved among area residents, engaging them in quiet conversations in hopes of eliciting tips.

Said the police spokesman, "Everyone's been looking, everyone's been putting up posters. She's a ten-year-old girl, you know. She's innocent."

New York City Mayor David N. Dinkins, apprised of the killing, stated, "Every loss of life is a tragedy. When it is a child of Jessica's age, the tragedy is magnified. Those responsible for this brutal waste of a person's life will be brought to justice."

Now the hundreds of cops who had searched tirelessly for the missing child, using helicopters and tracking dogs in their effort, began an all-out attempt to uncover meaningful clues which might lead them to Jessica's killer or killers. They were also searching the 43rd Precinct green book of open cases to determine whether Jessica's murder might be related to any other killing in the Castle Hill area.

Of particular interest were the killings of 13-year-old Nilda Cartagena and 15-year-old Heriberto Marrero, according to Detective-Sergeant John Kilvehan of the Fteley Avenue Station.

The two teenagers had disappeared on June 9, 1989, while on their way to Junior High School 129, in the Soundview section of the Bronx. Their bodies were found 11 days later off the Hutchinson River Parkway near the Whitestone Bridge—a mile from the spot where Jessica's corpse was discovered. Their naked bodies had been stuffed in plastic bags.

Sergeant Kilvehan would not elaborate at this point on the possible relationship between the two crimes. But other police sources noted that 29-year-old Alejandro (Alex) Henriquez, a Bronx cab driver and an uncle of Nilda Cartagena, had been interviewed by detectives following the deaths of the well-liked teenagers. The discussions had been triggered by information that on the day of the youngsters' disappearance, Henriquez had driven them to school.

According to Detective Irwin Silverman, who had led the search for Jessica Guzman, Henriquez had been interviewed along with numerous others in the Guzman case. Commented Detective Silverman, "He [Henriquez] was interviewed just as many other people were. He was cooperative at this point."

Of interest was the fact that up until 1989, Henriquez was said to have lived with his family in an apartment under the Castle Hills flat occupied by the Guzman family.

According to police sources and Guzman family members, Henriquez had told detectives that on the day Jessica vanished from Homer Avenue at about 4:00 P.M., he had come upon Jessica and two of her friends playing inside his car. The door of the vehicle was open. When Henriquez arrived at the car, the girls got out and spoke to him and then went off in separate directions.

In another coincidence, Henriquez had once dated Lisa Rodriquez, a 21-year-old college student whose body was found on June 19, 1990, near Bruckner Boulevard and the Hutchinson River Parkway. The site was only 100 yards from that on which Cartagena and Marrero had rested.

In addition, Henriquez was currently facing trial for the 1988 scalding of a former girlfriend's three-year-old son and for having injured the child further by throwing him down a flight of stairs.

By now rewards in the thousands of dollars were being offered for information leading to the slayer of Cartagena and Marrero and the one responsible for the Jessica Guzman homicide.

Despite these developments, police insisted that Henriquez was not a suspect in any murders at this time.

Nor were any other suspects being named. The only arrest in the Guzman case had concerned a woman who had been charged with fraud. According to Sergeant Edward Cremin of the 43rd Precinct, the woman had been soliciting funds which she had told donors were destined for the family of Jessica Guzman.

On Friday, October 19, 1990, the eagerly awaited autopsy report in Jessica Guzman's death was issued by the medical examiner's office.

It was said that the little girl had died of asphyxia resulting from either suffocation or strangulation. The manner of death appeared to be similar to that which had been suffered by Cartagena and Marrero.

However, according to Ellen Borakove, a spokeswoman for the medical examiner's office, Jessica's body had been so badly decomposed that it had been impossible to pin down exactly how the murder was committed. Borakove noted that no stab or bullet wounds had been found on the corpse.

For his part, Alex Henriquez decided to go public with his own statement. He told reporters, "I have a clear conscience. The police know where I was on those days."

"Why don't they arrest me, if they have any evidence? I know three other people that have been killed—why aren't they linking me to them?

"I haven't done nothing. Now I'm concerned about my loved ones. Someone could retaliate.

"My niece [Nilda Cartagena] was killed and I'm dying to find out who killed her. I mean, somebody killed my niece and somebody killed this little girl [Jessica Guzman]."

Possibilities other than Henriquez's involvement were receiving their share of police investigators' attention.

Being cited was a comment by Ms. Borakove who had speculated that Jessica's death might have "one of its possible causes" as chest compression. Some detectives believed that Jessica's killer or killers might have pressed

down on her chest with such force that the breath left
her body.

Death by chest compression was believed to represent
the darker side of the Santeria religion which has Afro-
Cuban roots and is a blend of Catholicism and voodoo.
Those familiar with the cult and its practices claimed
there were large pockets of Santeria believers in the Caribbean and Hispanic enclaves of New York City.

Said one knowledgeable police source, "There is a Santeria ceremony in which the killer breathes the last breath
of the victim. This gives them a sense of power over the
victim's soul."

On Sunday, October 21st, hundreds of mourners
jammed into St. John Vianney Roman Catholic Church
to pay their last respects to the slain honor student at
her wake. On Monday, October 22nd, John Cardinal
O'Connor officiated at a solemn funeral mass for little
Jessica Guzman. Said the noted clergyman, "We are related by pain, by suffering, by this common language of
sorrow, the anguish we all feel, every one of us."

Addressing Jessica's family, Mayor Dinkins stated, "The
entire city stands with you and shares your pain, for we,
too, have lost a child and a sister.

"Jessica, we love you and we miss you. Your glowing
face now lights up the heavens; your smile will shine up
the hearts of New Yorkers always."

As the 200-car cortege was moving slowly toward St.
Raymond's Cemetery (near the Bronx-Whitestone
Bridge) where the white coffin containing Jessica's body
would be lowered into her grave, police brass announced
the formation of a 20-person task force culled from several Bronx precincts as well as the major case squad, the
homicide task force, and the housing police to press forward in the frustrating investigation.

Admitting they were back "to square one" in their ongoing probe, sleuths noted that their stakeouts around

the Guzman funeral services had turned up no new suspects nor useful information. Moreover, the Santeria theory had gone nowhere.

In addition, it was learned that having not established evidence against the Bronx cab driver at this juncture, detectives allowed Alex Henriquez to leave the city on a Caribbean vacation. Sources said that during several questioning sessions, Henriquez had proved cooperative and established an alibi for the time immediately focused on Jessica's June 10th vanishing. Henriquez had told them that he had been with a friend, and detectives said the friend had confirmed Henriquez's statement.

Said Chief of Bronx Detectives Philbin, "We're really going back to the nuts and bolts of this investigation. I've never seen a case with so many coincidences and so little solid evidence."

The "nuts and bolts" aspects included reinterviewing neighbors, canvassing the area where Jessica was last seen alive, double-checking alibi witnesses and using computers to cross-index possible leads.

There still remained the distinct possibility that the killings of Guzman, Cartagena, and Marrero might somehow be linked. The prime theory was that the victims had been suffocated in plastic bags.

However, there were other equally viable scenarios. A pillow placed over the face or a rag shoved into a victim's mouth might have been the death implement. Then, too, the victims might have succumbed while imprisoned in the trunk of a car with no air supply.

Because of the proximity of the places the victims were abandoned, it didn't seem logical that the killer had been a transient. More likely, sleuths reasoned, the perp had been someone from the neighborhood, and the victims may well have known that person and willingly accompanied him without ever suspecting they were about to be slain.

Bedeviling the top detectives was establishing a motive for the murders.

To seek out the answers to these puzzling questions, police set up roadblocks on the Bronx River Parkway in hopes of finding a driver who would be able to tell them something.

Commented Captain Robert Martin of the Bronx Homicide Task Force, "There's a lot of concern in the community. You could see that by the number of people who showed up at the funeral. Hopefully someone will turn something up."

Perhaps the first break in the case was closer at hand than detectives had hoped. This came when Alex Henriquez told the cops that on October 17th, the day Jessica's body was found, he had traded in a cab to a company he managed, despite the cab being in perfect working order.

The car was impounded and underwent forensic tests on microscopic bits of fabrics that might have come from clothing Jessica was wearing at the time of her disappearance.

Then another name came to the attention of the police. And with its disclosure came the possibility of another connection between Henriquez and a young person who had died violently.

The case went back two years earlier to July 9, 1988. The crime scene was 100 yards from the police firing range near Pelham Bay in the Bronx.

Two officers on routine patrol had spotted a car speeding away on Rodman Road after somebody in the vehicle had dumped a large object onto the road.

Pausing to investigate, the two officers were sickened by the sight of the body of a young girl, naked below the waist except for her white socks and shoes. On top, she wore a red and white shirt underneath a blue jacket. A pair of jeans had been discarded near the body, which was lying face up.

It was not until three weeks later that investigators identified the youngster as 14-year-old Shamira Bello. The reason for the delay was that the teenager had a history of running away from home and her family had not reported her missing, figuring she would return on her own as she had done in the past.

For two years, the murder of Shamira Bello had caused little interest in a city that averages 2,000 homicides annually. Things could have remained that way except for one singular fact: Shamira Bello had dated a male relative of Alex Henriquez's.

On Tuesday, October 30th, Henriquez, his Caribbean cruise vacation behind him, was in State Supreme Court in the Bronx to answer the unrelated charges of child abuse.

Tanned and impeccably clad in a gray suit, white shirt, and print tie, Henriquez pleaded not guilty to the charges filed in the indictment. The charges said that in December 1988, Henriquez threw his former girlfriend's three-year-old son down a flight of stairs after having caused the child third-degree burns on his back by holding him under a scalding shower.

Later, Henriquez would change his plea to guilty and receive a four-year sentence for the act.

Now his attorney in the child torture case was advising Henriquez to maintain a cloak of silence concerning the ongoing homicide probes in which his name was continuing to surface. Said the attorney, "The police say he is not a suspect. But that statement seems to be inconsistent with the attention being paid him."

However, the embattled cabbie agreed to meet with reporters once again. The spot picked for the conclave was the Van Cortland Park stable where Henriquez kept his horse. The date was October 31st.

Once again, Henriquez complained that coincidence was the only explanation for the fact that all of the homicide victims had known him. Saying he enjoyed children, had two of his own, and that he and his wife were trying to have more, Henriquez stated, "There is nothing wrong with spending time with them. I play with them. I have fun with them. I enjoy children."

Of his troubles over the child abuse case, Henriquez blamed the child's father (who had once been married to Henriquez's wife) of "setting me up."

The child's natural father refused to accept that version. The man rebutted, "Me and him, we're like oil and vinegar. The truth is, he burned my kid. I don't have it out for him. I just want justice done."

As time slipped by, Henriquez's life in court became more and more complicated. On December 13, 1990, he found himself standing once again before the bar in Bronx Supreme Court and hearing himself indicated in a 1987 robbery during which he and an accomplice had stuck up the Manhattan Yacht Club.

According to police sources, Henriquez readily admitted the yacht club caper, telling them, "Okay, I did the robbery, but I didn't have anything to do with those kids."

Said one detective who preferred not to be identified, "We were hoping that people might feel less intimidated if we could show that his aura of invincibility was just a mirage. But now that he's behind bars [on the robbery arrest], and facing the prospect of some big time, we've had some people who are coming forward and being more cooperative."

Slowly the months slipped by as Alex Henriquez continued to proclaim his innocence in the killings and the task force went about their exhaustive and exhausting business of digging ever deeper into his tangled affairs. Their hope that new witnesses would come forward began to become a reality.

In April 1991, detectives reported that they had uncovered a witness who had seen Jessica Guzman and the cab driver together after 6:30 P.M., on October 10, 1990—the day of her disappearance. Henriquez told cops he had been watching television between 6:15 and 11:00 on that evening.

Detectives who had ranged from their Bronx command as far as Tyler, Texas, believed they had hit pay dirt when, with the help of FBI agents, they were able to track down a car that Henriquez had allegedly driven on the day Shamira Bello disappeared in July 1988.

Henriquez had lost the car when it had been repossessed. Subsequently, it had been bought by a Texas couple. When police approached the Texans, the couple feared that they had destroyed possible evidence accidentally when they replaced the mats on the vehicle's floors.

Said one source familiar with the case, "We thought all was lost, but when we checked near the screws which hold down the mats, there was all kinds of fibers."

Laboratory tests reportedly linked the fibers to clothing that had been on Shamira Bello's body.

The solution of Lisa Rodriquez's slaying seemed closer at hand. Although the young woman's body had been too badly decomposed for forensic experts to determine a cause of death, detectives operating under a court order had raided one of Henriquez's Bronx residences and found articles of clothing Lisa had been wearing at the time of her death.

Early in April 1991, there was speculation that Bronx District Attorney Robert Johnson would soon go before a grand jury to present evidence in at least three of the cases—the murders of Jessica Guzman, Shamira Bello, and Lisa Rodriguez. However, the action, which had appeared to be imminent, would be delayed for two months.

One investigator put the postponement in perspective, saying, "He's in jail. He's not going anywhere. Why should we go in and arrest him with forty cards in our deck when we could have fifty-two?"

Finally, on Tuesday, July 2, 1991, the word which had been so desperately awaited by those who had been close to the six young victims was given. It came from District Attorney Johnson who announced that a specially convened grand jury had acted.

The legal body had handed down an indictment charging Henriquez with second-degree murder and manslaughter in the slayings of Jessica Guzman, Shamira Bello, and Lisa Rodriguez. The suspect in these crimes had not been charged, however, in the deaths of Nilda Cartagena, Heriberto Marrero, and 17-year-old Annette Rosario, whose bodies had been found under circumstances similar to those concerning the others.

The grand jury action had been triggered by evidence presented to them on forensic matters—articles of clothing and textile fibers—community tips, witness testimony, and statements made by Henriquez that law enforcement authorities said incriminated him.

Chief of Detectives Joseph Borrelli noted that Henriquez was the sole suspect in the current case, but that he had not been "ruled out" in the latter three.

Borrelli said the length of time that had elapsed between the discovery of the murdered youngsters and the unsealing of the indictment was the result of a "wall of silence and alibis which had surrounded the suspect."

The detective chief commented, "When you're faced with a solid wall, you chip away at the foundation." He noted that Henriquez had been arrested on other unrelated charges. Slowly, the aura Henriquez had built around himself fell away, and information from his friends and acquaintances began to trickle in.

For his part, Defense Attorney Mel A. Sachs, who would represent Henriquez through more than a year of legal infighting, took strong issue with the statements of

Johnson and Borrelli. The highly respected trial attorney, who had won a reputation for aggressive and abrasive courtroom tactics, stated, "They waited an inordinate time before charging him [Henriquez]. There isn't any direct evidence in this case."

At issue was the question of whether Henriquez was a man who had overcome numerous hardships to become a success in his own livery cab company, or whether, as others believed, he was a cunning, fast-talking felon.

In the time between the unsealing of the indictment and the beginning of jury selection (on June 18, 1992), the positions of prosecution and defense were clearly outlined by a series of court hearings concerning the admissibility of evidence and testimony. Prosecutors continued to insist that Henriquez was the common link between victims Jessica Guzman, Shamira Bello, and Lisa Rodriguez.

The defense vociferously contended that the police had been under enormous community pressure to solve the case of the slain young woman and two girls and that to still the public outcry, they had made Henriquez the scapegoat.

For their part, relatives of the victims made a solemn vow that they would attend the daily sessions of the coming trial every day.

Said one, "I have to do this for [my daughter]. I have to try to be strong and do this. . . . To make sure that there is some justice that has been done."

"You couldn't keep me away from there," declared one father. "For the past two years we have been going through hell because she was our only daughter. That's not to say that the other parents aren't suffering with this loss, but at least they have other kids and they know they have to be strong for them, to be there for them. We don't have anybody but ourselves."

Noting that Henriquez had received a stab wound in

a prison altercation at Rikers Island, the man said, "When they stabbed him in the chest, a lot of people said, 'Why didn't they kill him?' Personally I don't want him dead right now. I want him to go to trial to find out what the truth is."

A third parent felt it was her responsibility to be on hand to help prosecutors in any way she could. "They have evidence, but they need more," the woman said. "I'm going to be there every day because we know he did it. He is the devil down there."

With 400 Bronx residents jamming the jurors' assembly room at the Bronx County Courthouse on June 18th, the voir dire process was set to get under way. Still there were some doubts as to whether the trial would go on as scheduled or a delay would be necessitated by the damage Henriquez had suffered in the jailhouse stabbing. He was said to be recovering from a collapsed lung. In addition, courtroom security had been beefed up due to threats made against Henriquez.

With the culmination of pretrial hearings, Supreme Court Justice Daniel J. Sullivan gave prosecutors a boost when he ruled that taped telephone conversations between Henriquez and the cabbie's former wife were admissible.

On Wednesday, July 15th, with the small and dingy ground-floor courtroom jammed with relatives of the victims and the 12 jurors and their alternates seated in the jury box, Assistant Bronx District Attorney Edward Talty, a lean, soft-spoken, and well-regarded prosecutor, rose to give his opening argument. He claimed that Henriquez was the only person who could have strangled Jessica Guzman, Shamira Bello, and Lisa Rodriquez. His remarks were brief and low-keyed as he outlined the evidence against the defendant.

"You will hear how each of the murders was carefully planned, how the defendant appeared to value setting up an alibi. What you are going to hear is some of the most clever, most murderous work."

In his 19-minute speech, Talty pointed out that all of the victims were "young, they were Hispanic, they were attractive. They had something else in common," the prosecutor continued. "They all knew Alejandro Henriquez, and they all wound up dead of asphyxiation."

Talty offered no motive for the slayings. He did say that the prosecution's case would be built from fiber and hair samples taken from Henriquez's house and one of his cars, the gray Mercedes police had recovered in Tyler, Texas. He also said the jury would hear from a young relative of Henriquez's to whom the suspect had revealed details about the murders and from Henriquez's former wife concerning the clothing Lisa Rodriguez was wearing when her body was found.

Defense Attorney Sachs took 25 minutes to blast the prosecution's case. He said it was weak and "comprised of unreliable circumstantial evidence like hair and fiber samples that offer no conclusive proof." He said his client was the innocent victim of a witch hunt in which the police, pressured by an angry community, were looking for somebody to blame for the heinous crimes.

Throughout the opening proceedings, Henriquez, neatly dressed in a gray suit, wearing eyeglasses, and clean-shaven, sat impassively staring straight ahead as he would throughout the six weeks of testimony.

Now, as the prosecutors began to flesh out their case with the more than 40 witnesses who would take the stand, a young woman testified that she had seen Henriquez pick up Shamira Bello twice in his livery cab on Taylor Avenue during March 1988. However, under cross-examination, she acknowledged that she had not seen the pair together from April to July of the same year, when the teenager's body had been discovered. She also noted that Bello had been dating a relative of the defendant's. Henriquez's name had not come up until two years later in connection with the other killings.

The prosecution produced Police Office Ellen Caiazzo, who told the court that on July 3, 1988, while driving along the road leading to the police firing range at Rodman's Neck, she saw a man in a gray car dump something along the road. The car recovered in Texas, the prosecutor pointed out, was a gray Mercedes. The officer told other police about the incident. That evening they returned to the spot and there discovered the body of Shamira Bello.

Linking Henriquez to Jessica Guzman, Housing Police Detective Randolph Mitchell testified that he had questioned Henriquez one day after the 10-year-old had vanished. Henriquez had told him that Jessica and two of her friends had gotten into his car at 5:00 P.M. on October 10, 1990, at Castle Hill Avenue. Henriquez had said that the girls playfully attempted to close the car windows and lock him out. Henriquez told detectives that the girls then left the car and went into a supermarket.

Detective Robert Sodine of the 43rd Precinct took the stand to report that he had questioned the livery cabbie in December 1990 about his relationship with Lisa Rodriguez. He asked Henriquez if he knew her, whether he had ever been to her home or she had visited him in his own home, or if the pair had ever dated.

"His responses to all of the questions was no," Sodine told the jury.

At this point in the interrogation, Sodine had told Henriquez he didn't believe him.

"I know you were on a date with Lisa Rodriguez," the detective then told him. "Lisa Rodriguez was in your home. I know you took Lisa Rodriguez [and another female relative] to a movie."

Sodine said Henriquez had stated, "Well, as far as the movie goes, that wasn't a real date."

The detective also testified that a woman who was a former companion of Henriquez had told the officer that she had given the defendant a shirt and pants that were the same color and brand as those found on Rodriguez's body.

On cross-examination, Sodine admitted that he had not recorded his conversation with Henriquez, nor had Henriquez signed any such statement. He said the defendant had not allowed him to record or write down statements.

The prosecution theory that sex had played a part in at least one of the three murders was buttressed by Dr. Zoya Shmuter, the medical examiner who performed the autopsy on Shamira Bello. Dr. Shmuter testified that semen had been found in the girl's mouth and vaginal area.

On Thursday, July 23rd, the court proceedings took a grisly turn as Dr. Yury Kogan, a city deputy medical examiner, described the state of decomposition of Jessica Guzman's maggot-infested body when he performed an autopsy on it. He noted that some body parts had been missing. He said the cause of the little girl's death had been homicidal asphyxia.

The afternoon trial session was thrown into near panic when the prosecution prepared to introduce into evidence the clothing Jessica Guzman had worn when her body was discovered. This was because a cardboard box containing the garment was opened in the courtroom and emitted such a foul odor of death and decay that it sickened court attendants and spectators alike.

Judge Sullivan hastily ordered all courtroom windows to be opened and the premises to be sprayed with antiseptic to get rid of the fearful stench, pending the jury's return. Sullivan then explained to the panel that because of the noxious odor, the clothing would not be put on view. (Both the prosecution and the defense agreed that Jessica had been wearing a T-shirt, jeans, socks and sneakers, and a bra and panties when her corpse had been found.)

Under cross-examination by Defense Attorney Sachs concerning details of the autopsy he had performed on Lisa Rodriguez, Dr. Kogan admitted that he had originally listed the cause of her death as "unknown," but had changed it more than a year later to "homicidal asphyxia." The pathologist contended that many parts of Rodriguez's body had been missing, including the neck area, so "asphyxia was the only alternative." There had been no other signs of lethal injury.

On Friday, July 31st, the thrust of the prosecution case shifted from official reports by law enforcement officials to the more intimate details of relationships that Henriquez had had with the women in his life.

This occurred when a young woman took the stand. For an hour and a half of preliminary testimony, she told the jurors of her association with the accused man. She said she had met Henriquez in September 1987 and had married him in March 1989. Later, she had learned that he was still wed to his first wife. She said Henriquez had told her he was a police detective and that he often flashed a police badge and wore a brown gun holster.

Her testimony was a prelude to the playing of four tapes of telephone conversations between herself and Henriquez which had taken place on January 22, 1991. In them, the woman told Henriquez that the police had shown her pictures of Lisa Rodriguez's body and that Rodriguez had been wearing sweatpants which had been taken from the witness's closet. The shirt that covered the upper portion of Lisa Rodriguez's corpse appeared to the witness to be one the defendant owned.

As Henriquez remained totally impassive in the courtroom, the jury and spectators heard the recorded surprise in his taped voice at what the witness had told him in the phone conversation. He denied knowing Lisa Rodriguez and insisted the clothing on the dead woman was not his or that of his former companion.

"I'm not going to give someone any clothes and then kill them," Henriquez said in the recording.

At another point, his recorded voice said, "What do you mean your pants? Did they have your name on them? Do you think they just make one pair of shoes, one pair of pants for you?

"I would never be stupid as to give another woman your clothes. What for?"

When the former companion told him she did not know what to think about his involvement in the murders, Henriquez answered, "I never in my life hurt anybody that way."

Yet, an hour later, Henriquez was back on the phone with a changed story and an elaborate explanation of how he had met Lisa Rodriguez and had given her a ride from the beach one day during the summer of 1990. He then took her to his apartment to shower because she had been covered with sand and oil from suntan lotion.

"I didn't want to tell you because I didn't think you'd believe me," he added. He continued to insist that he had had nothing to do with Lisa Rodriguez's brutal asphyxiation murder.

On the tape, the court heard Henriquez's recorded voice say, "I guess what you've seen created a big doubt in your mind. I've never killed anybody in my life, and I don't think I ever will. I'm not a murderer. I'm just a liar."

For his part, Defense Attorney Sachs objected vehemently against the playing of the tapes, charging that they told only about the couple's life together, which had nothing to do with the case. He was overruled.

On Wednesday, August 12th, the key witness, whose testimony was the linchpin of the prosecution's case, was sworn in. The man, a relative of the defendant, told a riveting story of what had transpired between him and the defendant during his three visits to Henriquez. The meetings took place in the winter of 1991 in the Brooklyn House of Detention, where Henriquez was being held on armed robbery charges.

According to the prosecution witness, Henriquez had concocted a plan which called for the family member to call news organizations and the police to convince them that the killer of the three victims was still on the loose.

"He wanted me to pretend like I was the killer," the witness said. "He told me to disguise my voice, to be careful not to get caught, to keep it a secret between me and him."

The witness then testified that Henriquez had devised a code that they could use on telephone calls that would inform the defendant of progress being made in the scam. "He would ask me, 'Did you take my pants to the cleaner?' I would say, 'yes, I took seven pairs,' for Channel Seven, 'two pants' for Channel Two."

The witness said he did not make the phone calls. Instead, he began cooperating with the police almost immediately. Under police instructions, he told Henriquez that news organizations said they would not believe his claim unless he disclosed details of the murders that had not been made public.

"He told me to tell them that Jessica's body was found near a small tree with her bra cut in the front and that Lisa was found on the other side of St. Raymond's Cemetery with a blue shirt and pink sweatpants and that Shamira had a bloody nose," said the witness. However, the young man noted that at no time had Henriquez confessed being the killer to him.

Cross-examining the witness, Defense Attorney Sachs tried to show that the young man was unreliable, a violent person who had turned against Henriquez. He also tried to show that there was no record of the House of Detention confabs because the witness had neglected to wear a recorder supplied by the police for that purpose.

The dramatic highpoint of the trial was reached with the young man's testimony. However, much bitterness between prosecution and defense still lay ahead as the opponents returned to the normally staid testimony of forensic witnesses.

The controversy swirled around the accuracy of tests conducted by the state's expert witnesses on comparisons between textile fibers found on the victims and fibers found in the defendant's home and between hair samples taken from Henriquez and hairs found on the victims.

Defense Attorney Sachs hurled thunderbolts of vitriol, charging that medical examiners and detectives assigned to the police crime lab had bungled and lost bits of evidence during the course of the investigation. Over and over, Sachs hit away at the lack of DNA testing which would have ruled out any other suspect.

With constant objections to points made by the prosecution, Sachs sought to make major gains for his client. Sachs's position was clearly stated in a three-hour summation. In it, the defense specialist argued, "The case against Alejandro Henriquez doesn't have evidence, evidence that had integrity, evidence that can be relied on." He charged that his client had been targeted by the police "wrongly and maliciously" as a suspect because of intense community pressure in the Castle Hill area, to find someone to pin the deaths on.

"If the police think they can come up here and do what they want to this person, they can do it to anybody," he charged.

Prosecutor Talty rejoined as he coolly assembled points of the prosecution evidence and testimony which he said "points like a compass to Henriquez." He appealed to the jurors' common sense, noting that the suspect had given details of the three killings to a relative and left behind incriminating bits of evidence including hair and fibers.

"This is the mind of the person we are talking about here," he said as he described one of the alibis Henriquez had used with the police. "This is not just a person who kills for emotion or greed. This is a person who *considers* murder,"the prosecutor declared, "who *plans* it—and plans it well."

After a final charge by Judge Sullivan on the legal ramifications of circumstantial evidence, the jury of eleven men and one woman went behind closed doors to begin their deliberations during the late afternoon of Tuesday, August 26th. As they did, speculation ran high among court watchers as to which way the panel would vote.

There were still a number of questions which remained to be answered. One was whether the prosecution was facing tough odds. It was pointed out by many that rates of conviction in Bronx Criminal Court were the lowest of the five boroughs. While juries in the other four boroughs had a 76 percent conviction rate, those in the Bronx showed only a 63 percent conviction figure.

Obviously, the prosecution case had been constructed purely on circumstantial evidence, which could make the going tougher.

On the other hand, the daily attendance of relatives of the three victims and the harrowingly graphic photographs of the decayed, maggot-invaded bodies of the three victims could have a tremendous impact.

Suddenly, on Thursday, August 28th, two days into the deliberations and as tension mounted in the courthouse, there was a sudden crisis, raising the possibility that the six-week trial had been for nought and the prosecution and defense would have to begin once again from scratch. It happened when a juror complained of severe stomach pains and asked to be removed to a hospital. If the illness proved serious enough and the man proved ill enough,

Defense Attorney Sachs let it be known that his client would refuse to accept the verdict of the remaining 11 jurors. The end result would be a mistrial.

The situation remained unchanged overnight. However, by Friday morning, the man was sufficiently improved to rejoin his fellow jurors.

At 2:55 on Friday afternoon, the grim-faced jurors returned to the courtroom. A packed group of victims' relatives and spectators heard the words that at long last brought a climax to the terrible months which lay behind.

Alejandro Henriquez, who showed absolutely no emotion as he listened, was told by the jury foreman that he had been found guilty of murder in the second degree in the slayings of Jessica Guzman, Shamira Bello, and Lisa Rodriguez. As the words echoed through the chambers, they were punctuated by the shrill scream of one of the parents of a victim.

"Bastard, I hope they kill you!" she shouted at the convicted killer.

In a posttrial statement, District Attorney Johnson said, "Henriquez's crimes were nothing less than animalistic. Getting a guilty verdict will give some measure of justice to these families. Their loss is never-ending. These three young ladies will never be brought back."

Defense Attorney Sachs commented, "We must believe in the jury system. All of the charges in this trial have to affect a jury. A jury sits in a courtroom with the pain of the families and felt the pain on a day-to-day basis."

The hardworking defense attorney said his client had made no mention of guilt or innocence following the reading of the verdict.

On Monday, September 21, 1992, Alex Henriquez was sentenced by Judge Daniel L. Sullivan to three consecutive terms of 25 years to life, to begin after he had served 4 years for the child abuse conviction and 5 to 15 years year for his armed-robbery conviction.

In addition, D.A. Johnson said his office is continuing its probe into the slayings of Annette Rosario, Heriberto Marrero, and Nilda Cartagena, in all of which Henriquez is a suspect.

However, Henriquez has not been charged in the murders and must be considered innocent of any involvement until and unless proven otherwise by due process, according to constitutional provisions.

"DERANGED DRIFTER'S BUS STOP BLOODBATH!"

by Bill Henry

The homeless man sat on a bench, two duffel bags beside him, at the bus stop at Young Circle in Hollywood, Florida. He was sipping a cold drink while patiently waiting for the Route 1 bus which runs from Miami to Fort Lauderdale to make its stop at the Circle in downtown Hollywood. But the homeless man did not board the first Route 1 bus to arrive. He had the look of just another homeless man with nothing better to do.

It was a warm but pleasant day, that July 23, 1989, when a third Route 1 bus arrived at the bus stop at 1:28 P.M. There was no need to hurry; several bus routes originated or crossed at the Circle so there would be a number of passengers leaving the bus to transfer to other routes and some passengers from other routes lining up to board the Route 1 bus which had just arrived.

Suddenly, the homeless man picked up one of his duffel bags, discarded his drinks, took out a pistol from a plastic bag, and fired several shots at the bus. If his objective was to disperse the passengers who were waiting to board the bus so he would not have to stand in line, his method was obviously effective. Everyone close to the bus ran as fast as they could.

While the passengers on the bus screamed and hid behind seats for protection, the gunman entered the bus and shot the bus driver, Sydney Granger, in the throat, killing him instantly. A passenger, Wesley Anderson, who had just dropped his fare into the box, tried to escape to the rear of the bus. The gunman shot him in the back three times. Anderson was dead by the time medical assistance reached him.

The gunman looked at the fallen man and at the frightened passengers and then calmly left the bus without the least sign of being concerned. Without hurrying or concealing his weapon, he walked east from the bus stop. No one tried to stop him; only a few people stood where they happened to be when the shots were heard and watched the gunman. No policeman heard the shots or arrived before the gunman made his escape from the scene of terror.

Two witnesses, Harold Butler and Betty Southerly, who were leaving a supermarket close to the bus stop with their purchases when they heard the shots, stood where they were, watching the gunman leave the bus and walk about 200 feet to Tyler Street. He carried his gun in full view of passersby, as if he didn't have a care in the world. Several cars had stopped on Tyler Street while the traffic light at the intersection of Young Circle was red. The gunman passed three cars and stopped at the fourth. He pointed his gun at the driver and told him that he had just killed two men and would kill the driver if he didn't get out of his car quickly and let the gunman have his vehicle. The driver, William Fenton, obeyed promptly but it did not save him. As Fenton walked away from his car, the gunman shot him in the back three times. The first bullet severed his spinal cord. As a result, Fenton would be in a wheelchair the rest of his life.

Harold Butler, the witness who had watched from the entrance of the supermarket, came to Fenton's aid in spite of his fear of the mad gunman. He asked Fenton what he could do for him. "You might call an ambulance for me," Fenton said.

As Butler started back to the supermarket to phone for an ambulance, he saw that the traffic light had turned from red to green, and the gunman drove away in Fenton's car. No one tried to stop him, and no policeman had arrived on the scene yet.

Sergeant Darron Castiglione of the Hollywood Police Department was the first policeman to reach Young Circle. He found that a crowd of witnesses who had fled from the scene were returning. They told Castiglione what they saw while they gawked at the two dead men in the bus and the wounded driver on the pavement. No one could tell the sergeant what had caused the killings.

When detectives from the homicide squad arrived at the scene, all the sergeant could tell them was that an unknown drifter, possibly one of the homeless men who were frequently seen loitering at Young Circle, shot and killed two men on a bus and then shot another man whom the killer had forced to surrender his automobile.

The witnesses who were interviewed described the murderer as a white man in his 40s, 5 feet 7 or 8 inches tall. He was thin, weighing about 120 to 140 pounds. He had dark hair which he wore in a ponytail. Some witnesses were sure the gunman wore glasses.

But no one knew his name or recalled anything more that would help identify him. With an accurate description of William Fenton's car and its current license plate, an all-points bulletin was issued in the hope that the killer would be apprehended in the automobile before he had gone far. But hours and then days passed with no report of the gunman being seen anywhere.

At the scene, one witness noticed the duffel bag left

on the bench at the bus stop and told the police about it. The bag was examined thoroughly for clues to its ownership, but it was not very helpful except for supplying the owner's name, Joseph Besaraba, and some medicines he took. They found no address where the owner had ever lived and no names or addresses of anyone who knew him. They did have, however, the name of the gunman. The police recovered no fingerprints from the bus or the duffel bag. They obtained a good description of the gunman from the many witnesses who had seen him up close, but no one remembered seeing him at any other place where the police might look for him or get any information to help them search for him.

Kevin Doyle, the lead detective from the Hollywood Police Department, was assigned to the case. He was convinced that the killer was a homeless man who would never return to this community. The police knew they needed more than Besaraba's name to begin a search for him. Of the three men he attacked, one survived but that man never saw the gunman before he surrendered his car to him.

The killer had attacked the bus first, firing several shots at it, but hitting no one. Might he be seeking revenge upon the bus company? sleuths theorized. Or was it only the bus driver whom he hated? Could Besaraba have known Sydney Granger and have been waiting for bus number 8702 just to kill him?

There was nothing to connect Besaraba with the other victims he shot, yet the gunman had waited at the bus stop while several other buses had arrived and departed, acting only when Granger's bus arrived. It seemed that Granger was the only possible enemy.

But before anything else was investigated, the police sent out the all-points "be on the lookout" for the 1986 silver Dodge sedan that Besaraba had taken to make his escape. The police supplied the license plate numbers to make it easy for any officer who saw the automobile to recognize it as the one taken by the gunman. It was possible the gunman would be caught in just a few hours, but hope of that soon faded.

If he was not arrested soon, sleuths knew there was little chance Besaraba would risk keeping the car for more than a day. He did not seem to be a stupid or confused man. He'd been incredibly calm and confident as he committed his crimes. Although it could have been prompted by madness, there was method in it. Yet Detective Doyle hoped Besaraba would keep the car. If he did, there was a chance he would be found because some alert policeman recognized the car or stopped it for some minor traffic violation. Besaraba might be as aggressive a driver as he was a killer. Only time would tell.

Yet the day passed, followed by the next and then another one, and the Hollywood Police Department received no word of Joseph Besaraba being found.

Detective Doyle could not put his investigation on hold and wait to see if Besaraba would be arrested in the stolen car. He and the Hollywood police worked at finding more witnesses and questioning everyone who knew Sydney Granger and who might know something about him that would provoke someone to kill him. It was tedious and time-consuming work.

Lawmen were told that everyone had liked Sydney Granger. He was a friendly, easygoing bus driver who was well liked by his fellow workers and judged dependable and trustworthy by his supervisor. He was fair, generous, and helpful. Passengers occasionally complained about other drivers, but none complained about Sydney.

One of Granger's regular passengers said of him, "Some of these drivers have nasty dispositions. This man was really a nice guy. Such a waste to do in such a nice guy."

Sleuths learned that Granger's home life was harmonious. His family was deeply aggrieved by his death.

The main hope of making any progress in the case was in finding the stolen car even if it was recovered without apprehending Besaraba in it. Sleuths felt they could possibly get Besaraba's fingerprints from the car once it was found. They believed that since Besaraba was so brazen in his murderous spree, he would most likely not have made an effort to conceal his activities.

Three days after the murders, the silver Dodge was found with Joseph Besaraba in it. There might have been still another killing had it not been for the lawman who spotted the Florida car parked beside state highway 80 in Brule, Nebraska, 1,900 miles from Hollywood, Florida. The officer, State Trooper Richard Cook, decided to radio his headquarters for a check on its Florida license plate, CWS 27R, before approaching it. The dispatch radioed back to Cook that the car had been stolen by a man who was wanted for two murders and other crimes. Cook and his partner approached the vehicle with drawn revolvers and tapped on its windows to awake a sleeping man on the rear seat. The man, Besaraba, opened the rear door and came out with his hands up. But when the officer holstered his revolver and tried to handcuff the prisoner, Besaraba ran back to the car and, diving into the driver's seat, reached for the gun he had hidden under the seat. Besaraba managed to get the gun but before he could use it, Trooper Cook threw himself on top of the prisoner and seized his wrists. The officer's partner threw himself on top of both men and for some time no one could move. Both the officers were big men; each weighed more than twice their prisoner. Besaraba had to release his hold on the handgun. Subsequent tests would prove that it was the same gun he had used to kill the two men in Hollywood.

Besaraba had his duffel bag in the car, and it proved

to have an unusual collection of his treasures. Among them was a United States passport and a permit to carry a pistol. That permit to have a handgun prompted a new drive to pass a law in the Florida legislature regulating the issuances of gun permits, but once more the gun-control measure failed to pass.

Detective Doyle took custody of the prisoner in Nebraska and brought him back to Broward County to be held for trial on the two charges of first-degree murder and the additional charges resulting from the assault upon William Fenton and the theft of his automobile. It was a strong case except for the lack of any known motive, normally essential in persuading a jury that the crime was premeditated and deserved a conviction of murder in the first degree.

The defendant denied his guilt and was uncooperative. He claimed he had been persecuted for years by the FBI and other unknown enemies. He said someone had poisoned him on the day of the murders, and he had no recollection of what he did on the Sunday of the murders up to the time he was arrested in Nebraska. However, Besaraba insisted he had committed no crime.

Assistant State's Attorney Charles Morton, who was assigned to prosecute, could be confident of a first-degree murder conviction only if he could discover Besaraba's motive. Without finding it, there was a good chance a jury might be persuaded that this senseless attack upon three men was the act of an insane man who should not be held accountable for his crimes. And months passed without Besaraba's motive for his attack being found out.

Prosecutor Morton had no doubt about the defendant's sanity. The defendant had been examined by psychiatrists as soon as he was returned to Broward County and was diagnosed as maladjusted and psychopathic but not insane. His behavior at the scene of the crime was indicative of an individual calmly performing a well-planned task. When he wanted a car for his getaway, he walked up to one stopped in traffic and ordered the driver to give it to him promptly or he would kill him.

But many a murderer has escaped conviction by persuading a jury he was insane, and then, after being committed to an asylum for the insane, the killer "recovered" his sanity and was released from custody. A.S.A. Morton was determined to resist such a ploy. He wanted to convict this defendant on first-degree murder and have him sentenced to death in the electric chair. It was essential, he knew, that he find the defendant's motive for attacking the bus driver. Morton was sure Besaraba killed because of some rational, human malice, however despicable and repulsive it might be, rather than because of a hysterical loss of self-control by a diseased mind. He knew there had to be a motive.

Besaraba continued to maintain his innocence. He said he had always been spied upon and mistreated by government agencies and he knew he would not get a fair trial. He claimed he was sane and would not tolerate counsel assigned to defend him to plead he was innocent because of insanity. Besaraba's objections to his lawyer ultimately prompted the lawyer to beg to be relieved of the assignment. A second lawyer was assigned and found that he could not prepare a defense because of Besaraba's uncooperative behavior. A third attorney, Dennis Bailey, was assigned, and when Besaraba asked to have him replaced—Besaraba also asked to have the judge replaced quite frequently—Judge Stanton Kaplan firmly refused. Yet it wasn't until January 22, 1992, that the trial finally began for the murders committed on July 23, 1989.

Some of the defendant's background was uncovered in those two and a half years that it took for the trial to get under way. Best of all, after the prosecutor had almost lost hope of learning Besaraba's motive for shooting the bus driver, a witness came forward to say that she was on the bus driven by Sydney Granger about an hour and a half before the murder when the bus was heading northbound to Fort Lauderdale. A man she now recognized from newspaper pictures as Joseph Besaraba was drinking something from a bottle he kept in a plastic bag. The bus driver told the man it was illegal to drink from the container, but the man refused to stop. Thereupon, the bus driver put him off the bus at a stop just short of Fort Lauderdale at Interstate 595.

When Besaraba was arrested in Nebraska, among the things found in his duffel bag was a bus ticket for that same trip from Young Circle to Fort Lauderdale with the time and date clearly stamped on it, proving that he was on the bus with the witness who belatedly appeared with the story of the killer's motive which A.S.A. Morton needed.

The other details of Besaraba's past showed him to be a man who could believe he was persecuted and would want to "get even." A gaunt man who weighed less than 100 pounds, Besaraba was born in Poland during the German occupation of that country in World War II, his parents having fled to Poland from Germany to escape Nazi persecution. Besaraba's older brother died of starvation during this period. When the war ended, the family suffered as much under the Russian occupation of Poland, so they hiked cross-country by night and hid by day, taking more than a month to reach the American zone, 80 miles away. Eventually, they were permitted to migrate to the United States.

Besaraba worked as a carpenter and did odd jobs for friends in his Boston neighborhood but rarely held a steady job for long. When he came to Florida, he obtained no work. There was no explanation of how he maintained himself except that he slept in various public parks and visited soup kitchens for his meals.

Just before the trial was to begin, Besaraba's attorney

asked the judge's permission to have the jury witness the electrocution of the next prisoner to die in the electric chair so the jurors would know what it meant to condemn a defendant to death. The lawyer also supported Besaraba's request that Judge Kaplan withdraw to let another judge try the case. The judge refused both requests.

The trial began on January 22nd as planned. Besaraba looked very different from the drifter who had killed the men on the bus two and a half years earlier. Instead of his long unkempt hair that had been tied into a ponytail hanging from the back of his head, his hair now was neatly trimmed. He was dressed in a conservative gray suit, wore a dark solid-color tie, had wire rim glasses, and comported himself as quietly as a librarian. Besaraba took extensive notes and frequently conferred with his two lawyers.

Assistant State's Attorney Morton described Besaraba's crime in lurid detail and told the jurors that he expected them to find the defendant guilty of murder in the first degree and recommend the death penalty.

Defense Attorney Bailey conceded that the defendant had killed two men on the bus that Sunday afternoon in July 1989, but insisted that these were not premeditated murders, and, therefore, he should be charged with murder in the second degree. He assured the jurors that there was no chance the defendant would escape punishment. Bailey asked only for an honest judgment of the evidence presented which would prompt the jurors to find Besaraba guilty of murder in the second degree.

The defendant was incensed by his lawyer's opening statement and repeated his request for another lawyer to be assigned to defend him. He told the judge and a newspaper reporter that he had never agreed to let his lawyer admit Besaraba's responsibility for the murders. Judge Kaplan felt that Bailey's opening statement was as good a defense of the man as could be made.

Bailey's conceding the facts of the killings did not relieve the prosecutor of the burden of proof beyond a reasonable doubt. The jurors still had to hear the testimony of all the witnesses to the crime and of the police and medical examiner and especially of the one victim who had survived.

In all, 29 witnesses were called to testify for the state. Some of the evidence showing gory pictures disturbed jurors. The descriptions of the bullet wounds in the corpses was given by a youthful associate medical examiner—Michael D. Bell, who looked more like a college freshman than a doctor. As he smiled a lot throughout his clinical testimony, grim expressions on all the jurors' faces could be seen. With photos to illustrate his explanations, Dr. Bell traced the course of the bullet that had entered Sydney Granger's throat and exited at the back of his head. The examiner believed Granger died within seconds of the injury. The other victim, Wesley Anderson, was shot three times, and the examiner recovered some of the bullets when he performed the autopsy.

William Fenton, who'd been paralyzed from the waist down as a result of the bullet Besaraba fired into his back, protested that he was too sick to leave his home in Georgia to testify at the trial. The prosecutor and the defense attorney agreed to show the jury a video recording of Fenton's testimony, but when the trial began after so many delays, Fenton decided he was well enough to appear. Defense Counselor Bailey objected to the state's calling Fenton to the stand after agreeing to use a video recording and advanced the defendant's claim that the judge could not be objective in his ruling.

However, Judge Kaplan ruled that State's Attorney Morton had a right to call the paralyzed Fenton to testify in person notwithstanding the prior agreement to use a recording.

No other witness appeared to have impressed the ju-

rors regarding the viciousness of Besaraba's shooting
spree as this young witness who was now confined to a
wheelchair for the rest of his life.

Then it was Bailey's turn to present his witnesses for
the defense and to plead that the defendant be found
guilty of murder in the second degree rather than subject
him to a life sentence or execution. Without claiming the
defendant was insane, Bailey tried to convince the jury
through a full day of testimony by a psychiatrist that Besaraba wasn't responsible for his violent behavior. The
persecution of his family, first by the Nazis and then Russian occupation troops in Poland, had programmed Besaraba to expect unfair treatment for the rest of his life,
the lawyer argued. For several years, Besaraba had been
so addicted to alcohol that he could not work, and he
became a vagrant. To get some spending money, he sold
his blood as frequently as he could manage it and served
as a subject for medical experimentation with new drugs.
His lifestyle made his claim that he'd "blacked out" on
the day of the murders credible. Bailey insisted the testimony of the state's witnesses did not prove that Besaraba
had planned his crimes, the essential condition for a verdict of guilty of first-degree murder.

Friends and neighbors who had known Besaraba when
he lived in Boston testified that he was a gentle man who
would not knowingly harm anyone. A member of his family who testified at great length said Besaraba had slowly
lost control of his life because of the hardships he'd suffered in his childhood.

Defense Attorney Bailey conceded that his client had
killed the two men on the bus but vigorously insisted that
he had not planned the crime and should therefore not
be found guilty of first-degree murder.

The prosecutor in his closing still demanded that the
jurors find Besaraba guilty of first-degree murder and recommend the death penalty.

After the jurors left the courtroom to deliberate, Besaraba asked the court's permission to read a statement that would be included in the transcript of the trial and be available to those who would consider his appeal from a possible verdict of guilty. Judge Kaplan warned the defendant that such a statement could harm his chance of a successful appeal, but he would permit the defendant to read his statement if he would allow his lawyer to see it and listen to any suggestions the lawyer made. Besaraba agreed to that and read the following:

"I've been under surveillance for thirty-five years by government agents, almost certainly the FBI. During this time, chemical substances were used on me for unknown reasons and purposes. These chemicals were illegally and unknowingly foisted upon me on the morning of July 23, 1989, before the murders in Young Circle, [which] caused me to have a complete loss of memory from the morning of July 23, 1989, until the time of my arrest in Nebraska on July 26, 1989.

"These government agents kept records and files of this surveillance and of the types and dosages they used on me. These files and records would prove my innocence and expose the wrongdoings and illegal acts of the government.

"I request under the Freedom of Information Act any file the FBI or other agency of the United States has on me.

"That is my statement."

The jury deliberated a little less than two hours. They found Joseph Besaraba guilty of all counts. They were released and instructed to return for a later hearing to recommend the sentence.

Once more, Defense Attorney Bailey pleaded for the jurors to mete out a life sentence rather than execution. After the jurors withdrew to deliberate, Besaraba again asked permission to read a statement for the record. It

"GUN-TOTING, WHEELCHAIR-BOUND KILLER"

by Steven Barry

Business was brisk at the Pine Watson Shopping Center almost every day of the week all year round. The shoppers came from every part of the borough of Langhorne, Pennsylvania, a suburb a few miles northeast of Philadelphia.

The Pine Watson Shopping Center was in the heart of town, at the intersection of Maple Avenue and Pine Street. It was thriving, yet peaceful. The auto thefts, stick-ups, and carjackings that plagued so many shopping complexes across the country seemed to bypass the Pine Waston plaza. Then, during the summer of 1994, all that changed for a few dramatic split-seconds.

The Langhorne Police Department first became aware of a breach of the peace shortly before 2:30 on the afternoon of June 3, 1994. A few minutes earlier, Patrick "Pat" Mooney had driven his fiancée to the shopping center. At 31, Mooney was young looking and muscular, a man of large stature, 6-foot-1 and 240 pounds, with dark, wavy hair. A union welder by trade, he'd started work that morning at 7:30—he was working on a big contract job at Graterford Prison—but he'd quit early, half an hour before noon, to come home.

Originally from South Philadelphia, Mooney came from a large family. He liked to hunt, fish, and play golf, and he liked to watch football on TV.

Roxanne Sullivan, Mooney's 39-year-old fiancée, was a brunette with shoulder-length hair. A divorced mother of three teenage children, she had reclaimed her maiden name three years earlier when her stormy marriage of 17 years ended in divorce. Sullivan's children lived with her ex-husband in the Highland Park section of nearby Levittown.

Mooney and Sullivan had been dating for 10 months and had been living together for nearly three months in the Country Manor Apartments in the 2100 block of Lincoln Highway in Levittown. They were planning to get married in the foreseeable future.

Once he arrived home on June 3rd, Pat Mooney took a shower and put on clean clothes: white athletic shorts, a T-shirt, gray socks, and white sneakers. Then Roxanne asked him to drive her to the Thrift Drug Store in the Pine Watson Shopping Center to get a prescription she had called in earlier.

At 2:23 P.M., Mooney pulled Roxanne's 1992 teal-colored Chevrolet Camaro RS up to the curb right outside the Thrift Drug Store and parked in the fire lane. Roxanne got out.

"I'll be right back," she said.

Mooney shut off the engine and rolled down the window.

At that moment inside the drugstore, a female cashier was punching out lottery tickets for a male customer who was in a wheelchair. The cashier glanced over the man's shoulder and watched as Roxanne Sullivan entered the store and went straight to the back, toward the pharmacy counter, without looking in her direction.

The man in the wheelchair asked the cashier about the triple-antibiotic cream that was on sale. She showed him a promotional display of the cream, and he bought two tubes and left the store.

At 2:26 P.M., a man was looking in the window of the gift shop that was next door to the Thrift Drug Store.

"I was looking for teddy bears for my daughter," the man would later say. "When I heard this noise, I looked over. This guy's wheelchair had hit the bottom of Thrift Drug's door."

The man in the wheelchair looked to be about 40 years old. He wore glasses and had long dark hair, a full beard and mustache, and he was wearing a dark T-shirt. After leaving the drug store, he rolled himself over to Roxanne Sullivan's Camaro and stopped next to the driver's door.

"Are you Pat Mooney?" the bearded man asked.

"Yeah," Mooney replied.

At that precise moment, a man who was standing inside a nearby pizza shop happened to look outside. Through the pizza shop window, he saw the man in the wheelchair pull something out of his pants.

"The guy in the wheelchair was about three feet away from the car," the witness inside the pizza shop recalled, "and his right arm was extended."

There was a pistol in the man's hand.

"No, no!" Mooney yelled at the man in the wheel chair. "Don't!"

The man in the wheelchair fired one shot into the car. The bullet drilled into the left posterior portion of Mooney's scalp, above and behind his left ear. It fractured his skull, which severely fragmented the bullet, then lacerated his meninges and brain before coming to rest in the frontal portion of Mooney's skull.

"After the first shot," the man inside the pizza shop continued, "the guy in the wheelchair opened the door of the car. The guy inside the car fell face-first onto the sidewalk and the guy in the chair continued to fire—it happened so fast. It sounded like an automatic, like a popping sound rather than the loud bang of a revolver."

"He was then shot four times," explained the man standing in front of the gift shop. "Point-blank. In the back. His body flipped over real fast and his head was straight up."

Of the last four shots, three struck the back of Mooney's left shoulder and passed partially through him, lacerating his second, third, and fourth intercostal muscle layers, his left lung, his pericardial sac, heart, and right lung, the right leaf of his diaphragm, and his liver. The fourth shot struck the back of Mooney's thorax on the left side and lacerated the underlying musculature. None of the five bullets exited his body.

At the sound of the gunfire, many of the shoppers in the parking lot ducked for cover, but one man kept walking across the parking lot. He was about 100 feet away from the Thrift Drug Store.

"I heard pop-pop-pop-pop," the third witness recalled, "just like that. It sounded like a car backfiring. Then I looked over and this guy in a wheelchair was motioning his hand downward with a gun in it. After he stopped firing, he wheeled his chair back a little bit and I could see the gun in his hand. Then he stuffed it into his belt and pushed himself away real fast.

"I started to go after him but, all of a sudden, I stopped—when I realized he had a gun."

Before the shooting started, Roxanne Sullivan was standing at the counter in the rear of the Thrift Drug Store, picking up her prescription for 30 doses of Xanex.

"How much?" she asked.

"Twenty-two ninety-nine," the pharmacist told her.

She paid in cash and was given the prescription. Then she heard the four rapid bangs exploding outside in the parking lot. Curious about the burst of gunfire, Sullivan walked up aisle two. About halfway to the front of the store, she could see outside through the store window.

"Oh, my God!" she said. "What happened?"

As Roxanne ran out, the pharmacist dialed 911 and reported the shooting.

"When I left Thrift Drugs," Roxanne Sullivan would later say, "I got up to the car and saw Pat. He was slumped on the ground on the driver's side and he was lying in a pool of his own blood. I saw blood coming out of his eye and out of his head."

Sullivan looked across the parking lot and caught a glimpse of the man speeding across the blacktop in his wheelchair, heading for the far side of the parking lot.

"You bastard!" she yelled. "Catch that son of a bitch! He shot my boyfriend!"

Overcome with emotion, Roxanne Sullivan dropped onto her knees on the sidewalk and cradled Mooney's head in her arms. "I love you, Pat," she repeated softly, over and over, her tears flowing freely.

A woman who was about to enter a nearby hair salon stopped and looked in the direction of the Thrift Drug Store. She saw Mooney and Sullivan on the ground, beside the Camaro.

"I ran over to the car," the woman would later recall, "and he was lying on his back. He was bleeding pretty bad. I started to give him CPR. He had a pulse, but he didn't respond. I kept up the CPR until the ambulance got here."

Less than a block from the shopping center, Officer Sean DiMeo was traveling south on Pine Street in a marked Langhorne Manor police car. At that moment, a police dispatcher's voice came on his car radio. By the time the dispatcher finished saying that a shooting had just taken place at the shopping center, Officer DiMeo's car was directly in front of the shopping center. DiMeo immediately turned right, into the busy parking lot, and saw a large group of people standing in front of the Thrift Drug Store.

"I observed a white male lying on the sidewalk in front of Thrift Drugs," Officer DiMeo would later say. "I got out of my vehicle and spoke with numerous witnesses at the scene. They stated that a white male, black hair, beard, and in a wheelchair [who was] heading toward the Meridian bank, had shot the man. I observed the actor going across the parking lot in his wheelchair."

"Meanwhile, a man had run inside the Shop'N'Bag supermarket and said, "Someone was just shot." A bag-boy who was on duty immediately ran outside. By the Thrift Drug Store, he saw a crowd gathering around someone who was lying on the ground.

"There goes the guy who shot him," a man said pointing at the bearded man speeding across the parking lot in his wheelchair.

The bag-boy chased after the man in the wheelchair and caught up to him just as he reached a black 1984 Chevrolet Monte Carlo parked in the last row of cars near Pine Street. The bag-boy grabbed the back of the wheelchair.

"I didn't do it," the man in the wheelchair told him.

"I can see the gun," the bag-boy replied.

"Leave me alone," the man in the wheelchair said. "He raped my daughter."

To the bag-boy, the man seemed pretty calm for someone who had just shot and killed someone. So he let go of the wheelchair, ran around to the back of the Monte Carlo, and wrote down the car's license number on a pack of cigarettes.

The man in the wheelchair opened the driver's door of the Monte Carlo, hoisted himself inside behind the wheel, then folded his wheelchair and tossed it on the backseat. Then he started the engine.

Less than a minute earlier, Officer Mike Jones of the

Langhorne Police Department had been dispatched to the Pine Watson Shopping Center. He was proceeding north on Pine Street, a few blocks south of the shopping center, with his emergency lights flashing and his siren wailing.

"I got on the radio," Officer DiMeo recalled, "and advised Officer Jones that I was on location with a person on the ground. I gave him a description of the actor and the actor's vehicle. Then I got back in my vehicle and went after him."

While DiMeo was turning on his emergency lights, activating his siren, and initiating pursuit, the Monte Carlo backed up, pulled forward, then turned left onto Pine Street.

"The actor is now leaving the shopping center in a black Chevy Monte Carlo heading north on Pine Street," DiMeo radioed.

At that moment, Officer Jones's car pulled into view and started to slow down.

"He just turned in front of you," DiMeo told Jones. "The black Monte Carlo right in front of you is the actor."

Officer Jones accelerated and quickly caught up to the fleeing Monte Carlo. He radioed the Bucks County dispatcher with the information that the suspect's tag number was Pennsylvania JMY-300.

DiMeo left the parking lot and moved his car into position behind Jones's car. From that point on, a high-speed chase began, twisting and turning through the residential streets of Langhorne.

First came a series of right turns: onto Winchester Avenue, onto North Flowers Mill Road, and onto Maple Avenue. Upon each change of direction, Jones advised the police dispatcher of his current location and the new direction of the pursuit. They were now heading west on Maple Avenue and were approaching a straightaway.

Jones swerved left, accelerated, and passed the Monte Carlo. He was trying to box the black car between his car and DiMeo's, which had moved into position directly behind the Monte Carlo. But the Monte Carlo made a quick left onto Cherry Street—foiling the lawman's risky maneuver—followed by a quick right onto Flowers Avenue that sent the chase back across Pine Street.

Both police cars were once again behind the Monte Carlo as it sped through stop sign after stop sign along Flowers Avenue before turning left onto Bellevue Avenue, heading south for a short distance, then turning right once again, at Gilliam Avenue. The three cars raced up and across an overpass. At the bottom of the downstroke of the bridge, the Monte Carlo turned left onto Highland Avenue, then right onto Hulmeville Avenue, then right again onto commercial Route 1, where it accelerated until it reached the entrance ramp leading onto Interstate 95.

While the chase through the borough was taking place, officers from the Langhorne, Middletown Township, and Lower Southampton Township Police Departments and the Bucks County Parks Department were monitoring its progress. Some of the officers drove parallel routes while others tried to get ahead of the Monte Carlo so that they could establish a roadblock.

"When I heard that the vehicle was now southbound on I-95, from Route 1," Detective Dan Baranoski of the Middletown Township PD would later explain, "I turned onto I-95 southbound and requested the dispatcher to contact the Bensalem police to also assist us."

Bensalem was the next township to the south, along I-95.

Traffic on I-95 was heavy at that time. For nearly three miles, the Monte Carlo kept cutting out of one lane and into another to avoid being overtaken from behind, its speed never dipping below 85 miles per hour and topping out at 105. But as the Monte Carlo neared the Street

Road exit, traffic up ahead had ground to a virtual stand-still—due to a roadblock of the southbound lanes that had been set up by Bensalem police officers.

"At this time," Jones would later explain, "the actor's vehicle proceeded onto the right shoulder of the roadway and continued until it came upon a Bensalem police officer. The actor's vehicle then came to a stop and the actor raised his hands."

Seconds later, Officers Jones and DiMeo braked their vehicles to a stop. With weapons drawn, they approached the black Monte Carlo with extreme caution. They suspected that the driver had just shot someone, they assumed that he was still armed, and they considered him extremely dangerous.

When Jones and DiMeo reached the Monte Carlo on foot, they noticed that a Bensalem police officer already had his gun leveled at the suspect. While Jones slowly maneuvered himself toward the driver's door, other police officers arrived at the scene and moved into position around the Monte Carlo to assist in the arrest. When Jones felt that it was safe, he opened the driver's door of the Monte Carlo.

"Step from the vehicle," Jones instructed the driver.

"I'm handicapped," the man responded. "I can't walk."

Jones pulled the suspect out of the car, placed him on the ground, and tried to handcuff him.

"Give me your hands," Jones told the suspect, but the man started thrashing around and grabbing the officer's arms with both of his hands. DiMeo, Ranger Tom Mumford of the Bucks County Parks Department, and Officer Andy Amoroso of the Middletown Township Police Department all moved in to help Jones.

"I saw a gun tucked in the front of the suspect's pants," Amoroso would later say, "and I took the gun at that time. The gun was a Smith and Wesson semiautomatic nine-millimeter, Model 5906, stainless steel with black plastic handgrips. The weapon was loaded with one round in the chamber and nine rounds in the magazine."

"That gun's pretty accurate, isn't it?" the bearded suspect commented to Amoroso. Then, suddenly, he asked, "Where's my thirty-eight?"

Ranger Mumford, who still had one knee on the suspect's back to immobilize him, looked down and saw the grip of a second handgun sticking out of the suspect's waistband, around back, on the right-hand side. The ranger removed it at once. The second gun was a Smith and Wesson .38-caliber revolver, Model 60. It was loaded with five live rounds.

Two of the officers then lifted the suspect and placed him against the car so that Jones could pat him down to see if he was carrying any more weapons. He was not.

When the suspect was handcuffed and no longer a threat, Jones advised him of his constitutional rights.

"Why didn't you do this to the guy who raped my daughter?" the suspect asked the officers in a loud, boisterous voice. "I did it because you guys couldn't take care of the problem. What would you do if someone raped your daughter? Do you have a daughter? What would you do? You would have done the same thing."

Two officers then carried the suspect to Jones's patrol car and placed him in the backseat. Moments later, Jones pulled away to take the suspect to a nearby state police barracks.

"By the way," the man said during the drive, "my name is Colson. What's yours?"

"Officer Michael Jones of the Langhorne Police Department."

"Man," the suspect said, "I'm really sorry I had to get you guys going like this, but I told Detective Kemmerer [of the Middletown Township PD] that if he didn't get this guy off the street, I was going to do it for him. It had to be done. It had to be done."

About 20 minutes later, at 3:15 P.M., Jones arrived at the state police barracks. Corporal Jeff Backenstoss and Detective Mario Battistini, of the Pennsylvania State Police, brought a chair outside and carried the suspect up a flight of steps and inside the Trevose Barracks, into the Criminal Investigation Office.

"Are you okay?" Corporal Backenstoss asked.

"Yes," the suspect replied.

"Do you need anything to drink?"

When the suspect said he was thirsty, the trooper got him a can of Pepsi. When the suspect indicated that he was uncomfortable because his pants were bothering him, the trooper helped him adjust them. When the suspect said he was cold, the trooper turned off the air-conditioning and got him a blanket.

The suspect gave his full name as Colson Derby Jr. A 40-year-old former steelworker, he'd been a paraplegic from the waist down ever since a commuter train hit him from behind while he was riding a motorcycle along the Conrail right-of-way about a half-mile east of the Langhorne station. He was also the ex-husband of Roxanne Sullivan.

At 3:23 P.M., with Jones and Detective Battistini acting as witnesses, Corporal Backenstoss advised Derby of his rights.

"We're investigating a shooting that you were involved in at the Pine Watson Shopping Center," Backenstoss informed Derby. He then asked, "What happened?"

"I went to Thrift Drugs," Derby began, "and bought Lotto tickets and triple antibiotics. I saw my ex-wife walk in and walk down an aisle. She was alone. I was at the checkout counter when I saw her, but I don't think she saw me. Everything just went blank after I saw her. I just lost it.

"I always carry a thirty-eight and a nine-millimeter semiautomatic. They're both loaded with hydroshocks. I have a license to carry. I carry the guns because I'm in the chair. I've had a couple of incidents where I was grabbed in the chair and beaten up. I don't know which gun I pulled out. I think it was the nine-millimeter because that's the one I always go to first.

"All I remember is, when I came out of the store I asked the guy if he was Pat Mooney. He said, 'Yeah,' and jumped out of the car and came at me. I grabbed his arm and pushed him aside, to keep him from jumping on me. I pushed him off me just enough to get the gun. I grabbed the gun and fired—I don't know how many times. I don't know what he did. I wheeled over to my car and left the area. It was parked on the other side of the parking lot, near the bank. I didn't see anybody in the parking lot when I shot—I blanked out. I didn't know where I was going. I saw the cops behind me around Flowers Mill Road. I don't know why I didn't stop."

The state trooper asked Derby if he and his ex-wife had been experiencing any sort of domestic problems.

"Not really," Derby replied. "There have been no problems between my ex-wife and me. I had a problem with Pat Mooney, though. He raped my daughter about a month ago. I just found out about it this past Sunday night. Detective Kemmerer from Middletown Township is investigating it. Since it happened, she's been screwed up. She's been cutting her hands and taking a baby bottle to bed.

"My wife started calling my house harassing me about the detectives coming around and invading her privacy and asking a lot of questions. I only got on the phone once, but she called a couple of times. The one time I talked to her, I told her off. She hasn't called back since. I haven't had any contact with Mooney since I found out about the rape. I didn't even know what he looked like—until today."

"Do you use drugs?" Backenstoss asked.

"I take a Valium on occasion, when my legs kill me—they burn all the time. I took a Valium last night, about ten-thirty or eleven, before I went to bed. I haven't taken any drugs today."

"What about alcohol?"

"I haven't had any alcohol to drink since Memorial Day weekend. I drank some whiskey mixed with soda or tea."

"When you said you always went for the nine-millimeter first," Corporal Backenstoss asked, "what did you mean?"

"When I go to the firing range," Derby replied, "to practice."

At 4:14 P.M., Backenstoss gave Derby a copy of his statement to review. Derby read it and acknowledged that it was accurate. When the interview ended at 4:23, Derby said he had a headache. The trooper then got him two glasses of water and two extra-strength Tylenol gelcaps.

"How's Mooney?" Derby asked Detective Battistini. "Is he dead?"

"I honestly don't know," Battistini replied.

Nearly two hours earlier, an ambulance had rushed Pat Mooney from the Pine Watson Shopping Center to Saint Mary Hospital. En route, paramedics did everything they could to resuscitate Mooney and prolong his life. The ambulance arrived at the hospital at 2:44 P.M.

"Apparently," a physician wrote on the emergency room consultation report, "the patient was pulled out of the car by bystanders and they were giving him resuscitation, but the patient did not respond. By the time paramedics arrived, the patient had no vital signs. He was completely unconscious. No breath sounds could be heard. No heart sounds, no pulse, no carotid pulse, pupils were fixed and dilated.

"The paramedics did an endotracheal intubation and with CPR in progress, they brought the patient here. When he arrived here, the patient was essentially DOA.

"His body temperature was cold and he was already purplish over his upper chest. . . . The patient was seen by the entire trauma team on his arrival. He was also seen by a neurosurgeon [who] immediately saw the gunshot wound [to the left side of his head] with the brain tissue coming out.

"The patient was pronounced dead at 2:52 P.M."

Some seven hours after the shooting had taken place, police investigators interviewed Colson Derby Jr. for the second time at the state police barracks in Trevose. This time, Troopers Bob Stroud and Ed Donorovich and Chief Jim McAndrew, of the Langhorne PD, conducted the interview.

At 7:25 P.M., Derby was read his Miranda rights. He waived those rights and agreed to make a statement.

"I got up at eleven or twelve o'clock," Derby told the investigators. "About two P.M., I went to Meridian Bank and withdrew two hundred dollars. Then I went to Thrift Drugs." From there, Derby described his actions almost exactly as he had the first time to Corporal Backenstoss, Detective Battistini, and Officer Jones: He said he came out of the Thrift Drug Store, saw his ex-wife's Camaro parked at the curb, saw a man sitting behind the wheel, and asked the man if he was Mooney.

"Why did you ask him if his last name was Mooney?" Chief McAndrew asked.

" 'Cause if I didn't," Derby replied, "I wouldn't have known who to shoot."

At 8:39 P.M., Officers Jones and DiMeo transported Derby to district court in Fallsington, where District Justice Jan Vislosky charged him with criminal homicide and related weapons offenses. Constables then transported Derby to the county jail to be held without bail until his preliminary hearing, which was scheduled for August.

"This is not a great whodunit," District Attorney Alan Rubenstein said afterward. "There is no question it was Derby's former wife and the deceased was Roxanne Sullivan's boyfriend. So the issue is not the what or how, it's the why?"

The *why* boiled down to whether or not Pat Mooney had raped one of Derby's daughters. Opinions varied.

"We have not seen the Middletown Township police reports," Corporal Petillo Jones, a state police supervisor, told the press. "There have been some swirling allegations, though unsubstantiated, that something to that effect might have been in Mr. Derby's mind. It remains to be seen if there is any credence to those allegations."

On Memorial Day, just four days before Pat Mooney was shot and killed, Colson Derby Jr. had accompanied one of his daughters to the Middletown Township Police Station to file a criminal complaint alleging that Mooney had sexually molested the girl.

"If you don't arrest him," Derby had told Detective Dave Kemmerer at the time the complaint was filed, "I'll take care of him myself."

"We told him that a thorough investigation was necessary," Detective Kemmerer told a reporter, "but he didn't seem to be interested in finding out the truth."

What was the truth?

"There was no rape," Roxanne Sullivan told a reporter. "My ex-husband was motivated by pure jealousy. His feeling was, if he couldn't have me, nobody else could either."

But one of Derby's relatives disagreed with Sullivan.

"She said it was a love triangle," Derby's relative told the same reporter, "but that isn't the case. If you want the truth, just ask the Middletown police."

The Middletown police, however, were suddenly refusing to make any comments regarding the rape investigation. Since the rape charges appeared to be related to the homicide charges and since both cases were open investigations, a gag order had been imposed. Detective Kemmerer issued a statement saying that he had been instructed by the district attorney's office not to discuss the case with the press.

Two days before his death, Pat Mooney had agreed to submit to a polygraph examination. The exam had been scheduled for 6:00 P.M. on the night of June 3rd, just a little more than three hours after he was killed.

"Pat Mooney did not deserve to die," Assistant District Attorney Terry Houck would say later, "but he's dead now and can't say whether or not [the sexual molestation] ever happened. What we have here instead is a willful, cold-blooded, and premeditated act.

"This is not an accidental killing. This is complete willfulness—putting a bullet into Pat Mooney's skull, then four more in his back."

Shortly after Mooney's death, one of his family members issued a statement to the press:

"Since Pat is not here to defend himself, we feel we must speak in his behalf. There were allegations made against Patrick. Naturally, we were distressed to hear this. However, the police informed us that they contacted Patrick and he denied the allegations.

"The police also informed us that he was very cooperative and volunteered to take a lie-detector test. He wanted his name cleared. We find it very suspicious that he was gunned down by Mr. Derby three hours before his appointment with the police."

With Mooney dead, the truth would probably never be learned about the rape allegations. However, the truth continued to be told about Colson Derby Jr.

A little more than two months after the shooting, on August 18, 1994, Derby's preliminary hearing was held at district court in Penndel. Prosecutor Terry Houck called an eyewitness who testified to seeing Derby pump five bullets into Mooney in cold blood. Houck also called Trooper Don Thomas, a forensic expert, who stated that the five 9mm shell casings that had been found near Mooney's body were consistent with the five 9mm slugs that had been removed from Mooney's corpse during the autopsy. Next, the trooper said that ballistic tests had verified that those five slugs had been fired from the 9mm semiautomatic pistol that Derby had been carrying at the time of his arrest.

The defense attorney called no witnesses.

District Justice Catherine Marks bound Derby over for trial and remanded him to the county jail without bail.

Derby's trial began three months later, on November 14, 1994, in Courtroom 3 of the Bucks County Courthouse in Doylestown, with Judge Edward Beister presiding. The trial lasted four days. On November 18th, the jury rejected the defense attorney's claims that Derby was insane at the time he killed Mooney. They found Derby guilty of first-degree murder.

"It won't bring Pat back," one of Mooney's family members said after hearing the verdict, "but it will clear his name. It confirmed our belief that he never raped the girl."

"It tells everyone in the community," the prosecutor said, "that you can't take the law into your own hands. Derby judged Mooney guilty, he sentenced him to death, then he carried out the execution."

For his crimes, Colson Derby Jr. was sentenced on November 29, 1994. Pending the results of any subsequent appeals, Derby will be spending the rest of his life in prison with no chance for parole. Ironically, Derby is currently being housed in the Graterford Prison, which is where Pat Mooney was working as a welder at the time he was murdered.

"PRETTY CABBIE'S ONE-WAY RIDE TO TERROR!"

by Chris Kelly

On Friday, February 19, 1993, the town of Tarboro, North Carolina, prepared for its first snowfall of the winter as the temperatures slid down into the 20s.

It was an extremely busy Friday night for City Cab, the largest taxi company in the small southern town. The harried dispatcher was busy fielding the numerous incoming calls, then radioing instructions to the cab drivers on duty that night. She recorded everything on the company manifest sheet, logging time, location, cab number, destination, number of passengers, and fare charged.

Mary Ann Lee, an attractive 26-year-old, was driving cab 103, a yellow LTD Ford station wagon. At 7:30 P.M., she received a radio message from the dispatcher that there was a "special" request for her cab. Lee picked up her fare at the Liberty Inn motel on West Wilson Street and took the young man to the Lakeside Trailer Park. She returned to the mobile home for the same man at 9:30 P.M. and drove him back to his motel, where he planned to attend a party. Two rooms, 31 and 32, of the one-story, cinder-block-and-brick motel had been rented that night for the shindig. As Mary Ann pulled away from the motel, she could still hear the loud music and the revelers' voices.

Paula Askew, another young Tarboro resident, was visiting friends at Pinehurst Homes, an area housing complex. Paula, who had a drug problem, was high from smoking crack cocaine, drinking numerous beers, and downing several shots of liquor. At 10:30 P.M., Paula called City Cab for a taxi to take her home. When she saw Mary Ann driving the cab, she recognized her as a former schoolmate and was delighted to climb into the front seat with her.

A few blocks from Paula's home, the two women saw fire trucks and police cars in the area—a local house was on fire. Paula asked Mary Ann to stop the cab—she wanted to join the gawkers gathered nearby. As she jumped out of the cab, she asked Mary Ann not to leave. Then Paula worked her way through the milling crowd, excited by the chaotic jumble of towering flames, flashing lights, screaming sirens, and people yelling. To Paula, it was just another loud party. As she made her way, she spotted a relative of hers and asked to exchange her lightweight coat for a warmer one in the frigid night air.

When Paula returned to the waiting cab, Mary Ann said she had to make another run to the Liberty Inn. Concerned about the possibility of being robbed, she asked Paula to ride with her, saying that she would feel safer. Although they were only a short distance from Paula's home, Paula agreed to accompany her friend.

When they arrived at the motel, Mary Ann and Paula realized that they were acquainted with the two young men waiting for the cab. From the rear seat, one of the passengers directed Mary Ann to a relative's home near Eason Farms outside the town. Meanwhile, the women began chatting about their children and old friends, ignoring the conversation of the passengers in the backseat.

Cab 103 proceeded down Main Street, then went past

the brightly lit hospital along Highway 64-Alternate, heading out of town. About eight miles later, the man sitting directly behind Mary Ann directed her to turn left onto Hart's Chapel Road. The two-lane paved road had no street lights, and because it was a moonless night, the darkness seemed to become deeper, ominously enveloping the cab.

As Mary Ann continued to follow directions, she turned up a narrow dirt road and was surprised to see no houses there. The cab was in the middle of a large field. Now the pretty cabbie slowly began to turn the low-slung station wagon around in the uneven, bumpy field. As she did so, she radioed her dispatcher to inform her that she was lost. "I think I'm at the Eason Farms," Mary Ann said.

City Cab owner Sam North was at home when he heard the radio transmission over his receiver. Always concerned about the safety of his drivers, North often monitored their calls, listening for indications of trouble. He heard the dispatcher inquire if Mary Ann needed any help, saying that another cab would be sent to find her, and Mary Ann's reply that it wasn't necessary.

It was now a quarter past eleven o'clock, and Friday night's business continued to be as hectic as usual.

Taxi dispatchers have special codes they routinely use for communicating with the drivers. Upon receiving a request for a cab, a dispatcher radios a driver using the driver's identification number to relay a pickup address. The driver then replies, "Ten-four," meaning that the message has been received. Then the driver radios back with the number of passengers and their destination. After the fares have been dropped off, the driver tells the dispatcher, "ten-twenty-four," which means, in effect, "I'm empty and ready for another assignment." It is also understood that drivers will notify the dispatcher when-

ever they leave their cabs so that pickups can be assigned
to other drivers.

About 1:30 A.M. on Saturday, the dispatcher on the next
shift became concerned when she realized that cab 103
had not been heard from since Mary Ann Lee's "Eason
Farms—I'm lost" transmission, nor had Mary Ann indicated that she was leaving her cab. Since drivers have
been known to stop calling in after several futile attempts
to reach a busy dispatcher, the night-shift dispatcher
wasn't unduly alarmed. But then she radioed 103 numerous times and got no replies, only silence. Any extended
break in radio contact is regarded as serious by the cab
company, so the dispatcher immediately contacted the
Tarboro Police Department. A search for cab 103 was
then quickly set into motion by both the city police and
the Edgecombe County Sheriff's Department.

Other City Cab drivers on duty that night became
concerned when they heard that Mary Ann Lee was
missing. One coworker told a police officer that she remembered see Mary Ann's cab at 11:00 P.M., when the
coworker had dropped off one fare at Heritage Hospital
and picked up a second one from nearby Glenoit Mills.
The cabbie said she had passed cab 103 at that time,
traveling in the opposite direction on North Main
Street. For a brief moment the two cabs had been side
by side on the well-lit street, and the other cabbie had
seen four people in cab 103.

"When I was getting ready to pass," she said, "a black
male put his head up to the glass and looked at me, and
there was a second passenger in the rear seat." The cabbie said that she and her passenger both had a clear view
of the two men, and also of the "figure and outline" of
a black woman in the front seat with Mary Ann.

Police officers concentrated their search on the streets
of the darkened city while sheriff's deputies checked the
area outside the city limits. Canvassing the Eason Farms

area were Sergeant Curtis Easton and an intern officer, 20-year-old Kristie Flynt Baity, an East Carolina University student who would later join the city police department of Winston-Salem, North Carolina.

As they drove along Hart's Chapel Road in the middle of the night, Officers Easton and Baity carefully scrutinized the blacktop for signs of anything unusual. Suddenly, they saw what looked like fresh tire tracks leading from a dirt path back onto the paved road. With only the cruiser's headlights to guide them in the darkness, Easton slowly drove up the bumpy path, following the muddy tracks. The two officers soon found themselves in a large, fallow field that fronted Hart's Chapel Road and extended to a stand of trees in the rear. As they looked around, they realized that they could not see the tall treetops from the paved road due to the lay of the land. The area had become a lovers' lane used by many amorous Edgecombe County couples.

The narrow road crested at the top of a gradual incline, then dipped down unexpectedly. As Easton hit the brakes, the heavy brown patrol car shuddered to a stop. The two officers stared through the windshield as the glaring headlights outlined a gruesome sight: a bloody, mangled body was lying in the middle of the muddy path.

The missing cab driver had now been found, but her yellow cab was nowhere to be seen.

Sheriff's Lieutenant Jerry A. Wiggs is in charge of all criminal investigations for Edgecombe County. At 3:45 A.M., the lieutenant received a call notifying him of the homicide and he quickly dressed and left his home. At the crime scene, he found the body of Mary Ann Lee lying face up on the cold, damp ground, naked except for her white shirt and her bra that had been ripped in half. Her once pale skin was covered with bloody lacerations from head to toe. Incredibly, her tennis shoes and socks remained on her small feet. One leg grotesquely twisted, was later determined to be broken in several places.

As the chief detective surveyed the field, he saw that numerous tire tracks had beaten down the brown knee-high weeds and surmised that the dead woman had been run over by a vehicle and probably dragged across the field. A tire-tread imprint was still visible on her bloody left cheek. But the most devastating memory the seasoned investigator of almost 50 homicide cases would carry away with him was the look of shock and horror frozen on the victim's face. Her eyes bulged, large and sightless, and her mouth was open wide in a desperate and soundless scream.

Meanwhile, just before 6:00 A.M., Detective Bob Davis, a 14-year veteran with the sheriff's department, left his warm bed, got dressed, and prepared to leave for work. As he drove out of his yard, the predicted snow began to fall. Davis joined his boss and other officers at the Eason Farm field as they began to search for physical evidence linked to the gruesome murder.

Dennis Honeycutt, a State Bureau of Investigation (SBI) agent, also joined the search. In charge of the Mobile Crime Lab for the SBI's Northeast District, Honeycutt was especially concerned about the worsening weather. He knew that fingerprints on the surface of any evidential items found could be washed away by the moisture of the snow. Among the objects the probers picked up in the lovers' lane were some condoms, beer cans, bottles, and even a pair of black panties. It was later determined that the panties did not belong to the slain cab driver.

Meanwhile, in downtown Tarboro, Police Corporal Jay Boykin was driving along Sorey Avenue when the first snowflakes softly hit his windshield. At that very moment, he spotted the missing yellow taxi parked on the street. It was just three blocks from the Liberty Inn motel, where Mary Ann Lee had picked up her last known fare.

Lieutenant Wiggs was in the midst of videotaping the crime scene out at Eason Farms when he was informed that cab 103 had been found. Before he could complete the taping, all traces of the muddy tire tracks, the beaten-down grass, and the gory trail were covered by a pristine layer of snow. Even the victim's body was lying beneath the blanket of snow until it could be removed by ambulance to Heritage Hospital for an autopsy.

When the investigators left the crime scene, they discovered a trail of paper and many of Mary Ann's personal items scattered along Hart's Chapel Road. It looked as though everything had been thrown haphazardly from a moving vehicle. Among the items found were one of the victim's earrings, a key, some money, and some receipts bearing the City Cab logo. Police Sergeant Rob Cherry even found Mary Ann's pocketbook and brown wallet lying in the middle of the highway.

Lieutenant Wiggs and Detectives Bob Davis and Gary Brady began to canvass the residents who lived within a three-mile radius of the crime scene. The sleuths knocked on each door and asked if anyone had seen or heard anything unusual on Friday night or early Saturday morning.

Most of the persons they questioned had been asleep, but one woman who lived near the Hart's Chapel Road turnoff said she remembered hearing a car drive into her yard around midnight. A horn blew, but she didn't go to the door because her "old man" was sick.

It snowed all morning, and by the time cab 103 was loaded onto a flatbed wrecker, it, too, turned white. Before it was wrapped in protective covering for transport to SBI headquarters in Raleigh, the state capital, the detectives performed a preliminary examination and photographed the vehicle. They found blood on the low-riding chassis, and spatters and streaks on the hood, front grill, fenders, and tires. Moreover, shreds of the black stretch pants Mary Ann had been wearing that night were hanging from beneath the taxi's framework, tangled around the driveshaft of the rear axle. On the front right seat, the officers found a knife, which they later learned was recently purchased by Mary Ann for protection after she'd been robbed by one of her passengers.

Now Detectives Davis and Brady began a house-to-house search in the Sorey Avenue area of downtown Tarboro. After interviewing several homeowners, the investigators determined that the cab had been abandoned on the street sometime between 11:45 P.M. and Friday midnight.

One resident said there had been no cab there when she turned off her porch light at 11:15 P.M., but when her son left the house at midnight, the yellow taxi was parked on the street.

Another homeowner told the sleuths that he heard a vehicle pull up in front of his home, immediately followed by the sound of two car doors slamming. Curious, the man peeked out a window and saw a cab parked there. When he looked again 15 minutes later, it was still there, so he went outside to ask that the cab be moved, but there was no driver.

In memory of Mary Ann Lee, a wreath was hung on the door of City Cab's Fountain Street office as her despondent coworkers attempted to cope with the company's first murder in its 24-year-history.

In remembering the 4-foot-10 driver, one of her fellow cabbies said, "She would have given anyone a free ride if they didn't have money. She was that type of person." He added that he had often scolded Mary Ann for giving too many freebies, thereby reducing her own income.

City Cab owner Sam North had become vehement over the senseless and cruel murder of his employee, who was short in stature, but big at heart. "When somebody is out there to serve the public . . . who's being a help to everybody—that's worse than bad!" he declared angrily.

North's taxi service operates around the clock, seven days a week. Most of the fares are people who need transportation to and from work, church, or doctor's appointments, and many have been his customers since 1969. Mary Ann's murder scared the hell out of North, but he vowed to continue his operation, because many townspeople had no other means of transportation. His 20 drivers always had the option of refusing any passenger whom they had reason to be wary of, and he hoped that each one would begin to think about working in a safer way. In an effort to assist with the murder investigation, North added $1,000 of his own money to the $5,000 reward already being offered for information that would lead to Mary Ann's killers.

The murder case was designated top priority by Edgecombe County Sheriff Phil Ellis, but it became temporarily sidetracked by two other homicides that occurred within his jurisdiction. The Tarboro taxicab murder investigation got back on track with Investigators Wiggs, Davis, and Brady working many long and frustrating hours to get the case solved.

Not quite 40, Jerry Wiggs, is a 19-year veteran of law enforcement. His red hair and mustache have darkened, but are also showing streaks of gray. His chocolate-brown eyes are stern, reflecting the seriousness and heavy demands of his job.

Darkly tanned, Gary Brady is a family man and a proud grandfather at only 40 years of age. He and his 36-year-old partner, Bob Davis, make a great team. Davis is a tall, gentle man who smiles easily and often, despite the somberness of his job.

In the course of the probe, the detectives began receiving many anonymous tips from the community, because the young and generous cab driver had been well liked. Still, it proved to be a difficult investigation. The sleuths often had to interview five or more people in order to turn up a single substantial witness. Sometimes they had only a nickname to work with, and only after questioning dozens of people were they able to find someone who knew the individual they were searching for.

Brady and Davis always interviewed each witness together to ensure that no one could accuse them of misquoting what was said. When it was necessary to establish the credibility of a witness, they would escort that person to the sheriff's office, located at the rear of the county courthouse. There, Lieutenant Wiggs would seat each witness in a wooden chair next to his desk, where all of his polygraph equipment was laid out. Wiggs would hook each person up to the paraphernalia to determine if that witness was telling the truth.

The three detectives met daily to discuss what progress they had made. It was a long, tedious process, but they gradually began to collect each piece of the puzzle—evidence which the lieutenant kept in his small office.

Many of the numerous tips led to dead ends. In one instance, the investigators went to question a man who lived in a white house in the Eason Farms area. He supposedly knew all about the murder. When Detectives Brady and Davis drove up the circular driveway, however, the found only an elderly man who had suffered a debilitating stroke, leaving him both deaf and blind.

Another man in nearby Orange County contacted the detectives one night after having read about the murder in a Raleigh newspaper. The caller said he was a member of a social club and he was convinced that one of his club friends was somehow involved in the killing because he'd been "acting strange."

Another tipster gave the investigators the name of a young woman, claiming she had been in cab 103 that Friday night and that her jacket was stained with Mary

Ann Lee's blood. But when Davis and Brady attempted to find this suspect, they learned that she had left town.

With the autopsy completed, the sheriff's office received a copy of the medical examiner's report. The M.E. was unable to determine the order in which Mary Ann's extensive injuries had occurred. All that could be said was that she had died from massive internal injuries.

The report listed "crushing injuries of the chest and abdomen" from having been run over and dragged by the cab—injuries so severe that her left lung was ripped from its position. The pathologist also found the liver and pancreas lacerated, and the vein that supplies blood to the heart destroyed. Abrasions covered the victim's entire body and head, and her face had been crushed, as had one of her legs.

A rape kit had been hand-delivered to the SBI lab. The test for sexual assault came back negative.

The slain woman came from a large family who now grieved at the untimely loss of their loved one. Their "Messy Ann," as they affectionately called her, had loved life and had even dreamed of becoming a famous singer. She had married young, but she was separated at the time of her death, and she drove the cab to support her two elementary school-aged children. Even though she was less than five feet tall, her family was sure the spunky woman had fought valiantly against her attackers in a desperate attempt to live.

Room 32 of the Liberty Inn motel became the focus of the investigation—it was where Mary Ann had picked up her last known fare. Detectives Davis and Brady questioned Charles King, a young, muscular black male who had rented the motel room at seven o'clock on the night of February 19th. King said that he had just received a $2,200 tax refund check and wanted to party with his friends and have some fun, so they spent the money on drugs, liquor, beer, and women. King, however, steadfastly denied that a cab had picked up any of his guests that night.

King's party, and one in the adjoining room, had become a "floating" affair, with everyone going back and forth between the two rooms. They even invited friends they encountered on the city streets to join in the merrymaking back at the motel.

When the detectives attempted to interview the persons in this long list of partygoers, they faced a wall of silence. Many of the group were related and not about to say anything incriminating about each other. Also, the guests knew they had broken the law by smoking crack cocaine that night, and they were afraid of being arrested if they admitted it to the investigators.

"We're not narcotics officers," Detective Davis told these individuals as he urged them to talk about the party. "We're homicide detectives. We're not interested in the drugs that were going on there—we only want to know about this murder. Tell us you were smoking crack . . . We're not going to charge you!" But the partygoers wouldn't talk. They knew that the motel rooms had been rented for illegal drug activities. They didn't want to go to jail.

Many of the anonymous tips received by the investigators indicated that a couple of guys named Artis Felton Johnson and Joseph Earl Bellamy were involved in Mary Ann Lee's murder. Johnson was one of Charles King's many guests. Bellamy was a party guest in room 31. Both men were well known at the county jail.

The 26-year-old Johnson had a long criminal record of violence, including assault on a female, hit-and-run, resisting arrest, and driving with a revoked license. In 1988, he received a two-year sentence for assault on a law enforcement officer. In addition, he was presently under indictment for rape, and had been questioned about an arson case that Detective Davis was investigating. Johnson worked as a plumber in a family owned business which had an excellent reputation. He appeared to be cooperating fully with the investigation, but he denied that cab 103 had picked him up at the motel after 10:30 that night.

Joe Bellamy was a 25-year-old who lived on the streets and made money by selling drugs. He had charges pending against him for breaking and entering of a motor vehicle, larceny of a firearm, assault on a female, and second-degree trespass. He was also wanted for violating the conditions of a current probation.

Both young men wore their hair short, were of medium height, and weighed 165 pounds. Bellamy had a short beard. Johnson was blind in one eye. The detectives obtained mugshots of the pair that had been taken several years before at the Edgecombe County Jail. They included the pictures in a photo lineup and had Mary Ann's fellow cabbie come into their office to look at the array. After carefully looking at the photographs a number of times, she was unable to identify the two black men she had seen in cab 103 in front of Heritage Hospital that Friday night.

Several weeks into the investigation, the probers finally managed to locate Paula Askew, the old schoolmate Mary Ann had picked up from the Pinehurst Homes complex at 10:30 P.M.

A friend of Paula's had contacted the sheriff's office, saying that he had some information they should hear. After giving him a polygraph test, the sleuths were very eager to interview Paula. When they brought her in for interrogation, however, she denied knowing anything about the murder.

Tall, thin, and eaten up by drugs, Askew had a checkered and volatile past. She was a crack-cocaine addict, and, after two suicide attempts, she had been committed to the psychiatric ward of Cherry Hospital in Goldsboro, North Carolina. Her children were taken from her by the

Department of Social Services—one was born with cocaine in its system.

Finally, though, the troubled young woman did agree to help with the investigation. She said that Mary Ann Lee had asked her to ride with her that night to the Liberty Inn motel, where they had picked up Johnson and Bellamy from room 32. She knew these two young men well. With Johnson giving directions, Paula said, Mary Ann drove out of town and turned off onto Hart's Chapel Road, supposedly to go to the home of a relative of his. When Johnson directed the cab driver to turn up a dirt road, they found themselves in the middle of a large field. Then, suddenly, Johnson got out of the cab and opened Mary Ann's door. Paula said that Mary Ann tried to fight him off, but Johnson, being much larger, grabbed her shirt and yanked her out of the cab. Then he threw the cabbie to the ground.

That was when Paula got out of the cab and asked Johnson what he was doing. She said, "He yelled at me—'Bitch, if you don't shut the fuck up, you're going, too!' "

Afraid that the two men were going to rape her friend and that she might be next, Paula began running toward the nearby woods. Glancing back, she saw Johnson kneeling on the ground next to the struggling Mary Ann. Then she saw Joseph Bellamy get into the driver's seat of the taxi and she heard some loud squealing noises, as though the car was "stuck on something."

Paula said she made her way back to Tarboro and immediately began receiving telephone calls from both men—and other individuals—with threats of death. Frightened out of her wits, she went to Rocky Mount to hide and, for a short time, even left the state. Paula told the sleuths that she was badly confused about her situation—she didn't know what to do or where to go. She was afraid to talk, but also afraid not to. She knew she was a danger to the murderers as long as she was alive. Finally, her confidant convinced her that her only safety lay in telling the detectives what she had seen that night.

The sleuths asked Paula if she'd ridden back to Tarboro in the taxi with Johnson and Bellamy that night. After all, eight miles is a long way to walk home. The frightened woman passionately denied having done so and never wavered from her account.

The probers brought Charles King, the host of the motel party, into their office for some more interrogation. Now he changed his story, saying that he had been drinking heavily that Friday, but he remembered that the "white girl" had picked up Artis Johnson in her cab several times. King said he even gave him cab fare, since Johnson was broke, but when he called City Cab just before midnight, he asked if Johnson wanted that white girl again. Johnson replied no, saying he "thought she had got off of work." This time Johnson had some money "rolled up," King told the detectives.

When Detectives Davis and Brady went to look for Johnson to bring him in for more questioning, they found him already sitting in a basement cell of the county jail, awaiting charges on another crime, unrelated to the current case.

The second suspect, Joe Bellamy, was being sought by the Tarboro police. Officers had attempted to serve an arrest warrant on him stemming from unrelated charges, but they had been unable to locate him. With the Tarboro warrant in hand, the sheriff's detectives went to the home of a relative of Bellamy's and conducted a thorough search. In one of the bedrooms, Davis crouched down to peer beneath a bed and discovered Bellamy hiding there. Bellamy crawled out on all fours and fell across the bed, apparently so frightened that he was unable to stand up.

With fresh mugshots of the two suspects, the investigators arranged another photo lineup for Mary Ann's fellow cabbie. This time, the woman was able to identify Johnson and Bellamy as the two men she had seen in the yellow cab just before the murder. Two days later, on Wednesday, March 10, 1993, both men were charged with first-degree murder, armed robbery, and larceny of the yellow cab.

Although they had two suspects locked up in jail, the investigators still had work to do. An anonymous caller reported there was blood on the coat Paula Askew had been wearing that night. The sleuths had it sent to the SBI lab to determine if Paula was also involved in the murder, but the blood turned out to belong to the relative from whom Paula had borrowed the jacket.

Meanwhile, an SBI technician was able to lift 24 identifiable fingerprints from the cab and from the other evidence collected at the crime scene. None of them matched the prints of either of the two suspects, and only one print belonged to the dead woman.

On Monday, April 11, 1994, the trial of Artis Johnson and Joseph Bellamy was held in the Edgecombe County Superior Court before Judge Frank Brown, with Assistant District Attorney Steve Graham prosecuting. Johnson's attorneys were Perry Jenkins and Bo Simmons; Robert Evans and Gene Muse represented the second defendant, Joseph Bellamy.

As testimony began on Thursday, April 14th, Judge Brown ruled that the jury could view graphic slides of the mangled corpse, even though the defense attorneys vehemently objected, claiming that the slides would only "inflame the jury." The defense objected again when the medical examiner was allowed to detail the extensive injuries that Mary Ann Lee had suffered from "head to toe." During cross-examination, Defense Attorney Simmons asked the pathologist if he could pinpoint the exact time of death. The doctor dryly replied, "Only pathologists who practice on TV can do that."

Paula Askew proved to be the most damaging witness against the two defendants. In attempting to discredit her testimony, the defense attorneys got her to admit to the court that she was a drug addict, that she had attempted suicide, had been in jail, and had been convicted of drunk driving, resisting arrest, and other charges. But from what she told the jury, none of that could change what happened the night she saw Johnson and Bellamy murder Mary Ann Lee, nor the fact that they had also threatened to kill her.

On Monday, April 18th, one week after the trial began, and 90 minutes after the state rested its case, one of the defendants' lawyers made a surprising move. Following close-door discussions, Defense Attorneys Jenkins and Simmons announced that Artis Johnson would accept a plea bargain of second-degree murder, so the state dropped all other charges pending against him, including rape. Judge Brown then sentenced Johnson to life in prison; he will be eligible for parole in 10 years.

On Tuesday, April 19th, a jury of seven women and five men were deliberating on Joseph Bellamy's fate. When they came back, they found him guilty of second-degree murder. He was subsequently sentenced to life in prison. He also received 20 years for robbery and 3 years for larceny of a motor vehicle. The sentences are to run consecutively.

Members of the victim's family were in court each day of the trial and, after it was all over, they indicated that they felt justice had been served. Nonetheless, they vowed to fight to keep Mary Ann's murderers in prison by attending all future appeals or parole hearings.

Currently, each Edgecombe County sheriff's detective carries a Polaroid camera as part of his investigative equipment. The sleuths believe that if they had been able to take an up-to-date picture of the prime suspects when they first questioned the pair, Johnson and Bellamy would have been identified from the first photo lineup. Mary Ann Lee's murder had been a complicated, difficult case to solve, but it was solved, thanks to the diligence and persistent work of Lieutenant Wiggs and Detectives Davis and Brady.

"CROSS-COUNTRY FUGITIVE'S LAST VICTIM WAS A COP!"

by Barry Benedict

It was the chilly Friday evening of November 26, 1993, when the dispatcher with Texas's Oldham County Sheriff's Office got word that there had been a shooting at Langergin's Truck Stop on Interstate 40, seven miles east of Vega, Texas.

Deputies hurried to the popular rest stop and discovered a woman weeping over the body of a bearded man who was sprawled in front of a gas-pump island. They learned that he was 35-year-old Gregory Croswell, a trucker from Eutaw, Alabama. He had been shot once in the back and was likely dead before he hit the ground.

The deputies checked the inside of the brightly lit office and found no one there. They observed that the drawer to the cash register was empty.

"It looks like they kidnapped the night manager," one of the deputies remarked.

When the lawmen checked the bathrooms at the rear of the rest stop, however, they discovered the body of a middle-aged woman sprawled on the floor, blood pooled under her head.

She was 48-year-old Pamela Gayle "Pam" Jackson.

She, too, had been shot once in the back of the head, execution-style.

Meanwhile, a team of detectives headed by Oldham County Sheriff Dave Medlin arrived at the scene.

The tearful young woman who'd been found bent over the dead trucker when deputies arrived was now seated in the back of one of the deputies' cruiser. She said she had been traveling with him on his cross-country haul and had been asleep in the back of the cab when the trucker pulled off the interstate.

She said she heard a "popping sound," followed by footsteps slapping on the cement. She sat up in the cab just in time to see two men running from the body of her trucker boyfriend and dive into a dark-colored four-door vehicle. The vehicle squealed out of the gas stop, back onto the interstate, and sped away.

The woman described one of the men as white, of medium height, and in his early 30s. She got only a glance at the other man, so she wasn't sure what he looked like.

The vehicle looked like a late-model Jeep or Ford Bronco. She didn't catch the license-plate number.

The police immediately issued an all-points bulletin (APB) with a description of the vehicle and the two men. It included the advisory that the men were wanted for questioning in a double murder and should be considered armed and dangerous.

In the meantime, crime scene investigators took photographs and inspected the rest-stop office and restroom for fingerprints and other evidence that might be present.

It appeared that Pam Jackson, the night manager, had been robbed inside the office, and then she was taken to the rest room where she was shot in the back of the head. If this theory was correct, the killer or killers must have been heading to their vehicle when Gregory Crosswell stopped his truck, got out, and was shot.

Crosswell's girlfriend had been asleep and was not seen

by the killers; otherwise she might well have been the third victim.

News of the double killing stunned the tiny town of Vega, with a population of 900, which is located 40 miles west of Amarillo in the Texas Panhandle. Just about everyone knew Pam Jackson, the affable night manager, who had moved to this tiny community with her family from Amarillo, in part because she'd felt that Amarillo was getting too big.

Although it sometimes got lonely, Pam had told friends and regular customers that she liked the job, and she was always eager to help motorists or truckers who pulled in to get directions or just to take a break from the long, often monotonous drive through the Panhandle. Her employers had instructed her that in the unlikely event that she was held up, she was not to resist, but to turn over the night's receipts.

Pam probably did as she'd been instructed, but she was killed anyway.

"We're after one twisted son of a bitch," one deputy remarked. "There was no reason in the world to shoot Pam. They did it out of pure meanness."

Regrettably, the detectives had very little in the way of clues that might help solve this crime of "pure meanness." The truck stop was fitted with a state-of-the-art video surveillance system that would record anyone entering or leaving the small, brightly lit office. But robberies on the interstate were so rare that someone had forgotten to load any videotape into the system.

The APB hadn't turned up any leads. Moreover, the crime scene technicians' search of the office and washrooms failed to turn up anything that might help identify the killer or killers.

The best lead the investigators had was the dead trucker's girlfriend. But she had been asleep when the shooting took place and had had only a brief look at the fleeting killer or killers.

Hoping to refresh her memory, Sheriff Medlin summoned a deputy in nearby Hutchinson County who had been trained in witness hypnotism. The deputy placed the witness in a trance and questioned her for three hours. Under hypnosis, the woman was able to provide more information about the two men she'd seen leaving the gas station.

She said she was sure that both were white—one was about 45 to 60 years old, with long gray hair and a round face; the other was a younger man, maybe 18 to 25 years old, with dark-blond hair, possibly wearing a red hood.

The new information was entered in an updated Teletype which was issued to all regional law enforcement officers.

Sheriff Medlin was not surprised that the updated APB did not get any responses. Three days had passed since the shooting. By now, the killer or killers could be anywhere.

Medlin also had reservations about the description of the two men provided by the hypnotized eyewitness. Hypnotism is a valuable tool in law enforcement, but not always an accurate one. The witness might have been describing the two men at the truck stop, or she might have been recalling two other men seen earlier in the day, bringing their images to mind in the confusion of the shooting.

The sheriff had the information broadcast anyway. It might prove accurate. And even if the descriptions were off, or completely wrong altogether, the update would keep reports of the double murder in the computer system.

Medlin was certain that anyone who would kill two people in cold blood at a truck stop for a couple of bucks would be heard from again.

A week passed, then another. Sheriff Medlin hoped his APB might produce an early gift for Christmas, but that holiday passed without anything turning up.

Then, in February 1994, Medlin got a call from the Nevada Division of Investigation. They had picked up a copy of his APB and read about the search for the two men fleeing the truck stop.

"We have good news and bad news," the detective said.

The good news was that they had a man believed to be the rest-stop killer in custody. The bad news was he had not been apprehended until after the life of a third victim had been notched on his gun.

On Tuesday evening, November 30, 1993, Nevada State Trooper Carlos Borland was patrolling a lonely stretch of Interstate 40, three miles north of Lovelock, when a red Chevy Blazer with Tennessee plates sped by. The vehicle matched one that had been reported as leaving a gas station in Trinity, a few miles west of Lovelock, without the driver paying for filling his tank with gas. The clincher was the distinctive orange Tennessee license plates.

Trooper Borland radioed the dispatcher his location and said he was in pursuit. Five minutes later, Borland reported that he had pulled the vehicle over and wanted a check run on the Tennessee license.

The dispatcher took the license number and then had to handle another call. When she finished, she heard a man's voice come on the line. "A trooper has been shot! A trooper has been shot!" the called said. "I'm calling from his cruiser." The caller gave his location as the eastbound lane of Interstate 40, about three miles from Lovelock.

Police vehicles quickly converged on the scene. A black-and-white cruiser was parked in the frontage lane, with the driver's door open and the radio on. Trooper Carlos Borland was sprawled in the beams of the headlights, 15 feet in front of the cruiser. He had been shot once in the face, but he was still alive, although unconscious.

The lawman was immediately airlifted to the Washoe Medical Center in Reno and admitted to the emergency room with a gunshot wound.

The man who reported the shooting was a long-haul trucker who'd been driving eastbound when he saw the trooper lying on the ground in the headlight beams and spotted a red Chevy Blazer leaving the scene. The trucker pulled off onto the frontage road and saw that the trooper had been shot. He called the dispatcher from the cruiser.

Lawmen from half a dozen different agencies began a search for the Chevy Blazer. A command post was set up in Nevada's Pershing County to take in the available information and coordinate the search.

Trooper Borland had been pursuing a motorist who was reported as leaving a gas station in Trinity, Nevada, without paying for filling his tank. The attendant described the driver as a white male, about 25 years old, with a slight build, and short, dark hair that was parted on the side.

The motorist had pulled into the station at 8:00 P.M. and told the attendant to fill the tank. After the tank was filled, the attendant turned toward the office to get a credit-card slip, and that was when the driver peeled out of the station.

The attendant said that the motorist was normal in appearance and his behavior was not belligerent or hostile. He did not appear to have been drinking or to be under the influence of drugs.

Yet, if the police were correct, this same "normal driver" shot a highway patrolman in the face after being stopped on the highway.

"There has to be more to this than a gas skip," one detective commented.

The search for the red Blazer continued all night. Roadblocks were set up. Motorists going both directions on the interstate were stopped.

Around 3:00 A.M., the investigators learned that Trooper Borland had died at the Washoe Medical Center without regaining consciousness. The easygoing, well-liked trooper was just 26 years old.

Borland was the second trooper to die by gunfire while on duty in the Nevada Highway Patrol's illustrious 44-year history. In 1975, Trooper Gary Gifford was gunned down in Lake Tahoe while trying to apprehend a bungling bank robber. The gunman was sentenced to life in prison and was later shot to death during a prison break.

The police had still not figured out what had prompted the motorist in the red Blazer to shoot Borland. A check on the Tennessee license plate revealed that it had been stolen from a car in the south. But the police were still dubious that a stolen car and a gas slip added up to enough motivation to gun down a state trooper.

The Nevada police continued their efforts to find the gunman. At eleven o'clock on Wednesday morning, they got a break when a search plane spotted a red vehicle in a gully in Churchill County. It appeared that the vehicle had gone off the road and become mired in a ditch. The driver had locked the doors, closed the windows, and attempted to hide the vehicle under some tree boughs before taking off.

The command post was moved to Dixie Road and a more intensive search for the gunman was set into motion. It appeared that after shooting Trooper Borland, the gunman had looped around and headed west on Interstate 40 before deserting his car.

The Blazer was abandoned in a spot between the Fallon National Wildlife Refuge and the Clan Alpine Mountains, a rugged area pocked with brushy ravines and canyons and offering excellent cover for deer and elk—and human beings.

Search parties composed of 60 officers from 10 different law enforcement agencies scoured the canyons and thick forests for the cop-killer. At midday, they discovered the remains of a campfire in the mountains near Dixie Valley, about five miles from the abandoned Jeep. The fire was still warm, meaning that it had been built on Tuesday evening, a fact that gave the fugitive a good lead.

Houses and businesses in the area were searched and the residents were evacuated. A roadblock was set up to inspect vehicles at the junction of U.S. 50 and Dixie Valley Road.

Trackers continued the manhunt until dusk, when it was called off. A helicopter equipped with sensitive infrared heat-seeking sensors was called in from the Naval Air Station in Fallon.

At ten o'clock that evening, the 'copter pilot reported what appeared to be a campfire four miles east of the command post. He took its bearing and flew back to the command post to pick up members of Nevada's Reno SWAT team who had volunteered their services in the manhunt.

The SWAT officers, equipped with night-vision goggles, were airlifted to a ridge that gave them a clear view of the campfire site. Peering into the darkness, they saw a tall man in a golfing jacket standing before the burning coals, hugging himself in the subfreezing temperatures.

The officers advanced to within 50 yards of the stranger, their steps cushioned by a carpet of needles covering the ground. When they got within 50 yards of the campfire, one of the officers snapped on his flashlight and ordered the man to put his hands in the air.

The stranger's face had the expression of a frightened deer caught in the headlights of a car as he turned toward the SWAT officers. He quickly reached inside his windbreaker, whipped out a small pistol, and raised it, placing its barrel against the side of his head.

In what seemed like a surreal moment, he told officers to shoot him before he shot himself.

"Drop the gun!" one of the officers barked.

"Shoot me!" the man called back, still holding the gunbarrel against his head. "It don't mean nothing." Then he waved the gun in the air, like a cowboy celebrating a Friday-night drunk. Finally, he brought the barrel to eye level and aimed at where the voices were coming from the darkness.

The SWAT officers were finished playing games. They fired twice. Both shots missed, but the potentially lethal slugs had a sobering effect on the gunman. He quickly dropped the pistol and raised his trembling hands.

"Don't shoot me!" he whimpered like a spanked pup. "Don't shoot!"

And so, 25 hours after the fatal shooting of Trooper Carlos Borland, the chase for the most wanted man in Nevada was over.

The fugitive was arrested and taken to the Pershing County Sheriff's Office, which was the nearest police station, and he was questioned about the shooting.

The suspect was identified as 25-year-old Michael Sonner, of North Carolina. He admitted to shooting the highway trooper and said he had done it because he was afraid. Then he asked if the trooper was all right.

The detectives looked at him without saying anything. Sonner screwed up his face into a question mark.

"He's not all right," one of the detectives said, finally breaking the silence. "He's dead. And *you* killed him."

Sooner's eyes filled with tears and he suddenly started beating the table before him with his fist. "No! No! No!" he wailed as he banged away.

The lawmen waited for Sonner to regain his composure before one of them put a hand on his shoulder and said, "Just tell us what happened, Mike."

The slender suspect nodded, but he said that first he wanted to make a phone call. The sleuths thought the call would be to an attorney, but they were surprised when he contacted North Carolina's *Greensboro News and Record*.

Sonner told a reporter who he was and said that he had murdered a trooper in Nevada. "I did it because I want to get the death penalty," he told the reporter. "I am going to ask for a speedy trial."

He said he shot the trooper because he had no reason to live. "My life is finished," he said. "I want to see what comes after life."

Sonner went on to tell the reporter that he escaped from jail in North Carolina, stole a red Chevy Blazer, and went on a cross-country joyride. His plan was to spend time at Lake Tahoe and enjoy himself, swimming in the fabled high-altitude lake and maybe gambling a little at one of the casinos. But he changed his plan and drove to the California coast, where he spent a week before deciding to return to North Carolina.

Sonner said he was heading homeward when he stopped at the service station in Trinity, Nevada, to gas up. He was low on money, so when the attendant turned his back, Sonner took off.

He had just passed Lovelock when the rear window of the Blazer was flooded with the flashing lights of the state trooper's cruiser.

"I pulled over and waited for the trooper," Sonner said. "He walked up to me and asked what I had in my hand."

Sonner was holding a small gun. He said that when the trooper saw the gun, he went for his own gun, only Sonner fired first.

"I beat him to the draw," Sonner said, obviously pleased with himself.

After shooting the trooper, Sonner headed west on the interstate, then took the turnoff south on Highway 50. He was planning to double back when he ran off the road, disabling the car. He hid the vehicle with some brush and took off on foot.

"I didn't think they would find the Blazer that fast," he said, his voice dipping with sorrow. "I thought I had a good chance."

It seemed that the confession, which was printed on the front page of the North Carolina newspaper, all but guaranteed a speedy conviction. But the reed-thin killer had more surprises up his sleeve.

On Wednesday, January 5, 1994, he notified the jailer that he wanted to talk to the police about two more murders he had committed before the trooper's.

The detectives hurried to the jail.

"It was in Texas," Sonner drawled. "It was a gas station attendant and another guy. I don't know who he was. I shot them both."

Sonner said he'd been traveling through Texas after escaping from the North Carolina jail when he stopped at an all-night gas station off Interstate 40, west of Amarillo. He saw that the woman was working in the office alone and he was the only customer.

After pulling his gun and cleaning out the cash drawer, he said, he marched the horror-stricken attendant into the women's bathroom, where he sexually assaulted her and then shot her once in the back of the head.

Sonner left the bathroom and started for the Blazer, when a man stepped from the cab of a long-haul truck parked at the gas-pump island and started walking in his direction.

Sonner said he nodded at the trucker and let him walk past before he lifted the barrel of the pistol against the trucker's head and fired.

Then Sonner got into the Blazer and continued on his way to California.

The detectives found one of the old APBs regarding the truck-stop murders in Vega, Texas, and contacted Oldham County Sheriff Medlin.

The description of the confessed cop-killer did not match either of the two men described running from the truck stop after the shooting. But Sonner gave accurate descriptions of the victims and how they were shot, and the locations of the bodies.

Three months after the police had been called to the Vega truck stop on that cold November 1993 night, Sheriff Medlin could now report that the murders of Pamela Jackson and Gregory Croswell were solved.

The murder trial of Michael Sonner began in Lovelock, Nevada, in September 1994 before Judge Richard Wagner and a packed courthouse.

Public Defender James Jackson did not contest the charge that Sonner shot Carlos Borland. "He did it," the public defender told the eight-man, four-woman jury. "He didn't want to. But it happened."

The defense lawyer asserted that Sonner was insane when he turned the gun on the surprised Nevada lawman and shot him once in the head. He said that Sonner had a history of physical and mental abuse as a child, and it was his past drug and alcohol abuse that was responsible for the tragedy that claimed Trooper Borland's life.

A relative of Sonner's testified that Sonner, the youngest of six children born to unwed parents, was repeatedly beaten and largely ignored as he was growing up.

Then the public defender introduced an audiotape of Sonner's confession, given shortly after his capture, in which he admitted shooting Borland, but indicated that he was unaware that the shot had been fatal.

"Michael Sonner was insane when he and Carlos Borland tragically crossed paths on November thirtieth," Defense Attorney Jackson said. "He didn't even know what he had done."

Special Prosecutor Brent Kolvet maintained that Sonner was not insane and knew exactly what he was doing when he pulled the trigger on that chilly November night.

"Mr. Sonner was desperate," Kolvet declared. "He might have been scared, but he also had resolved not to go back to prison. He was looking out for himself, and if someone got in the way—*anyone* got in the way—they were going to be the ones to get hurt."

Trooper Carlos Borland got in the way. He got hurt.

After hearing the final arguments, the jury retreated to chambers to deliberate. Eight hours later, the panel reached a verdict. They found Michael Sonner guilty of the cold-blooded, first-degree murder, rejecting the insanity plea offered by the defense. The jury also convicted him of possessing a stolen vehicle, being an ex-felon in possession of a firearm, and resisting arrest.

In the penalty phase of the trial, the jurors heard more evidence about the abuse Sonner underwent as a child and about how he had repeatedly sought help from mental health clinics only to be turned away.

But Sonner threw a monkey wrench into his own defense when he turned his attention from studying the round courthouse and told the judge that he wanted to speak to the jury himself.

Public Defender Jackson jumped to his feet and objected, saying that anything his client might say would be a "form of state-sanctioned suicide." The judge questioned Sonner out of the jury's earshot for 20 minutes before finally allowing him to speak.

Standing at the defense table, Sonner wiped a tear from his eye and apologized for causing so much pain to the family and friends of the victim. With that said, Sonner told the jury that he would rather die than go on living with himself.

"Since I pulled the trigger and shot that state trooper, there is something inside me that cannot be cured," Sonner declared. "Since that incident, it's just been getting worse. I would urge you to put me out of my misery."

At the conclusion of his brief statement, Sonner flashed a narrow, pointed-tooth smile and sat down.

On September 24, 1994, the jury gave Michael Sonner exactly what he had been demanding for over a year—the death sentence. They reached their verdict after just four hours of deliberations.

Michael Sonner stared impassively as each juror was polled and confirmed that the decision was unanimous.

By law, the death sentence will be automatically appealed to the State Supreme Court. Sonner is currently sitting in his place on Nevada's death row. Meanwhile, he must be presumed innocent of any other charges pending against him in Texas until and unless proven otherwise by due process of law.

"BEAUTY QUEEN WAS KILLED FOR HER RED CADDY"

by Bill G. Cox

A study in 1991 showed that 63 murderers and rapists given the death penalty in Texas in the last decade had been paroled. One of every four of the freshly released felons committed new crimes. Since that study, newspaper headlines day after day have blared "Parolee Charged in Murder." A case in point is Donald Leroy Evans, who was freed from a Texas penitentiary in April 1991—his first eligible parole date—after serving only 5 years of a 15-year sentence for aggravated rape. Later, he allegedly confessed to killing 60 people in 21 states!

The same terrible trend can be seen nationwide, but Texas's plight is ironic in that it is a federal court order that has led to the release of violent offenders on parole to kill and rape again.

Evans was one of those freed as a result of the court order that laced a 95 percent inmate population cap on the state's prison capacity, an order that made Texas the only state in America with a 95 percent capacity restriction.

At last report, Texas felons were serving on average only 10 months of a 10-year sentence. The state's law enforcement offices are left with a feeling of frustration toward the revolving prison doors that put violent criminals back on the streets in incredibly short order.

Such was the setting for the tragic events that started in Houston, Texas, on Tuesday, July 2, 1991. Cecile Ham, a beautiful, dark-haired 48-year-old former beauty queen, disappeared that afternoon while doing some routine errands. She was last heard from when she telephoned home and told her housekeeper that she would be there shortly after she made one final stop at a nearby bank. The call was received a few minutes past 4:30 P.M. Cecile said she was calling from the pay phone at a neighborhood pharmacy.

The pharmacy was located on Houston's west side, the area populated by the more affluent of Houston's residents. The Hams lived in one of the large manors in the area.

Cecile Ham was a former schoolteacher, a former model, and a representative for a national fashion magazine. In the early 1960s, she was named one of the 10 most beautiful girls at the University of Texas and was honored by former Governor John Connally in 1964 as the first Bluebonnet Queen of Texas.

For more than 20 years, Cecile had been married to one of the most respected talent agents in the country. His clients included the rock group ZZ Top and country singing star Clint Black.

Cecile Ham was reported missing by her husband, who called the Houston Police Department after checking everywhere he knew his wife might have been. Employees at the bank where Cecile had intended to stop after the phone call did not recall her being there that afternoon.

Police issued a missing-person's bulletin, with a description of the prominent Houston woman and the 1991 red Cadillac, bearing Texas license CJY-52N, that she was driving. Officers talked to employees at the drugstore where

Cecile was last seen, as well as other persons in the neighborhood. But no one recalled any unusual occurrences during that time. Investigators realized that the wet weather that afternoon would have lessened the possibility of people noticing anything unusual, since their primary interest would have been in getting out of the rain.

Always in the minds of detectives investigating the disappearance of a prominent and wealthy person is the possibility of kidnapping. But the woman's husband had not received any phone calls or ransom notes in the hours after his wife vanished.

Detectives questioned relatives and friends about the jewelry and clothing Cecile was wearing and what she carried in the way of cash or credit cards in case any of the items surfaced at pawnshops or unauthorized credit card transactions were made.

It was the latter that gave detectives their first clue as to what had befallen Cecile Ham. The information was ominous, to say the least. At 6:29 P.M. on that Tuesday, less than two hours after Cecile made the phone call to her home, a credit card bearing her name had been used by a man to purchase gas at a service station on the west side of town.

Detectives learned that a tall, muscular young man had filled the tank of the woman's red Cadillac. He had apparently been alone, which increased the official concern for the missing woman's welfare. The station attendant described the man as 25 to 28 years old, 6 feet to 6 feet 3 inches tall, weighing 190 to 220 pounds, and of large build. He had blond or light-colored hair, the station employee recalled.

Helicopters were added to the intense search for the missing woman and her sleek automobile in the general area of West Houston. The low-flying 'copters scanned fields and woods for the red Cadillac. But with no trace of the vehicle, the search was expanded over the state

within the next 48 hours as new developments on the use
of Cecile Ham's credit cards came to light in the massive
probe.

Shortly after the first credit card incident was reported,
Houston police, Texas Rangers, and members of the
Criminal Intelligence Division of the Texas Department
of Safety made arrangements with Cecile Ham's credit
card companies to report immediately all transactions
that might come through their records. The missing
woman's credit cards were put on the so-called "hot" list
of thousands of businesses in Texas.

Over the next week, it was like following an electronic
beeper trail for sleuths as the transaction duplicates came
in. Law enforcement agencies throughout the state were
on the alert for the muscular blond man who was living
the high life on the stolen plastic. But he always seemed
to be one jump ahead of the last place a card was used.
Amazingly enough, the sleuths noted, he was still driving
Cecile's red Cadillac. The officers found it hard to believe
that he and the bright red car wouldn't be spotted somewhere by searchers.

In all, the fugitive had used Cecile's credit cards at
least 60 times in an eight-day period, making purchases
after he left Houston in such cities as San Antonio, Pear-
sall, Devine, Austin, San Marcos, New Braunfels, Johnson
City, Blanco, and Round Mountain.

In San Antonio, the man had stayed three days, making
purchases with the credit cards on the north side of the
city. To officers this indicated that he had stayed somewhere in that part of town before moving on.

But after July 10th, the paper trail ended abruptly. No
more purchases were reported. This led detectives to
speculate that the suspect might have left the state, or
even the country.

At several of the businesses where purchases had been
made, surveillance cameras had luckily snapped photos

of the tall, heavyset blond man. Houston police released the photos to the newspapers and TV stations with a plea for public help in locating or identifying the subject. Investigators took to the road to follow the credit-card trail, interviewing clerks who had waited on the suspect. They compiled a thickening file but still did not have a definite identity.

"We think he may be either from Houston, Austin, or San Antonio because he has stayed for two or three days at one time in some of these places," said Houston Detective Bill Belk, who headed the Ham investigation for his department.

The sleuths were beginning to put together a profile of the suspect. Witnesses said the man talked a great deal, was a braggart, and wore designer sunglasses. Detective Belk said the young man had told one clerk he was the son of a prominent Houston man and owned a boat business.

It became apparent as the investigators gathered the credit card slips that the elusive card user had inscribed many of the slips with the number "12." At this point, they could attach no meaning to the numerical notation.

Among purchases he had made were cassette tapes of rap star Vanilla Ice (he affected the same style of sunglasses, too), gasoline, cigarettes, beer, and "detail" service to the red Cadillac. He was obviously taking personal pride in the expensive vehicle he was driving.

With public circulation of the surveillance camera photos, a witness came forward to tell where the tall, hulking suspect had been after the credit-card trail ended so suddenly on July 10th. Of all places, he had holed up in a Christian youth camp near Marble Falls! He told the youth campers that he had attended the camp previously and had come back to recall old times. He claimed to be an affluent boat company owner from Houston. While at the camp, the witnesses told officers, the blond man had performed odd jobs to pay for his stay. Most of the campers remembered him as a "nice guy," except one young woman who said that he had made unsuccessful sexual advances toward her.

Unfortunately, there were no daily newspapers, TVs, or even radios at the camp. Seclusion from the secular world to concentrate on spiritual matters was the main reason for the young church people being there. Not until the camp had ended and one witness returned to Houston did she see on TV a photo of the man being hunted nationwide as a suspect in the disappearance of Cecile Ham. She contacted the Houston police immediately to tell them that he had been the camp's arrogant and unwanted drop-in guest.

The widely published and telecast photos brought several calls from people, and by August 1st, resulted in the man being identified as Spencer Corey Goodman. When police ran the name through computer records of known offenders, they learned that one Spencer Corey Goodman, 22, had been released on parole on July 1st, the day before Cecile Ham and her Cadillac had vanished.

The records revealed that Goodman had first crossed with the law when he was given a two-year prison term on a burglary conviction in February 1989. Parole was granted after he served six months before getting into trouble again, this time drawing a five-year prison sentence for car theft. After three months in prison, Goodman was again released on parole. But he was arrested for violating his parole and sent to a parole violator's facility at San Antonio for 90 days.

It was from there that he was paroled once more on July 1st.

He had struck out three times with the law but had been given a "walk" every time!

Checking with officials at the violator facility in San Antonio, detectives learned still more about the loose reins kept on the paroled convict. They were told that Spencer Goodman and 23 other freed inmates were sent by bus to Houston and unloaded at a downtown parole office there. Given their paperwork and instructions to report to assigned halfway houses at various locations, they were told to wait for transportation to take them to their new homes.

But a parole board coordinator at the San Antonio facility said the parolees were literally on their own as far as the law was concerned after the stopover in Houston. He pointed out that the earlier warrants for their arrest on parole violation which had landed them in the parole violator facility were withdrawn after expiration of their confinement. The parolees would be under routine supervision at the newly assigned halfway houses.

Investigators' questioning of residents of the youth camp where Goodman stayed disclosed that he had stolen credit cards from one of the campers. A nationwide "hot" alert was put on the credit cards in the hope that Goodman's shopping habits would again pinpoint his whereabouts.

It happened on August 7, 1991, in a store in Basalt, Colorado. A merchant made a check on the card offered by the man in a red Cadillac. To his surprise, it came up as stolen. The store owner called the Eagle County, Colorado, Sheriff's Department.

As a patrol car approached, the blond man jumped in the Cadillac and took off at a high speed along a sharply curving mountain road that snaked through the forests. The wild pursuit at speeds reaching 100 mph went over 30 miles before the fleeing driver lost control on a turn and the car plunged over a 65-foot sloping embankment.

When pulled from the wreckage with only minor injuries, the driver admitted he was Spencer Corey Goodman. He was treated at a hospital and remanded to jail. Later, he voluntarily admitted to the Colorado officers that he had kidnapped Cecile Ham in her car and had killed her and ditched her body in Texas.

Goodman waived extradition and was flown back to Texas by two Houston detectives and a Texas Ranger. The suspect led Texas Rangers and other officers to the site where he left the victim's body on a ranch in Frio County, about 60 miles from San Antonio. The body had not been buried, and Goodman led them directly to the skeletal remains. Jewelry identified as Cecile Ham's was still on the remains, officers said.

Goodman was jailed without bond on a charge of capital murder.

In three confessions given to the Houston detectives, Goodman said that on the day of the murder, he did not wait for transportation from the Houston parole office. Instead, he started walking and had walked throughout the night and part of the next day before reaching West Houston. There, he saw Cecile Ham park her red Cadillac in front of a pharmacy and get out to use a pay phone outside.

When Cecile returned to the Cadillac, Goodman stepped to the unlocked door on the driver's side, knocked the woman unconscious with a single hard blow, shoved her over, and drove away. Before she regained consciousness, Goodman said he stopped somewhere in Houston and broke her neck. He then stuffed her in the car trunk. It was almost 20 hours later that he decided to dispose of the body.

Goodman's trial on the capital murder indictment began in mid-May 1992 in Richmond, Texas. In opening statements, the defense attorney told the jury that his client accepted "full responsibility for his actions" in killing Cecile Ham. But he did not mean to kill the woman, the attorney contended. Goodman's intent, the attorney claimed, was only to steal the woman's car. If that were true, Goodman would not be guilty of capital murder, which carries the death penalty.

The prosecution called law enforcement officers and parole officials to tell the jury that Goodman never arrived at the halfway house but instead killed the Houston woman for her Cadillac and breezed through Texas buying numerous items on her credit cards and bragging that he was a member of a rich family.

Under cross-examination by the defense, the parole officials testified that they had no legal way to make a parolee board the transportation provided to take him to his assigned halfway house.

The defendant's brazenness was further demonstrated in the testimony of a former parole counselor. With the body of Cecile Ham still in the trunk of the car, Goodman drove to San Antonio and asked to spend the night at the female counselor's apartment. The 28-year-old woman testified that she let Goodman sleep on her floor, unaware, of course, that he had just killed a woman whose body was in the trunk of the car.

The witness said Goodman gave her an Oriental wooden box and stand as a housewarming gift for the apartment into which she had just moved. She was unaware that the items had been bought by Cecile Ham only a short time before Goodman killed her.

Prosecutors introduced into evidence a five-page written statement by Goodman in which he related details of wanting the red Cadillac when he spotted it, of abducting and killing Cecile Ham with karate chops to her head and neck, and then trying to conceal her body with rocks on the remote ranch. In the statement, Goodman said he used a martial-arts technique to snap the woman's neck when he stopped a short time after abducting her. He also gave a videotaped confession to Houston police detectives after his arrest in Colorado.

Detective Belk testified that Goodman volunteered to

show him how he used his hands to kill Cecile Ham.
Goodman volunteered the term "martial arts" to describe
the method he used to kill the victim, the detective said.

In the statement, Goodman said, "I'm sorry for what
happened. I'll never know why I did it. It's something I'll
have to live with."

The Harris County chief medical examiner testified
that the victim's cause of death was blunt trauma, consistent with blows to the head and neck.

Goodman took the stand as the only witness called by
the defense. The defense had aimed its strategy at saving
the defendant from the death penalty by showing that
Goodman had no intent to kill the woman whose car
he'd stolen on impulse.

Building up to the main gist of his testimony, Goodman
told the story of his upbringing in a good Christian home.
He said he had been adopted when he was one year old,
and his adoptive parents had provided all his needs. But
his descent into another kind of lifestyle began after he
was kicked out of a private religious school in Oklahoma.

In recounting from the witness chair the events of July
2nd when Cecile Ham was abducted and slain, the burly
defendant strayed from the details he gave in his earlier
signed confession. He now told the jury that he had
planned to report to the halfway house "when I got
things straight."

Questioned as to what he meant, Goodman replied,
"To succeed and make something of myself—just to succeed and make my family say, 'He pulled himself out of
it.' "

About the murder, Goodman, sometimes in tears, testified, "I couldn't believe I'd done it. I just know that
something had happened that I couldn't walk away from.
Inside, I just knew I had killed this lady. I just didn't want
the lady to be dead."

He said that as he dumped her body, "I just kept saying, 'I'm sorry. I'm sorry.' "

Fighting hard to save his client's life and make it plain to the jury that he held no sympathy with the man's violent act, the defense attorney shouted at Goodman and demanded that he tell the community what gave him the right to take a life. Holding up a thick Houston phone book, the lawyer ordered the defendant to hit it as hard as he hit the murder victim. But Goodman hung his head and cried.

Under cross-examination by Prosecutor Frank Briscoe, Goodman admitted that he had a lifelong pattern of lying to those closest to him, including his parents and a parole counselor. He denied singling out Cecile Ham because of her car, claiming he wasn't aware what kind of car he was stealing.

But the state attorney argued that Goodman was after a car any way he could get it and would have attacked any unescorted woman driving a car he liked.

"Those bones out in Frio County could have been anyone's mother, daughter, or wife, couldn't they?" Briscoe asked.

Attacking the defense contention that Goodman was a contrite young man who never intended to kill, the state held that the defendant was a cold-blooded killer who thought he was playing a game with law enforcement officers during his month-long flight in the victim's car. Asked about the enigmatic numeral "12" that he had written on several of the credit card slips, Goodman claimed he wrote it because it reminded him of Christ's 12 disciples and his early religious training. He said that after the killing he went to the church youth camp to find God and peace.

Police witnesses said they believed Goodman went to the camp to hide out and that by writing the number 12 on the receipts he signed, Goodman was playing a game of "catch me if you can" by hinting at his identity.

After writing the defendant's name "Corey Goodman" on a blackboard, Prosecutor Briscoe asked him to count the letters. When Goodman answered there were 12, Briscoe asked, "Isn't it true you put those numbers on those tickets as a signature? You were telling the officers who you were and challenging them to find you, weren't you?"

Goodman answered with a denial.

In closing arguments to the jury, the prosecutor told the jury, "Goodman's story ought to send chills up and down your spine."

Showing the jury photos of the victim's skeletal remains and one of Goodman mugging for a picture taken at the church camp where he stayed after the killing, Prosecutor Briscoe declared, "This is an individual enjoying life. This is a photo of a cold-blooded killer who has already forgotten about his victim."

The defense attorney countered that Goodman was not the ruthless killer depicted by the state but a parolee full of remorse who was guilty of being "a penny-ante thief and a liar." Though guilty of murdering the woman, he wasn't guilty of capital murder because he lacked intent to kill, the lawyer argued.

Briscoe described Goodman's self-serving testimony of nonintent to kill as "a charade and a sham."

The jury agreed. After deliberating about three hours, they found Spencer Goodman guilty of capital murder. Goodman showed no emotion at the reading of the verdict.

During the punishment phase of the trial, the state called witnesses to show that Goodman had a violent nature and would be a threat to society, two of the legal criteria for obtaining the death penalty instead of life imprisonment. A string of witnesses testified about the killer's bad temper, boastfulness, and past criminal behavior.

A furniture deliveryman who was engaged to the parole counselor who had befriended Goodman told the jury that Goodman had threatened to kill him with a gun or with his bare hands. The witness said, "He told me that he had a gun, that he ought to just blow me away. Then he stated he wouldn't waste a bullet on me. Mister Goodman said he rather do it himself."

A former girlfriend testified Goodman was "a basically good person," but he stole her car one day and she never saw him again. Another girlfriend told of Goodman using her car without permission and also charging what she called "sex calls" on her phone bill—telling her he was part of a Colombian drug cartel and she could not force him to pay the bill.

Once, becoming angry at the prosecutor's questioning of a witness, Goodman rose from his chair and turned as if to leave the courtroom, saying, "The jury can do what they want to me." He was restrained by deputies and was returned to his chair. Prosecutor Briscoe moved his chair at the counsel table a few feet farther from the accused when the trial resumed.

The man who with his wife had adopted Goodman when he was only one year old said they did all they could to help him straighten out his life but did not succeed. "We put all the love and care and time and money into this that we knew how. We thought this child could grow up to be a really great person."

He related that Goodman's temper and failure to obey the rules resulted in his expulsion from the private religious school in Oklahoma and later his parents' home.

"We did everything we could," the witness said. "There was nothing more we could do. I hope we didn't do it—I hope it wasn't our home that turned out that person."

Aware of Goodman's previous convictions and prison terms, the witness said he and his wife did not feel that

Goodman should have been paroled at all in his earlier convictions.

The man said, "We love the memories of a child we raised. We love the time we spent with him. We love possibly anything that can be redeemed." But he added that they were heartbroken by Goodman's deeds.

On June 1st, the jury apparently failed to find any redeemable qualities in Spencer Goodman. They returned a verdict mandating that he be executed by lethal injection.

A Texas state treasurer who had attended college with Cecile Ham and was a personal friend, wrote to a Texas newspaper in September 1991, "I am writing both as a statewide official and as an outraged citizen who's had enough of Texas' revolving door criminal justice system. This senseless killing of innocent people must stop."

She urged the approval by Texans of a $1.1 billion bond issue to build more prisons to keep convicts behind bars.

She also suggested further legal action to remove the 95 percent population capacity imposed on Texas by the federal court order.

In November 1991, Texas did approve the big bond issue, and the construction of new prisons is under way. Meanwhile, the Texas Board of Pardon and Paroles indicated it would initiate measures that officials hope will cut down on the parole of violent offenders and tighten the supervisory control of parolees. Veteran police officers who have heard such promises before are just keeping their fingers crossed.

At this writing, Spencer Goodman was being held on death row while his case is appealed automatically to the Texas Court of Criminal Appeals.

"SLOW DEATH WITH A 4000-POUND WEAPON!"

by Joseph N. York

The fog hung heavy just before dawn along the coast of San Diego County. In a few hours the sun would burn off the mist that was suspended along the shore for a few miles inland.

Two night watchmen made their way along Torrey Pines Road in the affluent section of San Diego known as La Jolla. It was February 1, 1987, and the men would be getting off work in two and a half hours at eight o'clock. They had just finished checking one group of industrial buildings and were driving to check another when they saw something peculiar lying on the fog-shrouded road. The long, crooked form looked like a sleeping bag, but when they drove closer, they saw it had blond, flowing hair. They knew at once that they were seeing a body. They made a U-turn back to the buildings they'd just come from and called the San Diego Police Department.

The first patrol officer at the scene was puzzled by what he saw. He called for a supervisor and a traffic investigator. The body looked like it had been run over. A Mercedes was parked about 30 feet south of the female victim, and the officers assumed the vehicle had something to do with the body.

Sergeant Roger Michael of the hit-and-run detail decided to put in a call to homicide in order to pool their thoughts. Team I, headed by Sergeant Hank Olais, had the call-out duty. The crew consisted of Detectives Bob Lopez, Rick Hansen, and Vince Villalvazo.

The officers arrived about 6:30 A.M. in a fog that was still hanging heavy. Torrey Pines Road is very busy at that time of day, and it was necessary to divert the morning's commuter traffic.

Examination of the vehicle revealed a woman's purse on the front seat. The windows were partially rolled down, and the ignition keys were missing.

Impact evidence on the hood and windshield suggested that the body had made contact with the car at those points. Other signs on the road seemed to verify that the body had been struck and dragged to the place where it was found.

The car, police learned, was registered to Pamela Russ. Identification found inside the purse was also for Pamela Russ. The picture on the driver's license was of a beautiful blond woman, 33 years old. The officers thought she looked like the woman found dead in the street.

The body was stylishly dressed in high boots and expensive clothes. Her hair was long and flowing. Even in her death, the officers could tell she had been a beautiful woman. They agreed that someone must have been overcome with rage to do what had been done to Pamela Russ.

After a short meeting, the team of sleuths unanimously agreed that this was indeed a homicide rather than a traffic collision accidentally resulting in death. Sergeant Michael and his crew stayed around to help interpret evidence found in the road, but the case would be handled as a homicide.

Detective Bob Lopez was assigned to take charge of the crime scene. Lopez had worked a few homicides, but this was his first duty as the scene man. Detectives Villalvazo and Hansen were assigned to chase down leads.

Sergeant Olais had a newly installed cellular telephone in his car. This new technology was soon to become a valuable law enforcement tool, enabling detectives everywhere to call in to their headquarters without having to go through the regular police dispatchers on their busy patrol frequencies.

Some homeless people were sleeping under the sprawling pine trees in the area. Detectives Hansen and Villalvazo wanted to speak with them to determine if they had heard any noise. The sleuths also wanted to eliminate them from suspicion.

Seeming to rule out the homeless men as suspects, the victim's wallet, containing a few dollars, was still in her purse. An elaborate ring still adorned her tanned and manicured fingers.

Rich Hansen interviewed two scruffy homeless men who had staked out their territory just up an incline from where the woman's body was found. Each of them seemed to have shared their respective sleeping bags with a fifth of cheap vodka the night before.

Even if the men had been sober, the heavy fog and lack of street lights in that area would have prohibited them from seeing anything.

One of the men said he thought he heard some screaming at about five o'clock. The skeptical detective asked the man what time it was now. The man looked at Hansen strangely. "I don't know. I ain't got a watch."

Meanwhile, Detective Lopez reported that there were signs of a struggle near where the car had been parked. Several hundred feet away were even more signs of disturbances on the roadway. It looked as though the victim had been run over at a slow speed.

The medical examiner would do an autopsy and determine the exact cause of death later. The detectives noticed a gash on the woman's head. A large amount of blood stained the left front tire rim of the Mercedes. There was also a trail of blood leading from the car to the body. What appeared to be human tissue and hair was clinging to the undercarriage of the vehicle.

The detectives theorized that Pamela Russ had stopped her vehicle for some reason. She either climbed out or was dragged out and beaten. She started to run, and the killer got into her vehicle and chased her. The killer then apparently hit her, and she flew up onto the hood and hit the windshield. There was a braking skid, and Pamela rolled off the hood onto the pavement. Then, the killer drove over her, slowly, crushing her to death with the Mercedes.

As Olais and Lopez were sharing the crime scene information with Hansen and Villalvazo, a call came over the cellular phone that Pamela's husband was at Central Headquarters reporting Pamela as a missing person.

Sergeant Olais was a homicide detective for many years before he was promoted to sergeant. He did a short stint in patrol and rotated back to homicide as a supervisor. He was viewed by his fellow lawmen as a "cop's cop."

The detectives liked to work for Olais. He was not like some guy who had read a few books on homicide and then started telling veterans how to do the job. He had actually "been there."

Experience told Olais that the first place to look was the immediate family. Money, lust, and jealousy were usually the main reasons for homicides. Olais told the officers that their first job was to clear the husband as the killer.

One detective asked Olais, "What do you mean, we have to 'clear' the husband?"

"Just what I said," Olais retorted. "The odds are that a family member was involved. Before we start running around looking everywhere, we have to make sure we have eliminated the husband. Once we do that, we can investigate elsewhere."

Detective Hansen was assigned to interview the husband, who was waiting at the downtown station. The veteran detective had been a cop long enough to know that you never rush to judgment on a case. The good detectives watched, listened, and analyzed what they saw.

As soon as he saw Charles Russ, however, Hansen knew he did not like him. Russ was a "pretty boy" to be sure. He had the confident air Hansen had seen on too many con men. Russ's smile was too pretty, his hair done too expertly. Hansen knew this guy had never done a real day's work in his life.

Russ appeared distraught at what had happened to his wife. He haltingly explained to the detectives that the two of them were preparing to leave for Australia later that day. They had planned to see the America's Cup sailboat races, Russ said.

Pamela Russ was an aspiring artist as well as an accomplished Hawaiian dancer. She rented a loft studio in the gaslight district of downtown San Diego, an artsy area of restored buildings and "in" restaurants.

Russ explained that Pamela had gone to the studio to finish up some last minute details before the trip.

When she did not return, Russ told the cops, he became alarmed and went looking for her. He went to the studio after calling there several times. Russ said the phone at Pamela's studio was disconnected. Next, Russ said he drove the streets looking for Pamela. Finally, at 6:30 A.M., he called the police. He went to Central Headquarters and made the report.

The interview was cordial and nonconfrontational. The sleuths took notes and asked all the usual questions. Detectives Hansen and Villalvazo drove Charles Russ home. Once there, the detectives went inside the stylish condominium, continuing their almost casual questioning of Charles Russ. Hansen asked to use the bathroom. While in there, he took note that the shower stall was still wet. The conversation moved into the bedroom. The sleuths noted that, while there were suitcases outside the closet, there were no other signs that anyone was packing.

Detective Villalvazo asked to see the airline tickets. Russ said he did not have them yet. The detective asked to see the visas necessary to stay in Australia. Russ said he had not picked them up yet. Russ volunteered that his wife had $28,000 in travelers' checks.

The detectives asked Russ if he would be willing to take a polygraph exam whenever one could be set up. Russ did not hesitate. "Of course I will," he said. He seemed almost exasperated that the detectives even had a question about that.

On their way to headquarters, the sleuths stopped by the security guard's post at Russ's apartment complex. By plain old good luck, the guard was pulling a double shift and was the same one who had worked the night before. He said that Russ left in his Mercedes between 5:25 and 5:45 A.M. The guard noted that Russ's hair was wet at the time he left. He had not seen Mrs. Russ leave, he said.

The detectives went back to the station to confer with Sergeant Olais about what else they'd learned from the crime scene.

Olais sat on the edge of his desk slowly running his index and middle fingers around the lip of his coffee cup. The sergeant usually had a funny quip, or at least a smart comeback, to anything anyone had to say. This afternoon, however, he was quiet.

"Can we clear him yet?" Olais asked.

"Not even," Hansen replied. "I'll bet anything that little twerp did her in. We sure can't prove it. We sure can't clear him, either."

Later, Detective Lopez returned from the autopsy performed by Deputy Medical Examiner John Eisele. Beautiful Pamela Russ had had her head smashed into the steering wheel of her car while she sat in the front seat. She was dragged outside, and her head was knocked into the tire rim. She got up and ran. Her killer jumped behind the wheel and followed her. Pamela was struck and went flying up on the hood with her face next to the windshield. The killer slammed on the brakes, sending Pamela sliding to the pavement. Then, the killer drove over Pamela slowly, finishing her off with the sheer weight of the car.

Pamela Russ suffered a fractured skull, a broken neck, and several internal injuries. It was a horrible ending for anyone.

Detective Lopez said the investigators found some shoe prints at the scene. At the moment, he did not know what kind of shoe it was—probably a sneaker—but he would know soon enough. They also found some tire impressions that were like those of Pamela Russ's tires but were not from her car. Interestingly enough, Charles Russ had a Mercedes almost identical to Pamela's.

Olais said, "Since we can't move on and look at anyone else, we need to stay with Charlie Boy. We need to get the phone records from their place and from Pamela's loft. We need to arrange the polygraph for Charlie and check with the airlines. Find out where they had reservations in Australia and when they were made. Check with Pamela's relatives and find out what they thought of Charlie.

"It's six o'clock now. Let's get some rest because we'll be hitting it hard tomorrow; probably go a long time."

The detectives checked with Pamela's relatives the following day. They all loved "Chuck," as they called him.

The couple met when Pamela was 16 and Charles was 20. She had never loved anyone else, the relatives swore.

Charles was a wealthy businessman. He had been into

many ventures over the years. Most recently, he was into telemarketing and was more successful than anyone could imagine. In fact, one of Pamela's relatives had invested her retirement savings with Charles only a few months before. The amount was over $80,000. Her return was going to be phenomenal, she claimed. She would never have to think about money again.

Detectives Lopez and Olais went to Pamela's art studio and looked around. Nothing seemed out of order there. For sure, no murder or struggle had taken place there. They looked at Pamela's work. Neither sleuth was an art critic, but they liked what they saw.

The detectives listened to the phone answering machine. There were a few calls from the female relative who had invested all of her money with Charles Russ.

"Wait a minute," Olais said. "I'm sure Hansen told me that Russ said the phone here was disconnected. Yet there are messages on here that leave dates and times *after* he said he called her."

The answering machine seemed to be in good working order. Sergeant Olais left the studio and called the supposedly out-of-order machine from a pay phone. The machine picked up and Olais left a message. The officers seized the tape and machine as possible evidence.

When they arrived back at the station, a police communications supervisor, Herb Kelsey, told Olais that he had spoken with Charles Russ when Russ came to report his wife missing. Russ told Kelsey that he'd heard that his wife's body was found on Torrey Pines Road. Nobody knew this information at the time. The story hadn't made the news yet, so no one but police and the killer should have known where the body was found.

Olais assigned Detectives Hansen and Villalvazo to go back to speak with Charles Russ. This interview would be at Charles's house. They took a portable tape recorder with them.

Once again they had Russ go over in detail his actions when he went looking for his wife. This time instead of saying that he thought the phone was disconnected, Russ said he got a busy signal, making him think the phone was off the hook.

When the detectives pointed out that the phone would not keep ringing because there was an answering machine, nor would he have had a continuous busy signal, Russ said that he might have been dialing the wrong number. The detectives could only roll their eyes incredulously.

As they were leaving, the sleuths spotted an open book on the kitchen counter. The title was *Telling Lies*. The book was opened to the chapter entitled, "How to Lie on a Polygraph."

By now, the detectives were sure they were not going to eliminate Charles Russ as a suspect. But they were also sure that they were a long way from proving in court that he killed his wife.

When they phoned Charles to tell him the time of his polygraph examination, they were not surprised to learn that his attorney had told him not to take the polygraph.

To the detectives, this refusal said loud and clear that Charles was probably guilty. But, his refusal to take a polygraph exam could not be used in court.

The detectives knew it was time to dig in and come up with solid proof. What they really needed was a motive.

From outward appearances Pamela and Charles Russ were an ideal couple. The first help sleuths had in establishing a motive came about when they learned that Russ had an insurance policy on Pamela for $600,000. The detectives went out snooping to see what else they could find out about financial wizard Charles Russ.

Their search took several months of calling, writing, and phoning all over the country. Charles Russ was not a man you would want to fork over your life savings to and wait for the grand return.

Charles Russ had started out in his early 20s running a family business, an aerospace engineering and electronics firm. It folded.

In 1975, Charles and Pamela moved to Gallup, New Mexico, to work for a trade publication dealing with Indian jewelry and artifacts.

Charles was able to persuade several investors to give him money so he could become a partner in the publication. He would be responsible for handling the advertising section and would take care of the financial responsibilities.

The profits did not come in as everyone anticipated. When the investors decided to examine the books, they could not find them, let alone find out how the business was doing.

Charles was confronted. His response was to offer to resign if they would buy him out for $9,000. The investors wanted to sue him, but they ended up buying him out as he had asked, just to end the matter so they could recoup their losses in other ways. In other words, Charles skated.

Charles and Pamela moved back to San Diego in 1976 to start a small beachwear business. That venture was characterized by bad check after bad check and constant phone calls from creditors.

Charles borrowed $33,000 from the parents of a friend and moved into a lavishingly furnished office, complete with the finest furniture and accessories.

In 1978, the beachwear business folded. The friend went to the office to check on things and found it padlocked. Charles had moved to Montana without a word of apology or explanation: a fine way to treat parents of a friend.

After moving from odd job to odd job in Montana,

Charles scraped up money—other people's, of course—and bought a small weekly newspaper. He sold the newspaper for $3,500, a $3,000 loss, three years later in 1982. The new buyer learned that Charles still owed $4,000 of the original purchase price.

Charles had told the locals he had to move because he had developed a heart condition and had to live at a lower altitude. Everyone felt sorry for the dapper young man. Some locals went over to his house with food and a few farewell gifts. They found that Charles had taken the $3,500 he made on the newspaper sale and bought a truck. His house was empty and standing wide open. Apparently, he had packed and vanished in the middle of the night.

The original seller of the paper sued Charles and won a judgment of $7,000. He has not received any money yet. The "sucker list" continued to grow the more the San Diego police officers looked.

A Montana print shop owner said Charles Russ owed him over $10,000. Another "friend" in Montana said she gave Charles $7,000 in a deal for 10 acres of land. She had paid him that large sum down and $200 a month for three years. When Charles skipped town, the friend learned the land was in foreclosure for nonpayment.

Back in San Diego, Charles started up where he had left off in Montana, wheeling and dealing. He somehow became the fund-raising chief for the Paralyzed Veterans Association. He also became the owner of a telemarketing business that had a plush office in one of the up-and-coming areas of San Diego. Charles was on a roll, everyone thought.

Charles told a relative of Pamela's that he needed a Mercedes 300D as a car for work. He told her he dealt with a lot of "high rollers," and they would respect him more if he had an impressive car. The relative helped him lease that car and later even cosigned for a $69,000

Mercedes 560SEC for him. The relative said Charles was successful not only in appearance, but in reality, as well.

Pamela's relative told the officers that Charles approached her sometime in 1985 and offered her a deal that he claimed would yield a 24 percent return on her investment. The relative knew nothing about Charles's Montana adventures or any of his local problems. So, she mortgaged her home and handed over $75,000 to Charles. Later, she liquidated an IRA account and gave Charles another $8,150.

For Pamela's relative, the first hint of Charles's financial problems came to surface a few months after Pamela's death when Charles was sued by authorities in San Mateo and Santa Clara Counties in northern California. The charitable organizations that Charles collected money for there only received about 10 percent of the donations that honest, hardworking people gave. The rest went into the pockets of Charles Russ. The problem was that the people who gave money believed most of it went to the disadvantaged people they hoped to help.

Soon, the relative learned that Charles had no money. *None.* None of the money that was to be returned with 24 percent interest. Mortgage and balloon payments were soon due. Charles had nothing. Pamela's relative decided that it would be necessary to sue Charles to get something back from him. The only problem was that Charles had vanished.

By now it was August, six months after the death of Pamela Russ. Sergeant Olais had been to the district attorney. No case had been issued. Lieutenant Phil Jarvis of homicide told the press that his officers were still looking for the killer of Pamela Russ. In reality, they were only looking at one person, and that was Charles Russ.

District Attorney Investigator Joe Santibanez was called in to help. This was now a high-profile case from the standpoint of the media's interest. Pamela Russ's beautiful picture had been run several times in the newspaper, and public interest was running high.

Santibanez worked a pretrial team and did whatever was needed to get a case ready for court. The honchos at the district attorney's office agreed that the San Diego police had done a good job on this case. But, more attention was now needed—meticulous attention to fine, minute details.

Homicide Team I just did not have the time to perform these tasks. The homicide team was likened to a group of M*A*S*H surgeons. Investigator Santibanez was needed to do the slow, precise work of a resident specialist surgeon.

Santibanez tracked Charles Russ to Taos, New Mexico. Theft warrants had been prepared and extradition papers were ready. After surrounding the condominium in New Mexico, the authorities moved in. The place had been picked clean. Russ was gone, without a trace, an apparent repeat of his Montana vanishing act.

A few months later, Santibanez found evidence that Russ had gone back to Montana. The pickup scenario was repeated, with the results being the same as they'd been in New Mexico. Russ had scampered.

In January 1988, Deputy District Attorney Mark Pettine was assigned the case. Until then it had been floating around with several deputies looking at it, and then handing it off as soon as they could.

Investigator Santibanez was overjoyed when Pettine took the case. Pettine had been a deputy district attorney for over 15 years. He handled his first homicide case in 1981. Since then he had so many, he could not remember the number.

Pettine took the case home over the weekend. He spread the reports over a large desk in his study and made notes on his computer. He ate while working and only slept a few hours. The case consumed him.

Pettine knew he did not have one thing alone that clinched the guilt of Charles Russ. But he *did* have many little things to indicate Russ's guilt.

An arrest warrant for embezzlement from Pamela's relative was issued. Investigator Santibanez continued tracking Russ, without luck. This being the age of electronic media, the San Diego searchers decided to enlist the aid of the television show, *America's Most Wanted.*

Three times during the course of 18 months, the handsome face of Charles Russ adorned the television screen. Finally, in August 1989, someone in Hollywood, Florida, who had seen the television show, called the local authorities about a dapper young man who lived in a house on the beach. Soon after, Charles Russ was arrested.

Items were seized from the place Russ was renting, including a pair of Reebok shoes that had a similar pattern to ones that left tracks at the death scene.

Russ was extradited back to San Diego, and the legal battle was officially on.

The murder trial was held on January 24, 1991, in the courtroom of Superior Court Judge Michael D. Wellington, one of the most respected jurists in San Diego.

The trial took two months. Russ was represented by Deputy Public Defender Bill Youmans. Cynical onlookers laughed quietly at the so-called wealthy financial wizard having to be represented by the same "firm" that handles indigent cases.

Pettine and Santibanez set out methodically presenting the case. Pettine called 93 witnesses and introduced 240 exhibits of physical evidence. None of these were extraneous or "padded" exhibits. Each exhibit had independent significance.

The Reeboks from Florida were "consistent" with the shoe tracks found at the scene. The tire tracks from his Mercedes were consistent with tracks from the scene.

Investigator Santibanez discovered that just prior to

Pamela Russ's death, Charles had ordered over $400,000 worth of stock. Yet, at that time, he had no money at all. Was he anticipating receiving $600,000 worth of insurance benefit money?

The flight to Australia had Sydney as its destination. Yet, Sydney was on the opposite side of the country from where the America's Cup was being held.

Four months before Pamela's murder, Charles went to Colorado to buy some property. He told the seller he was separated from his wife. This was clearly not true.

The prosecutor speculated that Pamela became aware that Charles was cheating her relative out of her retirement money. This was too much for Pamela to bear. No one knows if Pamela was aware of Charles's financial history—or of his cheating everyone with whom he came into contact.

Prosecutor Pettine theorized that even if Pamela knew how Charles operated, she would not condone his cheating her relative. The speculation was that Pamela was going to cause trouble for him. He became enraged and killed her.

Even the wet shower floor in the Russ apartment came into play. The guard testified that Charles left between 5:25 and 5:45 A.M. Pettine theorized that after the struggle of killing Pamela, Charles returned to the apartment, cleaned up, and left again, discarding his bloody clothing somewhere.

Judge Wellington did not allow Pettine to say that Russ was on the lam so long that it took three stints on *America's Most Wanted* to actually nab him.

Charles Russ chose to testify in his own defense. He took the stand appearing confident and charming. His stylish clothes, furnished by his family, caused journalists covering the story to refer to him as "dapper."

His story was pat and reasonable. But, it was obviously contrived and rehearsed. Charles Russ testified for a day and a half. It was one thing to have Defense Attorney Youmans leading him along by the hand. Now it was Prosecutor Pettine's turn.

Pettine had the defendant on cross-examination for three and a half days. They went over every detail Russ had mentioned. Pettine caught him in one misstatement after another. Russ tried to change gears about statements he had made to the police. In changing gears he only appeared foolish.

For example, the defendant said initially that he could not get through on Pamela's answering machine. Then, on the stand, he said he called and hung up without leaving a message because he longed to hear Pamela's voice.

That was a pretty good statement. The only problem was that about a week earlier, a close relative of Pamela's had said the same thing as she tearfully recounted how much she missed Pamela.

The discrepancy did not go unnoticed by the astute jurors.

Russ told police that on the day of the murder, Pamela had $28,000 in traveler's checks when she was killed. Prosecutor Pettine proved that both Pamela and Charles probably only had $400 to their name when she was killed.

And on it went. Pettine picked Russ apart like a surgeon doing a delicate operation.

At the start of the trial, Defense Attorney Youmans said Charles Russ was not involved in theft or murder. In his closing argument, after seeing Pettine's case, even Youmans had to say that his client was a thief, but was not a murderer.

The jury returned with their verdict after a day and a half of deliberations. Later, it was learned that they examined and discussed all of the evidence. Then, after only one vote, they convicted Charles Russ of first-degree murder.

On April 26, 1991, Judge Michael D. Wellington sentenced Charles Russ to life in prison. Russ is currently serving his term in the California prison system.

For his work on this case, and other cases, Mark Pettine was chosen as the San Diego County prosecutor of the year for 1991.

"2 MOMS HITCHHIKED TO RAPE-MURDER!"

by Adam Register

Contentnea Creek Trailer Park in a rural area near Grifton, North Carolina, was home to 29-year-old Bernadine Parrish and her three children. During the summer of 1991, Bernadine's 23-year-old brother and his 19-year-old girlfriend, Bobbie Jean Hartwig, were also living in the mobile home. Recently, though, Bobbie Jean had talked about moving back to nearby Bridgeton. The divorced mother of two small children missed her large, close-knit family.

On Friday, August 24, 1991, temperatures soared during the day, and nightfall brought little respite from the heat.

While Bernadine, her brother, and his girlfriend were having some drinks with friends, Bernadine got a call from an old boyfriend in Ayden, about 10 miles away, asking if she wanted to come over for the night. Bernadine still carried a torch for the man, and she was willing to make the trek. The problem was, she had no car. She would have to walk or hitch a ride. It was already after midnight, so Bernadine's brother and his girlfriend decided to walk with her to keep her safe.

It was not unusual for the group to walk or hitchhike when visiting friends, but when a small, light-colored car stopped for them, the hitchhikers turned down the ride. Something about the three men in the car didn't feel right. They were drinking, apparently heavily, and seemed rude and obnoxious. Besides, the car was too small to hold six adults.

The car's driver pulled over a few yards ahead and parked. When he got out of the car, the three hitchhikers were unnerved to see a shotgun in his hands. The driver ordered the frightened trio to hand over their possessions. Unhesitatingly, Bernadine, her brother, and Bobbie Jean handed over the only two things they had with them: a cigarette lighter and a foam-rubber can cooler. They had no real valuables or money on their persons.

Keeping the shotgun pointed at the trio, the driver ordered Bernadine's brother to walk away and the two women to get into the car.

Trembling, the young man turned and walked toward a ditch at the side of the road. Three shots rang out in the still, dark night. The young man screamed with pain as shotgun pellets hit him in the back and he fell into the ditch. As he lay on his face, severely wounded, the young man heard the car drive off, leaving him to die.

Dazed and bleeding, Bernadine's brother somehow managed to crawl out of the ditch and stagger back to the dark highway. He desperately needed help. Bernadine and Bobbie Jean also needed help. He hoped a passing motorist would see him and stop, but none came by.

Meanwhile, a nearby resident who had stepped out for a breath of fresh air heard the gunshots. He first thought that hunters were illegally "spotting" deer—blinding them with bright lights and shooting them. Deciding to investigate, the man drove his truck toward the direction of the gunshots. Instead of hunters spotting deer, however, he found an injured man wandering across the highway. A car with several young women traveling from Greenville stopped at the same time. While the homeowner remained with the wounded man, the women went for help and notified the Grifton police and rescue squad.

Sergeant Virgil Malpass, an 11-year veteran of the Grifton Police Department, was the first law enforcement officer to reach the shooting scene. It was the most violent crime the lawman had ever dealt with in this town of only 2,400 residents.

The victim was treated by the rescue squad medical technicians on the scene, then rushed to a Greenville hospital, where he underwent surgery.

Because the robbery, shooting, and kidnappings were committed in the Pitt County sheriff's jurisdiction, Sheriff's Investigator Mac Manning was called out of his comfortable bed around 2:30 on Saturday morning. He arrived at the hospital a short while later. There, Bernadine Parrish's brother, who was recovering from his surgery, told Manning and other deputies about the crime. He gave a brief description of the strangers and the car they were driving. Investigators needed more substantial information. Did he hear the men using each other's names, they asked, or did he see the car's license plate? Everything had happened too quickly, the shooting victim replied. It was dark on the deserted highway, and fear and alcohol affected his recollection of the events.

Pitt County Sheriff Billy Vandiford, a 30-year veteran lawman, had been handed a difficult case to solve. With random acts of violence, detectives have no clear motives or immediate suspects to help in their investigation.

While Bernadine's brother recuperated in the hospital, officers of the sheriff's department and agents from the State Bureau of Investigation (SBI) joined forces to search for the two missing women. On Tuesday, a helicopter hovered over the crime scene from the air. Nothing was discovered that would assist the sleuths.

Greenville Police Sergeant Doug Jackson, a spokesman for the local branch of Crime Stoppers, used local media outlets to offer on behalf of the nonprofit organization up to $2,500 for information about the violent crime. One caller provided the names of possible suspects, but without additional information, the sleuths' hands were tied.

Detectives visited Bernadine Parrish's gray trailer hoping to find some clue to her whereabouts, but it was just as she had left it on that Friday night. Toys littered the yard and porch. A light beckoned from inside the home, but the house remained silent. Bernadine's three children were staying with close relatives. No one was home.

Several trailer park residents expressed anger at the senseless violence and pessimism that Bernadine Parrish or Bobbie Jean Hartwig would be found alive. One resident said it was time for "a good old-fashioned hanging" when the three suspects were caught.

Investigator Manning, just a few years older than Parrish, said he hadn't lost all hope, but, the 6-foot 9-inch chief investigator conceded, "It does look grim."

Several weeks passed with no further clues to help in the search. Friends and relatives remained vigilant in their prayers and hopes, but the law enforcement officers knew the probability of finding either the suspects or the victims decreased with each passing day.

On Tuesday, September 11th, nineteen days after the abductions, the probers got their first breakthrough in the case: It was not good news.

A maintenance man at nearby Pitt Community College was checking on a construction site in a remote part of the campus, when he came upon the bodies in a canal-like water-filled ditch. The worker immediately reported his frightful discovery to Sheriff Vandiford's office.

Two dozen sheriff's deputies, SBI officials, and college security officers converged on the crime scene about 100 yards off an unpaved entrance to the small campus. There, in the ditch, the investigators found the badly decomposed bodies of two females, one completely nude, the other partially clothed. After SBI technicians thoroughly photographed the crime scene, the bodies were removed to the morgue.

Aware that Bobbie Jean Hartwig's driver's license was found lying near the bodies, Sheriff Vandiford called off the massive search for the missing women. But the sheriff would wait to offer positive identification to the victims' relatives until after autopsies were performed on the bodies at a local hospital.

Deputies and other officials combed the half-acre site where the bodies were found, hoping to find evidence that would help them determine if the women had been murdered on the campus site or were killed somewhere else and then dumped in the ditch.

The search did not go unrewarded. Detectives found scattered about the area some aluminum ladders, some metal construction parts, some cement blocks, and a wooden door or tabletop. Detectives also found keys, an empty brandy bottle, a cassette tape box, and assorted articles of clothing.

Investigators put together a hypothesis based on the evidence to explain what had happened to the hitchhikers that August night. They surmised that the three kidnappers were unfamiliar with the area. After shooting Bernadine Parrish's brother and abducting her and Bobbie Jean Hartwig, the kidnappers drove toward the campus. They probably found the remote road into the campus an attractive place to commit their intended crime, but when the road ended, they inadvertently drove the car into a ditch and got stuck. The three young men then apparently constructed a makeshift ramp from items taken from the nearby construction site and successfully drove the car out and over the campus to a paved road.

The way in which the "bridge" was constructed led investigators to believe the suspects had military engineering training.

Other evidence seemed to support a military connection. The set of keys found at the scene was stamped with a government seal, and the cassette box bore the emblem of the United States Marines. Suspecting that a price code on the brandy bottle would tell them where the bottle had been purchased, the detectives contacted the manufacturer. They learned that the brandy had been bought from a store at Camp Lejeune, a Marine base in Jacksonville, some 45 miles south of Grifton. A trace of the keys led sleuths to the same base.

In 1991, more than 49,000 military personnel were assigned to the Marine base at Jacksonville. Marines, looking for action with the opposite sex, frequented the many bars and clubs in Greenville, about 60 miles away. From Jacksonville, they would drive North on Highway 258 to Kinston and then take Highway 11 into the college town. Greenville is home not only to Pitt Community College, where the bodies were found, but also to East Carolina University and its school of medicine.

Military police and the Naval Investigative Services (NIS) now joined the hunt for the three suspects in the August 24th robbery, kidnapping, and murders.

While investigators worked around the clock searching for the perpetrators of the horrific crimes, autopsies were conducted on the two victims. Dr. M.G.F. Gilliland, a Pitt County Memorial Hospital medical examiner, confirmed Sheriff Vandiford's opinion: the bodies were indeed those of the two missing women.

Bobbie Jean Hartwig had died of a gunshot wound to her chest, the pathologist said. But Dr. Gilliland was unable to determine the exact cause of Bernadine Parrish's death. She could only report that Parrish had died "by an undetermined form of violence." Because both women's bodies were unclothed, Dr. Gilliland assumed that they had been sexually assaulted, but the condition of the bodies precluded the doctor from being able to deny or confirm that assumption.

Relatives of the two women could now bury their loved ones and begin the grieving process.

A cooperative effort between the Pitt County Sheriff's Department, the SBI, the Camp Lejeune military police, and the NIS quickly reeled in the three suspects. One, Kendrick Wayne Bradford, was already in the custody of the Onslow County sheriff in Jacksonville, North Carolina, on an unrelated armed robbery charge. The barracks' keys found at the crime scene opened Private Bradford's room at Camp Lejeune. Interrogation of Bradford led detectives to a second marine, Warren Gregory. With the assistance of an attorney, Richard Gonzales, also a marine, turned himself into authorities.

Private Bradford, sleuths learned, was from Gilmex, Texas. A field artillery specialist serving with HQ Battery, the 20-year-old leatherneck had not even completed his first year in the Corps. Lance Corporal Warren Robert Gregory, from Chicago, Illinois, was assigned to S Battery in the 5th Battalion. The 22-year old marine had served his country in Operation Desert Storm in the Persian Gulf. Corporal Richard Gonzales, the oldest suspect at 24, was with HQ Battery and also a Desert Storm veteran. Originally from Long Beach, New York, Gonzales was a field artillery operator and had been a marine for several years.

After questioning the suspects, detectives learned the three young men were probably intoxicated when they borrowed a fellow marine's car to go barhopping in Greenville on the night of August 24th. A few hours later, violence had radically changed six young lives forever.

The accused murderers were to be held in the Pitt County Jail in Greenville without bond until their trial dates. On November 7, 1991, however, while attempting to escape from the jail, Warren Gregory assaulted a guard. The incident landed him a six-year term in Raleigh's Central Prison, where he resumed his wait for the Parrish/Hartwig murder trial.

Kendrick Bradford, not Gregory, would be the first to be prosecuted by the state of North Carolina. On January 19, 1993, 17 months after the crimes were committed, jury selection for Bradford's trial began.

The state had a good case against Bradford, who, if found guilty, faced a probable death sentence. Not only did the prosecutor, District Attorney Tom Haigwood, have all the evidence found at the murder site, he had a key witness. One of the three marines, Richard Gonzales, had turned state's evidence and agreed to testify against both Bradford and Gregory. In exchange, Gonzales would plead guilty to lessor charges of murder: the other charges would remain the same. Rather than take his chances with a jury, Gonzales hoped to receive a lighter sentence from the judge.

Kendrick Bradford's attorneys, Graham Clark and Terry Alford, had attempted to plea-bargain for their client, too, but prosecutors weren't receptive. They needed only one eyewitness to the crime to turn state's evidence and would throw the book at the other two men.

The capital murder trial was held in Superior Court in Greenville, the county seat, with Superior Court Judge Cy Grant presiding. During pretrial motions, Judge Grant ruled that the prosecution could use Bradford's confession during the trial, but could not show the jury all the photographs taken of the murder scene. Many of the pictures were unusually gruesome.

On Monday, February 1st, after two weeks of jury selection, ten women and two men filed into the jury box. Finally, the public would learn the horrifying violence the hitchhikers had suffered.

Bernadine Parrish's brother, the surviving victim of the random violence, took the witness stand to tell what he remembered of the crime. He admitted, however, that he could not identify the man on trial as one of his attackers.

The Pitt Community College maintenance employee who found the bodies described the murder scene to the jury. In addition to the two gruesome bodies in the ditch, he said he found ladders, cement blocks, and something that looked like a door or tabletop. The maintenance worker also testified to having seen a cigarette lighter, a can cooler, jeans, T-shirts, and women's underwear at the scene. It looked as though the clothing had been run over by a car, he said, because the items were embedded in muddy tire tracks.

On Tuesday, forensic pathologist Dr. M.G.F. Gilliland took the witness stand. She testified that Bobbie Jean Hartwig had died from a shotgun blast to the chest. Shotgun pellets were found in the body. Bernadine Parrish may have been strangled to death, Dr. Gilliland said; she found no evidence of firearm or cutting injury of any type on Parrish's body. Extensive decomposition of the victims' bodies led her to conclude that the two women had probably been killed shortly after they were abducted.

Finally, on Wednesday, February 3, 1993, Richard Gonzales, the state's star witness, took the stand. In 1991, Gonzales testified, he was a young man with great prospects. He had plans to make a career in the Marine Corps and raise a family, but everything changed on August 24, 1991.

The ex-marine gave the jury the first full account of what happened that star-filled night along a deserted stretch of Highway 11. According to Gonzales, the three friends left the base at about 11:00 P.M., intending to go to a Greenville nightclub. Along the way, they spotted three people hitchhiking and stopped the car. But when the hitchhikers refused the ride, Gregory grabbed a shotgun and got out of the car. After robbing the hitchhikers, Gonzales said, Gregory ordered the women into the car and told the man to run for his life. Gonzales recalled that Gregory then fired his gun at the man three times, and the man screamed as though in great pain. With the two hysterical women in the backseat with Kendrick Bradford, the group continued toward Greenville.

Gonzales testified that Gregory turned onto another road, and when the road suddenly ended, they found themselves stuck in a ditch. Gregory remained in the car while Gonzales and Bradford attempted to push it out of the ditch, but the car wouldn't budge. Gregory then ordered everyone out of the car.

Telling Gonzales to grab some shotgun shells, Gregory directed the women over to a stand of trees and ordered them to undress. The two desperately frightened women obeyed. Bradford and Gregory then raped the two victims. Subsequently, Gonzales said, Gregory turned the shotgun on him and ordered him to rape Hartwig. Then, according to the witness's tale, Bradford and Gregory switched places and raped the women again. "It wasn't a voluntary-type situation," Gonzales said of the women's cooperation. "It was more like they didn't want to be hurt."

Gonzales said that a short while later, as the older woman was lying on the ground, Gregory tried to choke her and snap her head back. But Parrish did not die easily. When she suddenly regained consciousness, Gregory strangled her and tried breaking her neck again. This time, he succeeded.

"I asked him why did he choke the girl," Gonzales testified, "and he said because he didn't want to go to prison."

With her friend dead, Bobbie Jean Hartwig became hysterical and started screaming. At Gregory's command, Kendrick Bradford picked up the shotgun, walked over to where Hartwig was lying, and fired point-blank into her chest. Hartwig's screaming stopped.

The marines then turned their attention to the stuck car. They used aluminum ladders, a tabletop, and the women's clothes to get enough traction to drive out of the ditch.

As they were driving back to Camp Lejeune, Gonzales testified, "Someone said, 'What are we going to do to top this?' I remember Mr. Gregory laughed."

During cross-examination the following day, Bradford's attorney, Terry Alford, asked Gonzales, "Mr. Bradford followed what Mr. Gregory told him to do, didn't he?"

"Yes, sir," Gonzales replied.

"And earlier, you had done what Mr. Gregory told you to do, didn't you?"

"Yes, sir."

"And you didn't do anything to stop it, did you?" Alford asked.

"No, sir, I did not try to stop it," Gonzales admitted.

In his testimony, North Carolina SBI Agent Jim Wilson read for the jury Bradford's confession to police after he was arrested. Bradford said he told one friend that he had committed an act so horrible, no one, not even God, would ever forgive him. Bradford did not tell his friend about the crime, Wilson said, but he did recount to police how he had first raped the two women and then killed 19-year-old Bobbie Jean Hartwig. "He closed his eyes and fired one time," the witness testified.

Kendrick Bradford eventually took the witness stand in his own defense. Facing a possible death sentence if found guilty, the 21-year-old ex-marine hoped to play on the jury's sympathy in order to save his own life. Bradford told the court he was drunk that fateful night in August and could not remember many of the details. He claimed to have followed Gregory's orders because he feared he would be killed if he refused.

During closing arguments, Graham Clark, Bradford's other defense attorney, attempted to separate his client from Gregory and Gonzales. Clark told the jury that none of the marines had discussed committing rape or murder when they stopped for three hitchhikers. He argued that the horrific acts of violence had been masterminded by Gregory. Clark asked the jury to discount Gonzales's testimony, arguing that Gonzales was under intense pressure from the prosecution, and the story he told them was not necessarily the truth.

Prosecutor Tom Haigwood said in his closing argument that Bradford was guilty of all charges against him and deserved nothing less than the death penalty.

On Wednesday, February 10th, just eight days after his trial had begun, Kendrick Bradford was found guilty of Bobbie Jean Hartwig's murder. The jury also found him guilty of two counts of first-degree rape and two counts of kidnapping. Bradford could have received death, but his attorneys were successful in persuading the jury to be lenient. He was sentenced to life in prison after the mitigating circumstances of drug and alcohol abuse were considered. Bradford received a total of three life sentences plus 18 years.

On Thursday, April 29, 1993, Warren R. Gregory, the accused ringleader, went on trial for his life before Superior Court Judge Cy Grant in the same Greenville courtroom. Richard Gonzales again testified as the state's star witness.

Gregory's former Camp Lejeune roommate told the nine-man, four-woman jury that around the time of the kidnapping-murders, he saw Gregory remove a shotgun from behind a ceiling tile and a .25-caliber pistol from a nightstand in their barracks room. The witness said that he and Kendrick Bradford used the same two guns to pull an armed robbery in the Jacksonville area, a crime for which they were caught and punished. Later, the witness said, Gregory admitted to him that he had abducted and killed two women hitchhikers.

No witnesses were called by the defense attorneys. On Friday, May 4th, after only two hours of deliberation, the Pitt County jury found Warren Gregory guilty of all charges against him.

Prosecutor Tom Haigwood said he would seek the death penalty for Gregory.

At the sentencing hearing, Gregory finally took the witness stand. During hours of testimony, the Chicago native told of having a nervous breakdown in 1990 after a failed marriage. He testified that he had psychological problems caused from the stress of having participated in the Persian Gulf War and began to drink heavily after returning from Saudi Arabia. He told of hallucinations and sleeplessness and said he had problems distinguishing between reality and fantasy and that he suffered from nightmares. The worst, he said, concerned the Greenville rapes and murders.

Gregory claimed that his signed confession was inaccurate and denied having committed the crimes for which he had been found guilty. Instead, he pointed the finger of blame at Kendrick Bradford.

A psychiatrist testified that stress, heavy drinking, large does of caffeine, and fatigue probably contributed to the manic episode Gregory suffered at the time of the murders. According to the doctor, Gregory was already suffering from mental illness when the two women were killed, and since the accused was significantly impaired in his ability to appreciate the criminality of his actions, he did not have a normal ability to tell right from wrong. The Gulf War, the psychiatrist said, was a major source of the defendant's stress. After deployment, Gregory suffered from posttraumatic stress disorder, which resulted in sleeplessness and constant fear.

In the doctor's opinion, the defendant's manic symptoms began to subside after he began a treatment of strong medications. But, he told the court, he had no way of determining if Gregory's psychosis would recur or if the murders were a one-time episode.

A close relative of the convicted man took the stand, hoping to save Gregory's life. She described him as a former Boy Scout, who had often helped the elderly in their neighborhood by shoveling snow and raking leaves. But, the relative admitted, Gregory did have behavioral problems in school, had belonged to a Chicago street gang, and was often involved in fights. She said she noticed he had serious problems after returning from the Persian Gulf War, and that he drank heavily and suffered from sleeplessness.

After hearing all the testimony, the Superior Court jury took only five hours to decide the ex-marine's fate: Warren Gregory was sentenced to die for the two murders. In addition to two death sentences, he was given two life sentences for the rapes, two 30-year sentences for the kidnappings, and 15 years for the attempted murder of Bernadine Parrish's brother. Warren Gregory was only 24 years old.

On May 20, 1993, Richard M. Gonzales, the last to be sentenced, was allowed to plead guilty to two counts of second-degree murder, two counts of first-degree kidnapping, and one count of first-degree rape.

The 23-year-old could have received a maximum sentence of three life sentences plus 100 years, but Judge Grant was lenient. Gonzales received two life sentences for the murder charges and a third life term for rape. In addition, he was given 30 years for kidnapping and for being an accessory after the fact to first-degree rape and assault with a deadly weapon with intent to kill. All prison terms are to run concurrently.

During his sentencing hearing, Gonzales apologized to the victims' families, and to his own relatives, for their loss, pain, and suffering. "I never wanted anybody to get hurt," he told the families. "I never wanted anybody to die."

"MIAMI PERVERT BUTCHERED, THEN DEFILED A WOMAN AND A MAN!"

by Michael Sasser

In August 1992, South Florida simply ceased to exist as it had. Hurricane Andrew blew through town, leveling homes, businesses, infrastructure, and much of the area's subtropical vegetation. The effects were chilling and largely permanent.

Following the devastation of Hurricane Andrew, thousands flocked to South Florida to help rebuild the fractured community. Some were modern-day saviors to hurricane victims. Others were predators.

The hurricane still dominated the news on September 29, 1992, when Detective John Parmenter of Florida's Metro-Dade County Police Department received a phone call from dispatch. There was a report of three dead bodies found in a car on the campus of Florida International University (FIU) in Southwest Miami. The dispatcher said that the scene was a grisly one.

This was something to knock the hurricane out of the news.

At 9:30 A.M., Detective Parmenter arrived at the scene

on the campus. FIU, though located in the middle of urban clutter, is a large, handsome campus that takes full advantage of the tropical Florida environs. Once on the campus, Parmenter had no problem finding the scene of the crime.

Located just to the west of a pond and just east of a parking lot, a late-model blue Toyota Camry was the center of interest. The area around the car was sectioned off with crime scene tape. A number of other Metro-Dade police cars, as well as campus police vehicles, were parked nearby, and the officers walked inside the perimeter. A large crowd of civilians pressed against the yellow tape. Whatever happened was attracting a lot of attention.

Parmenter found the lead officer and asked for a briefing.

"About nine A.M., a campus police officer found the car here, thought something must be wrong, and stopped," the officer said, pointing the campus officer out to Parmenter.

"What did you see in the car?" Parmenter asked.

"Bodies," the campus officer replied. "And a lot of blood. I didn't want to touch anything—they were obviously dead—so I secured the scene and called police."

"Did you see anything else of interest?" Parmenter asked.

Unfortunately, the officer said that he'd seen nothing and no one to help in the investigation.

Officers on the scene told Parmenter that so far there were no witnesses. The mobile crime scene unit arrived and began photographing the car's interior and exterior and began looking for physical evidence. As they walked around the car, the investigators noted what they saw.

On the passenger side of the car, a few feet from the door closer to the pond, was a large pool of blood. The bloody area was wide and deep. Evidently, something had happened here.

"There's more over here, toward the car," a forensic investigator told Detective Parmenter. Several more areas of blood led, more or less, from the blood pool to the side of the car.

Detectives also worked several patches of crushed grass in the turf beside the car. These were possibly areas where a struggle had occurred—although this would have to be verified by other forensic evidence, since there were any number of other possible explanations.

As the technicians began collecting blood specimens from the ground and looking for other clues, Parmenter approached the car for the first time and peered inside.

Most notable about the car's interior was the blood. It splattered and soaked the dashboard, the seats, and the three bodies in the car. The first victim the sleuth observed was a young man with his head on the passenger floor and his legs crossed near the driver's window. The angle and the position made it appear as though the young man had been pitched headfirst into the car.

Two bodies were in the backseat, one on top of the other. On top was a female, face up, with her head jammed into the seat. The victim, who appeared to be in her teens, was partially undressed and covered in blood.

Beneath her was a young male. Although he was obscured partially by the woman on top of him, the third victim's face was visible between the two seats, facedown with his legs folded in.

All the victims had obviously died violently. Even from a careful distance, Detective Parmenter could see wounds in various parts of the victims' bodies. It was a bloodbath in the car—the kind of scene that made even a veteran homicide detective wince.

Parmenter checked with the crime scene team to see if they had discovered anything else around the car.

"We've found an automatic teller card from a bank, in the name of Andrew McGinnis," the technician said.

Parmenter believed the card probably belonged to one of the victims. That and the car's license plate were the best leads yet in search of identifications for the victims. Parmenter checked to make sure that the car's registration was being traced.

Careful preservation of the scene would be vital to the investigation, Parmenter knew. He worked with the crime scene team, a serologist and a blood splatter expert, advising them on what to take samples of. They wanted as wide a variety of samples as possible. Because they didn't want to jeopardize the integrity of the evidence inside the car, the investigators concentrated their efforts on the exterior. Working on the inside of the car would be tricky. A decision was made to tow the car on a flatbed to the medical examiner's rear lot, where a controlled environment could be maintained.

Detective Parmenter ran the Dade County plate and discovered that it was registered as a leased vehicle to 20-year-old Ronny Quisbert. There was no way to know yet if Quisbert was among the victims, but it was an excellent place to start.

In the late morning, the car was towed to the medical examiner's office. There, over a period of time, the interior was photographed, samples of various kinds were taken, and evidence collected. Fortunately, there was plenty of evidence in the car.

On the driver's seat was a gold, two-finger ring, covered in blood, which bore the name "Steven." Steven was the third male name to appear in the investigation, and there were just two male victims. It was obvious from observing the ring that it had probably been pulled off the owner.

Also inside the car, sleuths found numerous fingerprints, some clean and some bloody. The blood splatter evidence would be helpful in creating a scenario for the crime.

On the front passenger seat a bloodied buck knife was collected for examination as a possible murder weapon.

Finally, about 3:00 P.M., investigators removed the bodies carefully, one at a time. Although a thorough autopsy would be done on the three victims, it was obvious that each had sustained multiple stab wounds in various parts of their bodies. When the two bodies in the backseat were separated, investigators discovered that the young male in the back was also partially undressed.

By midafternoon, the first news reports of the grisly discovery on the campus were broadcast. Following news accounts that featured pictures of the car, the Metro-Dade Police department was flooded with calls.

All the witnesses said largely the same thing.

"I think I recognize that car in the report," a caller said, reflecting the statements of others. The caller said that the driver of the car was young Ronny Quisbert, a student at Florida International University. Callers had various ideas on whom the driver had been associating with in the past 24 hours.

Finally, one female caller, Sabrina Collins, said she had direct knowledge of circumstances the night before.

"I was out with Ronny and other friends last night before they dropped me off," Collins said. She proceeded to detail the events of the night before.

According to Collins, she and Quisbert were out with two other friends, Andrew McGinnis, 21, and Regina Rodriguez, 15. McGinnis was a senior at the University of Miami from Pennsylvania, and Rodriguez was a Miami Beach native.

"We were at a bar near the school," Collins said. It was the kind of bar frequently found near colleges—with a reputation, deserved or not, for serving alcohol to underage students.

Collins said they saw a number of friends at the bar and generally had a good time, with no sign that anything was wrong. The group did some drinking, and, Collins said, they met another young man there.

"He was a National Guardsman," Collins said. She gave a physical description of the young man. "Other people must have seen him there with us, too."

Around 2:00 A.M. the group, including the guardsman, left the bar.

"They took me home and said they were going out to another bar, the four of them," Collins said. "That's the last time I heard from them." She named the second bar the group was headed toward.

"Did you catch the guardsman's name?" Detective Parmenter asked.

"No, I'm sorry I don't remember," Collins answered. However, she could describe the man and remembered some personal information. She described the man as black, in his early 20s, and said he was wearing camouflage gear.

"He said he was in from Tampa and was down here doing hurricane relief," Collins said.

Several other callers, including the victims' friends, contacted Detective Parmenter with similar information. Some had seen the National Guardsman and gave similar descriptions.

Now Detective Parmenter had a good idea who the victims were—but not a positive identification. That came from a surprising source inside the police department.

Working for the forensics department of the police complex was a young assistant photographer. When he, like everyone else, went to see the course of the investigation, he got a look at the car and reported to Parmenter.

"I think I know that car," the photographer said. He added that if he was right, he would recognize the victims, as well. Parmenter arranged for the young man to view the bodies.

"I know who they are," the photographer said. The victims were indeed Ronny Quisbert, Andrew McGinnis, and Regina Rodriguez. The victims' relatives would eventually have to verify the identifications, but for all intents and purposes, Parmenter finally knew who the dead trio were.

The photographer provided home contact numbers for the victims, and several detectives were assigned to visit the families, give them the bad news, and request possible additional information.

Meanwhile, calls continued to come in from people who'd seen the young victims with the National Guardsman. Amazingly, no one knew the guardsman's name.

"He was playing pool and drinking a little," said one caller who had seen the guardsman at the first bar. The caller said that the guardsman didn't seem to be drunk.

Other callers added to the portrait of the guardsman.

"He was hitting on every woman in the bar—hitting on them hard," a caller said. Several others said the same thing, though all added that the young guardsman had not been very successful.

Detective Parmenter knew who the victims were and had some idea how they were killed and how they spent their evening before the killings. He was missing one important piece of information. Who did it? Parmenter had a description and perhaps one other piece of information that could help reveal the killer's identity: the name "Steven" on the ring found in the car.

Was the guardsman named Steven? Was he the killer?

Under normal circumstances, that would be an excellent lead. However, at the time, South Florida was swarming with guardsmen who were working hurricane relief. Parmenter could only hope that some of the other personal information was true. Otherwise the killer of the young trio might go unpunished forever. People in South Florida had suffered enough. Investigators did not want to add an unsolved triple homicide to the local collective conscience.

By that afternoon, detectives had successfully contacted the victims' next-of-kin. Unfortunately, the grieving families had no information to help in the investigation.

With a handle on the victims, Detective Parmenter traveled to the Army National Guard encampment at the Tamiami Park, located next to the campus of FIU. It was a full-frontal assault in the investigation, if something of a longshot.

In Parmenter's experience, a knife-wielding assailant was often cut in the process of delivering his blows. Parmenter went to the sick bay at the encampment and asked if a guardsman named Steven had sought treatment for cut wounds on his hands or arms. Amazingly, the staff at sick bay said one had.

"We had a young soldier come in this morning with lacerations on his arm," a medic said. "His name is Steven Coleman." The medic said he bandaged both arms and that the wounds were not terribly serious.

"Did he say how he was injured?" Parmenter asked.

"He said he cut himself on a fence," the medic replied.

It sounded like a good lead. Detective Parmenter contacted the commanders of the guard unit. He explained that this was a delicate situation, and he needed their help. The officers agreed. Soon Detective Parmenter was face to face with Steven Coleman.

Coleman had bandages on one arm and a Band-Aid on the other hand's thumb. Parmenter asked Coleman if he would accompany him back to the police station. Coleman was friendly and jovial and readily agreed.

At the station, Coleman was Mirandized. He consented to let investigators search his tent, have his fingerprints and photo taken, and to speak to Parmenter.

Steven Coleman started off by talking about his background. He lived in Tampa, Florida, but was originally from the Bronx, New York, and had lived in North Carolina, as well. He said he worked various office-type jobs and was unmarried.

"What did you do last night?" Parmenter asked.

"Some other guys and I went out to a bar, played pool, and drank some beer," Coleman said. *"Monday Night Football* was on, and we wanted to watch it. We went back to the tent, split a case of beer, and watched more of the game."

Later that night, Coleman said, he returned to the bar and drank yet more beer.

"I met some people there, two guys and a girl. We dropped one of the girls off and went to another bar. We played quarters. I lost a lot, so I drank a lot—maybe seven, eight more beers."

At closing time, Coleman asked for a ride back to his unit. The three agreed, but they turned into the college campus instead.

"I asked why we were there, but no one told me," Coleman said. He said he was in the rear right seat of the car, next to one guy. The other man was driving, and the girl was next to him.

"The guy next to me asked me how much money the guard paid me," Coleman said. "It was very strange."

Then the driver allegedly said, "I'm tired of this shit."

"I tried to get out of the car, but they locked the doors." Coleman said he asked what was going on but received no answer.

"Then this fight just happened."

According to Coleman, the man in the back hit him first. A fight ensued, and eventually the driver stabbed him. Coleman said he used the man in the backseat as a human shield. He then fought all three of the young people with his own knife, "until the girl screamed and slumped over," Coleman said. Next, he disabled the driver and finally the man in the backseat. When it was over, all three were dead.

"I saw the sun rising, and a police car driving by," Coleman said. He waded into the pond about halfway, but the police car did not stop. "Then I walked back to camp and saw the medic a little later."

Detective Parmenter told Coleman that the physical evidence did not verify this story—specifically the location of the bodies.

"Everything was true up until when I said I went into the water," Coleman said. He said he looked back, saw the girl sitting up too high in the car and returned to push the girl down farther.

"Tell me some truth," Parmenter said. "You're not even close."

Coleman then said that when he was rearranging the girl's body, her shirt was inadvertently pulled off to her waist. That, Coleman said, excited him, so he proceeded to have sexual intercourse with her.

Parmenter said that Coleman was still not telling the entire truth. But Coleman, for the moment, had nothing more to add.

"Why did this happen?" Parmenter asked.

"I'm not sure," Coleman replied. He added that when the driver said he was tired of "this shit," he, Coleman, was worried and told the people that he'd "kick all of their asses."

Parmenter changed his line of questioning once again and asked Coleman if he had a two-finger ring engraved with his name.

"Yes, I did," Coleman said. "But I don't know where it's at or what happened to it."

Parmenter knew. He pushed Coleman again, maintaining that the guardsman's story still didn't match the facts.

This time, Coleman became very emotional. Up to this

point, he'd been friendly and helpful. He now became distraught.

"Listen, I'm not gay," Coleman insisted. However, he said that with the one victim's position in the car, he became aroused, stripped the young man's pants off, and sodomized him.

With Coleman's final story, the claim pretty much matched the scene of the crime. Parmenter was done with his initial interviews, although Steven Coleman refused to give a formal recorded statement.

Coleman was arrested for the crimes and booked into the jail.

In the next few days, Parmenter worked on Coleman's story. He discovered there were still some discrepancies in it. For example, witnesses had said that Coleman didn't drink anywhere near as much alcohol as he claimed.

On the other hand, Detective Parmenter could find not one person who said anything bad about Coleman. He had no significant criminal record and had a nondistinguished but perfectly acceptable National Guard record. People who knew Coleman said that he was a friendly, decent man.

Meanwhile, autopsies revealed that the three victims had been butchered with a knife. Rodriguez and McGinnis were sodomized, McGinnis after death and Rodriguez probably just as she died. Only McGinnis had serious defensive wounds—which was unusual given Coleman's statement.

The blood in the car belong largely to Quisbert. The blood droplets outside the car belonged to Coleman. Test results on the one-foot-by-18-inch pool of blood revealed that it belonged to Regina Rodriguez. With this information, Detective Parmenter realized that Steven Coleman had left out a major part of the story.

Most perplexing was that Andrew McGinnis's blood wasn't found anywhere on the scene.

Parmenter and the crime scene investigators returned to examine the car. In a complex series of blood splatter tests, the investigators came to the conclusions that at least two of the victims had not been murdered in the car.

Also significant was that only one knife slash was found in the car—beginning at the center of the backseat and moving toward the driver's side seat. There was no way that a two-party knife fight occurred in the car.

The forensics information helped the sleuths form a theory about what happened. Coleman may have been left alone in the car with Quisbert while Rodriguez and McGinnis got out of the car for some reason. There was no way to know what happened, but Quisbert may have been killed in the car without his friends knowing anything was wrong.

Detective Parmenter theorized that Rodriguez and McGinnis were killed at the same place in the grass—near the pool of blood. One theory was that McGinnis's blood was beneath Rodriguez's and didn't show up because only one sample was taken from that pool.

Both victims were then sodomized and tossed back into the car with their dead friend, according to this theory.

There was no way to prove the theory, and it was largely moot. Physical evidence and Coleman's own statement were enough to lay the blame on him. The fact that Coleman lied about the events only made him appear more guilty.

More evidence came in during the subsequent investigation. The medics at sick bay said that Coleman was sober and jovial when he got treatment for his arms. There was no smell of alcohol on or around him.

Detectives searched Coleman's tent and found yet more corroborative evidence. In the otherwise fairly neat tent, sleuths found a pair of camouflage pants and shirt that were soaking wet. Inside the pants, they found a bloody knife with grass on it.

There was no way to know which knife—the one found in the car or the one found in Coleman's pants or both—was used in the murders. One of the victims might have had a weapon. This, however, was irrelevant.

The case against Steven Coleman was solid, even though investigators could only conjecture about what really happened.

Research on the three victims revealed that none of them had violent backgrounds or histories of mayhem.

For almost two years, defense attorneys tried to come up with a defense for Coleman. Apparently, they could not. In September 1994, Coleman pleaded guilty to avoid the death penalty.

Steven Coleman will serve three consecutive life sentences for the murders. With state sentencing requirements, that amounts to at least 75 years before Coleman can be considered for release.

"VICIOUS CAREER CRIMINAL ESCAPED TO CARJACK & KILL!"

by Barry Benedict

San Diego patrol officers were in light traffic on Monday evening, October 22, 1992, when they got a call about a shooting at the intersection of Fifth Avenue and G Street in the heart of the city's Gas Lamp District.

Although downtown shootings are not rare, the address of this one took officers by surprise. The Gas Lamp is a gentrified rectangle of trendy restaurants, swanky shops, and hip dance clubs that form one of the city's most popular entertainment districts. Heavily patrolled, Gas Lamp residents worry less about shootings than panhandlers who cling to the streets.

It took less than a minute to punch through the red lights and around jaywalkers before the officers arrived at the intersection. Witnesses, including several outdoor diners from a nearby restaurant, formed a circle in the intersection. In the middle of the circle was the body of a man in his mid-to-late 20s. He was sprawled on his side, with the back of his head blown away.

More police arrived, followed by a homicide team

headed by Sergeant Mike Hurley. By then, the shooting scene was cordoned off with barricade tape and ringed with enough television camera crews to film a TV series.

The victim was 29-year-old clerk Michael Champion, of Hillcrest. Investigators questioned the patrol supervisor at the scene and several witnesses, including Dave Marsh, a friend of the victim's.

Their statements formed a bizarre scenario.

Champion, a 10-year Navy veteran and employee at a car stereo shop, had spent the evening with Marsh at a bar in the Gas Lamp District, playing darts and watching *Monday Night Football*. After the game, the two stopped for a beer at Brewski's, a popular microbrewery on lower Fifth Avenue. They then continued to Champion's maroon 1989 Honda Civic.

They drove up Fifth to G Street and stopped for a red light. The corner is wall-to-wall restaurants, and both sides of the street were thick with pedestrians.

Suddenly, a man in an orange jumpsuit yanked open the Honda's back door and jumped in behind Champion.

"Give me your car!" the man ordered.

"Mike told the guy to get out of the car," Marsh told detectives. "Then the guy shot him."

Marsh said he was unaware the man had a gun until he felt the concussion from the muzzle. He turned in horror and saw Michael slump forward, the back of his head blown away. Marsh said he fumbled with the lock on the passenger side of the car and got out. He then ran to a nearby bar and called 911.

Meanwhile, the gunman grabbed Champion by the front of his shirt and pulled him out onto the street. Witnesses saw the gunman jump inside the car and speed north, weaving around startled pedestrians who were crossing the street. He went through a red light and disappeared around the corner.

The shooting took place in front of Trattoria La Strada,

one of the most popular restaurants in the downtown area. Diners who packed the sidewalk tables had witnessed the shooting.

The gunman was described as a black man, about 6 feet 4 inches tall and 240 to 250 pounds with a tight haircut, and wearing a jail-issued jumpsuit.

Detectives had no trouble identifying the brazen gunman.

Minutes before the shooting, a green sheriff's van transporting inmates from a San Diego County Jail in El Cajon to the Metropolitan Correctional Center downtown stopped at Fourth and Market.

As the driver, a 58-year-old female San Diego deputy, waited for the light to change, one of the inmates, Johnaton George, kicked out the rear door and dove out of the bus.

George, a former football linebacker, sprinted through the streets to a car parked at a stoplight. He pulled the female motorist out by the neck and jumped behind the wheel. But the motorist had the keys in her hand and refused to let go.

George then ran to a Radio Cab one block away and tried to commandeer it. He struggled with the reluctant driver and bit him in the face but didn't get the car.

During the struggle, the 5-foot 2-inch female deputy who had been transporting the prisoners in the green bus, caught up with George and jumped on his back, knocking him to the pavement. George beat her senseless and stole her service revolver. He ran another block to the Fifth and G Street intersection, where Michael Champion waited at a red light, heading home to Hillcrest and his wife of just four years.

As pieces of the bizarre shooting fell into place, more shots rang out.

Police sped to an apartment at the 400 block of South Euclid and found a young woman and her four children cringing in terror. A middle-aged man who had also been inside the apartment during the incident appeared dazed.

The woman was Johnaton George's former girlfriend. She said George had pounded on the front door, demanding to be let in. When she refused, he tried to knock the door down. When that didn't work, he tried to rip the bars off one of the front windows. Finally, he pulled a gun and shot four rounds into the house. One of the slugs came within an inch of striking the dazed man who had been asleep in the front bedroom.

George then got back into the stolen Honda and fled.

George's ex-girlfriend told police that she had been scheduled to testify as a defense witness when George was scheduled to stand trial on a shoplifting rap in the South Bath area. But at the last moment, she decided not to testify.

She said George had threatened to kill her for not appearing in court. But she didn't think she had anything to worry about because he was locked up in jail. The four shots fired through her home made her think again.

At police headquarters, detectives pulled Johnaton George's lengthy criminal file. It listed an address in Southeast San Diego—the home of his parents. Police staked out the residence, but the jail escapee never showed.

The search for George was one of the largest manhunts in the city's history. San Diego police and sheriff's officers checked out dozens of sightings. One call came from Escondido, 30 miles north of San Diego. A man fitting George's description was seen pedaling a bike in the north end of the city known as County Club Lane. Police and a sheriff's helicopter searched the area.

A man fitting George's description was also briefly detained at the U.S.-Mexican border.

Sleuths questioned friends and former criminal associates of the 240-pound fugitive. George was a career criminal, well known to patrol officers who worked the city's crime-plagued southeast side.

George's story was revealed in court documents detailing a string of rapes dating back 15 years.

It began June 7, 1997, when a 19-year-old woman returned to her Southeast San Diego apartment after seeing a movie at the College Grove Shopping Center. As she opened her front door, a man pushed her from behind, picked her up, and took her into the bedroom, where he raped her.

The victim described her attacker as black, well over 6 feet tall, and more than 200 pounds.

Over the next 10 days, a rapist matching that description struck three more times. One of the victims was an 18-year-old housewife who was attacked in her Euclid Avenue apartment. Another was a 14-year-old girl who was assaulted in an alley after she left a friend's home.

One of the victims said she tried to keep the man out by locking a large solid oak door and pushing a heavy refrigerator behind it. But the rapist managed to break the door down and push the refrigerator back.

It was not until June 20th that the police got their first break. A patrol officer was poking along 49th Street when he spotted a large black man in a skin-tight white T-shirt breaking into a ground-floor apartment. Police chased the suspect two blocks and saw him break through the front door of an apartment. Officers poured in after him and arrested Johnaton George.

George, then 19 years old, had a rap sheet for drug possession, car theft, and assault. He denied raping anyone, but he was picked out in separate lineups by two victims who identified him as their rapist. And in a search of his Ocean View Boulevard apartment, detectives found a jeweled purse that had been stolen from one of the victims after the assaults.

George pled not guilty to multiple sex counts, claiming

he was innocent. But at his attorney's urging, he later agreed to a deal and pled guilty to two of the rapes, one charge of lewd and lascivious conduct with a minor, and one count of first-degree burglary.

Before sentencing, George was admitted to Patton State Hospital in San Bernardino County to undergo psychiatric evaluation. He escaped but was caught two weeks later and sent to Atascadero State Hospital for the criminally insane. While there, George romanced a transsexual and the two became engaged.

The romance ended when George was returned to San Diego in 1980 to be sentenced for the rapes he'd committed three years earlier. George told Judge David Gill before sentencing that he had sexually assaulted the women but said it wasn't his fault. He claimed he sought revenge after a white man raped his girlfriend.

"I was engaged to her for four years," he said. "After that white man raped her, I hated all white people and wanted to strike back."

George said he misdirected his rage on his victims, something he learned in his stay at Atascadero State Prison. He said the insight from counseling sessions had made him a better person. While in prison, he planned to get a college degree in physical education and try out for professional football.

Prosecutor Mike Carpenter urged the judge to give George the maximum sentence, noting that George was an intimidating, vicious, and violent criminal who had never shown the slightest regard for the welfare of his victims. Carpenter said he doubted George had gained anything during his stay at Atascadero State Hospital except perhaps to learn the professional language necessary to convince people that he was cured.

"He learned that language during his stay at the California Youth Authority where he was committed for robbery, and he learned the language as a result of his stay at Chino prison," Carpenter noted. "Mr. George is telling us what he thinks we want to hear, that he is rehabilitated and can be released back into society. But it is only language. I submit that Mr. George should be sentenced consecutively on all counts before you because of the very nature of the charges themselves."

Judge Gill concurred with the prosecutor and ordered George imprisoned for five years to life. "Mr. George is a conman. He knows how to shine people on," Gill noted. "I think by and large that's what he is doing here and this is by and large what his testimony amounted to here."

Judge Gill enclosed a letter in George's file, warning officials at the Vacaville State Prison that the inmate was a menace to others and deserved the maximum incarceration.

But George was released on parole in 1985 after serving just five years behind bars, the minimum sentence required. He was paroled to San Diego. That same year, he was arrested for beating a man to a pulp and stealing his wallet. Six months later, he was arrested for failure to notify authorities he was a mentally disordered sex offender after he moved out of the county.

George had compiled a list of arrests and parole infractions when he was arrested outside a supermarket in South San Diego. Security guards at the market told the police that they had observed George as he stuffed baby food under his shirt, then went through the checkout lane without paying. When guards confronted him, he tried to walk away.

George gave police false identification and was allowed to go when a computer check did not turn up any warrants. When a second computer check revealed that the fictitious name George gave police was an alias he frequently used, a warrant was issued and George was arrested.

At a preliminary hearing in South San Diego County Court, George claimed he was innocent and said he had witnesses who could verify that he was nowhere near the market when the shoplifter was apprehended.

During a lunchbreak, George was put in a holding cell. Inexplicably, the door was left unlocked, and George escaped by walking down a corridor and through an empty courtroom to the front door.

A warrant was issued for his arrest.

Four days later, George walked into a pet store in North Park to purchase supplies for a pet parakeet. The owner recognized the powerfully built ex-con as the man who had stolen a car from in front of his store four days earlier. He called police.

It took five officers to subdue the belligerent George and take him to jail. He was charged with the escape from the holding cell and suspicion of car theft.

As an ex-con on parole, George faced up to seven years in prison on the shoplifting rap. The federal government had also decided to try George as a career criminal, which could put him behind bars for the rest of his life.

It was while he was being transferred to the Metropolitan Correctional Center that George overpowered the female deputy, shot Michael Champion, and fled in his Honda.

A task force of 30 investigators under the direction of Sergeant Gordon Redding focused on locating George and having him returned to jail. This time the charge was murder.

The task force investigators sorted through hundreds of tips and leads. One of those tips came from a retired San Diego deputy sheriff, who learned that a man matching George's description had visited a man in Spring Valley. The man told task force investigators that he knew George when they were both growing up in Southeast

San Diego and that George had visited him on the night of the shooting.

"I thought he was in jail," the witness told detectives. "Johnaton said he was, but that he broke out."

George said he was going to get out of San Diego and meet with some friends back East. He said he first had to get some money together.

The witness said he gave George a few bucks, and he left that night. He hadn't seen him since. George didn't say where he was going, but he got the impression it might be Los Angeles.

Investigators continued to question George's friends and former inmates who might have information that would lead police to George's whereabouts. One inmate was a 49-year-old longtime convict whose trouble with the law included burglary and assault convictions and who, like George, faced heavy prison time as an armed career criminal.

The inmate said they were housed together in the federal jail when George described an intricate plan to escape from a sheriff's van, commandeer a car, and hunt down those he blamed for putting him behind bars.

"He said he would kill anyone who got in his way," the inmate told detectives. "I knew he had gone off the deep end. Something had to have snapped in his mind."

The inmate said George had noted that a single deputy had escorted him to and from the jail in El Cajon where he was being held. He said George had fashioned a homemade handcuff key, but about five or six days before his escape, he lifted a real key from a jailer's key chain, which had been left lying unattended in a common area of the jail.

The inmate said George had also studied the double-sided doors of sheriff's vans, and he noticed that if you kicked it with enough force, it would open.

"He said after he got out of the van he was going to

take the first car he could and go," the inmate said. "He said he was going to do it even if he had to bust the window open with his hand and pull someone out by the throat.

"George said if he had to, he would take the officer's weapon. He didn't want to do that, because he figured they'll get him for it, but he would do it if necessary because he wasn't going back to prison."

Inmates talked about escape plans all the time, the witness said, but George actually sounded serious. "I knew he had escaped from the lockup in South Bay and Atascadero. And the plan sounded good."

The inmate said he was shocked, however, when he learned that a motorist had been killed during George's escape and that this was partly the reason he was coming forward.

Investigators checked out the inmate's story, but they were unable to determine if George had stolen a key from a deputy's key ring, or how he was able to slip out of his handcuffs and the waist belt he wore while being transported to the Metropolitan Correctional Center.

Meanwhile, task force investigators continued sifting through leads hoping to zero in on George. Detectives learned that George had friends in Murphysboro, Illinois, and Chicago, and that he might be trying to contact them.

It was also learned that George had a family friend who lived in Compton, California, a suburb of Los Angeles. Compton police were alerted by San Diego police that George might be in their city.

The search soon focused on "Fruittown," a working-class neighborhood, so called because the streets are named after fruit trees.

On October 13th, the search focused on a home on West Cherry Street, where a man matching Johnaton

George's description and going by the name of Sampson had been spotted.

Compton officers went to the door of the home using the old ruse that they had received reports of a domestic fight at the house. As they talked to the female home-owner, one of the officers looked behind the woman and saw a large, heavyset man bolt out the back door. Seconds later, an officer at the back of the house yelled, "Police! Get down, Get down!"

The officers at the front door ran past the woman into the backyard where Johnaton George lay facedown in the dirt, held at bay by two shotgun-wielding officers.

San Diego police were notified that George was in custody. A caravan of police cars arrived in Compton to take the suspect back to San Diego. He was shackled hand and foot and seated in the middle of the backseat of one car, with police officers on each side flanking him and two other officers in front.

George offered no resistance in the two-hour drive to San Diego. He was booked into the San Diego County Jail, charged with suspicion of murder.

On October 16th, the 240-pound escape artist made a brief appearance in municipal court. George beamed with pleasure as he entered the packed courtroom to be charged with multiple felony counts in connection with Michael Champion's murder.

One of the spectators was Dave Marsh, who had sat next to Champion during the shooting and would be a key witness in the upcoming trial.

George was impassive as he was ordered to stand trial for Champion's murder. The district attorney's office later announced it would seek the death sentence.

First, however, George would stand trial in federal court on weapons charges and for being a career crimi-nal, which carried an automatic life-without-parole sen-tence. A federal jury heard evidence that George had stolen a handgun from his grandmother's apartment on South 36th Street, and that he had been convicted on 19 major felonies that included strong-armed robbery, assault, and rape. He had also escaped from jail or county institutions four times.

George was found guilty on multiple federal charges. On September 23rd, he was sentenced to spend the rest of his natural life behind bars.

George was returned to the county jail where he received a celebrity's welcome from other cons. George celebrated the occasion with an illegal snort of methamphetamine. He was caught doing it and charged with another felony, bringing the tally to an even 20.

George was scheduled to stand trial on murder charges in February 1994, but the trial did not begin until June.

Key witness Dave Marsh took the witness stand and told jurors about that fateful night when an evening of darts with his good friend Mike Champion turned into a nightmare. He said that George jumped into the car and demanded the keys, and when Champion refused, George pointed a handgun inside the car.

"All I saw was a chrome revolver in the hands of Mr George pointed square at Mike's head," Marsh said. "There was a deafening explosion and everything was quiet after that."

Marsh said he thought the shot had missed Champion until he saw all the blood. "It was the most blood I had ever seen in my life," the witness said, breaking into tears. "It was running out of Mike's head."

George, however, said he didn't mean to shoot Champion and blamed the victim for his own death. Taking the witness stand, the defendant said his intention was to steal the car and that he had pointed the cocked weapon at Champion only to scare him.

"The gun went off when the driver raised his hands,"

George said. "If had just gotten out of the car, he wouldn't have gotten shot."

Johnaton George was found guilty of first-degree murder. But jurors split seven to five on the death penalty. By law, George was automatically sentenced to life without the possibility of parole, but Prosecutor Robert Phillips said he was considering pursuing the death penalty for George in a retrial of the penalty phase.

In any case, George must first serve his federal term of life-without-parole before being transferred to a California prison.

"ARIZONA'S REST STOP KILLERS SNUFFED THE IVY LEAGUE LOVERS"

by Barry Benedict

One of the strangest and most shocking criminal cases in Arizona history began late on the Tuesday evening of September 10, 1991, when a motorist called the Yuma County Sheriff's Office. He said he had pulled into a rest stop off Interstate 8 about 30 miles east of Yuma city limits when he saw two persons sprawled on the pavement beside a car.

"They weren't moving," the caller said. "I think they might be dead."

Deputy Richard Johnson went to investigate. Pulling into the rest stop, he saw a dark blue Chevy Chevette nosed into one of the parking slots. A woman was sprawled beside the passenger side door, her motionless body pressed against the charcoal black asphalt. Blood matted her hair and formed pools beneath her on the pavement.

On the driver's side of the car, the deputy found a young man lying facedown on the pavement, moaning.

"Have you been shot?" Johnson asked.

"I think so," the man replied.

"What happened?"

"We were attacked," the victim replied. "He threatened me with a gun."

"Can you identify him?"

"No, I don't know who he was."

Paramedics arrived at the scene. They checked the woman, but she was dead. There was nothing they could do for her. Her companion, however, was alive, though just barely. They worked on him at the scene and en route to the Yuma Regional Medical Center, where he was admitted to the emergency room suffering from a gunshot wound.

Detectives Leon Wilmont and Ken Lindsey headed the investigation into what would come to be called "The Rest Stop Murders." They arrived at the scene to find barricade tape stretched across the entrance and exit to the rest stop. In the middle of the rest stop, the sleuths found the late model Chevy Chevette and beside it the dead woman, who was now covered with a sheet.

The woman appeared to be in her early 20s, of medium height and weight, and with thick, dark brown hair that hung to her shoulders. She was wearing a blouse, dark brown shorts, and sandals.

After examining the corpse under the sheet, detectives focused their attention on the car. The 1986 Chevette bore New York license plates and had a roof rack packed with luggage. Boxes containing college books and papers filled the backseat. A sticker for Cornell University was on the left side of the bumper.

In the glove compartment, detectives found registration listing Bryan Keith Bernstein, 22, as the owner. They also found identification for Laura Bernstein, who was also 22.

The crime scene search continued well into the morning. Deputies explored around the car and searched the asphalt, looking for tire tracks and physical evidence that might tell them more about the crime.

The victim's body was taken to the medical examiner's office, where an autopsy was scheduled.

Investigators scratched for leads. The motorist who called the sheriff's office said that the Chevette was the only car in the rest stop when he pulled in to stretch his legs. He said the whole scene looked mighty strange.

"I would have called from the rest stop, but there wasn't a phone," he told detectives. "I stopped the first place I could."

Apparently, the Bernsteins had been resting when they were shot. Both were fully clothed, and there was no evidence to indicate they had been sexually assaulted. The motive, detectives suspected, was robbery.

Police hoped that Bryan Bernstein might be able to tell them more about the shootings. After his condition stabilized, he was flown to the prestigious Barrow Neurological Institute in Phoenix. Initially, doctors thought the young man had a slight chance to pull through. But Bernstein quickly took a turn for the worse and slipped into a coma from which he would never awake. Within hours after his arrival, Bryan Bernstein was pronounced brain dead.

Bryan and Laura Bernstein, police learned, had been a gifted young couple. They had met at Cornell University in Ithaca, New York. Bryan grew up in Texas, the son of two professors. Laura was raised in Puerto Rico in a family that was also academically inclined. The Bernsteins were bright, hardworking students. While attending Cornell, Bryan worked at a pizza parlor and Laura at the university library. During the summer of their senior year, they were interns in Washington, Bryan at the U.S. Justice Department, Laura at the Smithsonian Museum. In July 1989, the couple were married at Buttermilk Falls State Park

near Cornell, the third generation of Bernsteins to be
wed while attending school there.

In 1991, both Bryan and Laura won fellowships to
UCLA for graduate school. It was a free ticket that included room and board and meant the couple could de-
vote their full time to their studies and not have to worry
about part-time jobs.

They leased an apartment in married-student housing
near Westwood campus.

Bryan planned to study political science, then go into
law. His dream was to be a U.S. Supreme Court justice.
Laura was majoring in library science. Her goal was to
do research for the Smithsonian.

After graduating, the couple spent the summer at the
campus of Auburn University in Alabama, where Bryan's
parents taught. They did research, hung out, and went
to movies. On Labor Day, they piled their stuff into
Bryan's aging blue Chevette and headed for California.

It was a leisurely trip that included a stop in Texas to
see relatives and a side trip to Carlsbad, New Mexico, to
visit the famous Carlsbad Caverns. On September 9th, the
Bernsteins toured Old Tucson and spent the night at a
Best Western Motel. Early the next morning, Bryan called
his parents to say he and Laura were leaving that morning
and would call once they arrived in Westwood.

The couple got as far as the outskirts of Yuma where
two bullets put an end to their dreams and their lives.

Police learned that the Bernsteins were not in the habit
of picking up hitchhikers, and that Bryan had said nothing on the phone about giving anyone a ride. Detectives
suspected that the Bernsteins had encountered the gunman after they pulled into the rest stop.

Thirty miles from town, the rest stop was an isolated
spot that offered no bathrooms or drinking water. Travelers didn't spend much time there. It was the perfect
place to hold up the occasional unsuspecting motorist.

From the examination of the crime scene, detectives figured that the Ivy League couple had been shot while sitting in their car and never had a chance to defend themselves or get away.

"It was a cold-blooded killing," Detective Leon Wilmont noted glumly. "Those young kids never had a chance."

Police were still searching for leads when they got word that someone had tried to use one of the couple's stolen credit cards at the local Kmart store.

On September 11th, the day after the murders, a young man had entered the store and tried to pay for a T-shirt and blue jeans with the Bernsteins' Discover card. Although the card had not yet been entered as stolen, the store supervisor refused to honor the card because the signature on the back didn't match the young man's handwriting.

"I told him that the bearer of the card would have to sign for the purchase," the supervisor told detectives. "He said the card belonged to his dad and he would be right back."

She said the boy left the store and returned a few minutes later. He said his dad didn't want to sign because the jeans and shirt cost too much. The supervisor said she tore up the credit slip and the boy left.

She described the youth as white, 18 to 20 years old, thin and short, perhaps no taller than 5 feet 4 inches. He had hazel-colored eyes, a pug nose, and medium-length brown hair that hung over his forehead.

She said she watched him climb into a yellow pickup that was driven by an older man. They both drove away.

Store employees went to the police station to help create composites of the young man and driver. They also looked through mugshot books of pickup trucks and decided the vehicle was a faded yellow half-ton pickup, a 1962 to 1966 Chevy or GMC Fleetside. It had a square

steel tubing over the bed and a toolbox that ran length-
wise along the side rails.

A description of the vehicle was later released to the
media. It produced a few calls, as did a Silent Witness
reward of $1,000, but none resulted in any solid leads.

In mid-October, Yuma County Sheriff John Phipps announced plans to run for reelection in 1992. The an-
nouncement scotched rumors that Yuma County's top
lawman might run for county board of supervisors or
the Arizona legislature. Phipps said that one of his top
priorities would be finding the killer or killers of Bryan
and Laura Bernstein. Like others, the affable sheriff had
been outraged by the senseless killings of the Ivy League
couple.

Phipps said that he had assigned two detectives to work
the case full time, as long as there were any leads to follow. He admitted, however, that rest stop crimes were
hard to solve, and that this one had been particularly
tough.

"We don't plan to give up on it, though," Phipps said.
"We plan to do everything that is humanly possible to
find who did it and bring them to trial."

In December, deputies distributed 2,500 fliers with
drawings of the two men seen fleeing the Kmart store in
the yellow truck. The fliers were sent to law enforcement
agencies in Arizona, California, and New Mexico and distributed locally to the telephone, cable, and utility companies. Sheriff's Deputy Ralph Ogden said the aim was
to have a flier in every utility vehicle that traveled the
service alleys in the Yuma area.

It was good, dogged police work, but like other efforts,
it did not produce any usable leads.

The Rest Stop Killings made the news one more time
in 1991—when the *Yuma Daily Sun* ran a selection of the
year's top 10 stories. The big story, of course, was Opera-

tion Desert Storm, but the murders of Bryan and Laura Bernstein came seventh on the list.

At the police station, the order of the stories was, if anything, reversed. But without a hit on the yellow pickup or the suspect sketches, detectives had little to go on.

It was not until three months into the new year that new life was pumped into the dormant investigation.

On Saturday March 22, 1992, San Diego Detectives Gerry Kramer and Terry Burgland were completing the paperwork on an investigation of an assault with a deadly weapon. It was a small potatoes sort of crime that rarely makes the headlines.

On Friday afternoon, 16-year-old Travis Wade Amaral, from the suburban town of Santee, California, stole a car from home and headed for the beach with an older friend, 26-year-old Gregory Dickens of Lakeside. Amaral's family notified the sheriff's office that the youth had run away.

Later that evening, a relative of Amaral's and her boyfriend had traced Amaral to a Pacific Beach neighborhood, when they spotted him standing near the idling car in the middle of an alley. Dickens, who was driving, spotted the couple and hit the gas. The car roared down the alley, nicked the boyfriend, then stopped only to collect Amaral before disappearing down the street.

A few hours later, Amaral called home to say he and Dickens were holed up in a motel in Oceanside. He said he was tired of hanging out and wanted to come home.

Police arrived at the motel and arrested Gregory Dickens. Amaral went home, while Dickens went to jail, charged with assault with a deadly weapon.

On Saturday afternoon, Detective Kramer took a statement from Amaral, which would be used in the case against Dickens. At the time Amaral was considered as much a victim of Dickens as the injured boyfriend was.

That changed after Amaral casually mentioned that he had shot two people in Arizona.

"What two people?" Kramer asked, astonished.

Amaral said he didn't know who they were. "They pulled into a rest stop outside Yuma," he said matter-of-factly. "I had a gun and I shot them." He said killing the two people was no big deal. As he put it, "I'd rather kill a human being than step on a dog's tail."

Detective Kramer stepped from the interview room and contacted the Yuma County Sheriff's Office. Detective Wilmont was punching through the paperwork when he got the call. Kramer told Wilmont Amaral's story. Wilmont told Kramer about the murders of Bryan and Laura Bernstein and the six-month search to find their killers.

Kramer returned to the interrogation room and pumped Amaral for information. The pumping went on for almost 12 hours, with occasional breaks so Kramer could relay information to Wilmont and Yuma County District Attorney Conrad Mallek, who had been called to the police station.

Later, Detective Wilmont arrived and took another statement from the eager-beaver teenager, who seemed happy to tell all.

"I shot them both," Amaral beamed. "But it wasn't my idea. I just pulled the trigger."

The brains behind the cold-blooded killings, Amaral said, was his old buddy, Gregory Dickens. "It was the quickest way to make money," Amaral explained.

Afterward, Amaral said, he was dropped off at the bus station, still carrying the murder weapon in his knapsack. Someone called the cops, and he was busted as a runaway.

"They took the gun," Amaral said. Later, a relative came to take him home. But he never got his gun back.

If the kid was telling the truth, that meant Yuma police might still have the gun. Wilmont made a few telephone calls.

They had the gun, all right.

On September 12th, two days after the Bernstein shooting, Patrolman Jack Guinn had been called to the Greyhound Bus Station to investigate a report of a runaway juvenile. He questioned Amaral and was later given a Ross .38-caliber revolver by an adult who said the gun had come from Amaral's backpack. Guinn put the gun in the police locker, where detectives found it nine months later.

At the time, the gun wasn't tied to the Bernstein killings because the serial number for the weapon had been incorrectly fed into the computer. Had the number been entered correctly, it would have shown that the gun was reported stolen from a San Diego security guard—a co-worker of Amaral's friend, Gregory Dickens.

Dickens and Amaral were returned separately to Yuma. In April 1992, a Yuma County grand jury indicted both men on multiple felony counts in connection with the Bernstein shootings. The indictment charged Dickens with four counts of first-degree murder, two of armed robber, one of conspiracy to commit murder, and one of conspiracy to commit armed robbery. Both men pled not guilty at their arraignments. They were held on $4.5 million bond each.

A trial was scheduled to begin in January 1993, with Conrad Mallek as chief prosecutor and Michael Donovan as defense attorney for both men.

Shortly before jury selection, Travis Amaral cut a deal with the D.A.'s office in which he agreed to testify against his former pal in return for a reduced sentence.

Dickens turned livid once word of the agreement reached him behind bars. "If Travis is guilty, the D.A. doesn't have the right to offer him a deal," Dickens told a reporter in a jailhouse conversation. "Imagine how the family will feel when they are told of this."

He claimed that the D.A. had squeezed Amaral to make him tell the story the D.A. wanted to hear. "It's damn wrong," Dickens said. "Justice can't work with deals. Justice works when the truth is told. Our court system is based on truth and justice, not on deals."

Dickens gave the public an open invitation to attend his trial, saying, "I have been proclaiming my innocence since the beginning. Let the people come and hear the evidence for themselves."

The trial began on January 26th. Jurors heard from sheriff's deputies who discovered the bodies and pathologists who examined them. They also heard tapes which Dickens had made to police following his arrest.

The most dramatic evidence was reserved for February 3rd, when Travis Amaral swaggered to the witness stand.

Under Prosecutor Mallek's gentle questioning, the pint-sized killer riveted the court's attention as he gave a chilling account of events that led to the execution-style murders of Laura and Bryan Bernstein.

He said he met Dickens in the spring of 1990 while he was in a court-ordered treatment center in Temecula, California. Dickens was officially a counselor. After he was released, Amaral said, he stayed in touch with Dickens and often went to visit him in Carlsbad, California.

In September 1991, Amaral said he was hanging out in San Diego, bored out of his mind, when he got a call from Dickens. His old pal was in Yuma, working on a relative's home.

"He said he was lonely," Amaral told jurors. "He asked if I wanted to join him. I told him I was broke, but he said he would pay for the bus fare. So I went."

Amaral said he and Dickens spent the days hanging out at the house and the nights cruising downtown Yuma.

On September 10th, after a day spent on the Colorado River, they went to a fast-food place and hatched an idea to make some money.

"Greg wanted to do a robbery," Amaral said. "I wanted to do it, too, but I wasn't so determined to do it."

They finally flipped a coin—robbery won.

"I was committed," Amaral said. "I didn't have any choice."

They talked about robbing a convenience store or rest stop. Amaral said they picked the rest stop because it was secluded, and there would be no witnesses.

They headed 20 miles east of Yuma and pulled off into a rest stop on the south side of the interstate. He said Dickens waited in the car while he ran across the highway to the rest stop on the north side. They kept in contact through a walkie-talkie that he carried hooked to his belt.

Amaral said he passed up several cars, including one with six Iranians in it. He said he had nothing against Iranians, only the number of them. "There were six of them and I only had five bullets in my gun," Amaral told jurors. "If something went wrong, I wouldn't have enough bullets to handle the situation."

He said he waited until a blue Chevette pulled in. There were two people in the car, a man and a woman.

"It was a perfect situation," Amaral said. "They were an easy target. One would have been even better, though."

Amaral testified that he relayed the information to Dickens, who was waiting at the south side rest stop. Dickens instructed him to be careful and "to leave no witnesses."

Amaral said he approached the woman on the passenger side of the car. She turned away from him. He raised the .38 revolver Dickens had given him and fired once. The gun roared, and the woman dropped out of sight. The robotic killer then turned toward the driver and fired again. The driver slumped forward.

Two shots, two hits. Amaral said he grabbed the victims' wallets and ran to the highway. Dickens had made a U-turn across the interstate and picked him up. They headed back to Yuma, looking in the rearview mirror. No one followed.

Amaral said they had committed the perfect crime, but it was hardly worth it. "They [the victims] only had a few bucks," he whined.

He said the next day, they tried to use the couple's credit cards at a Kmart, but a store employee got wise and they had to leave without getting anything.

Amaral said he was bitterly disappointed. He had killed two people, yet he was as broke as he was before he pulled the trigger. He said he was sick of Yuma and decided to return to San Diego.

At the bus station, he got busted for having a weapon in his knapsack. He said he thought the cops might tie the gun to the killings and arrest him for murder. Instead, the gun was confiscated, and he was turned over to the custody of his family.

Amaral spent the next six months running away from home and doing drugs, until the encounter in the alley led to his being put behind bars for good.

From the defense table, Dickens steamed like a boiling tea kettle as he watched his one-time buddy blame him for the killings. He got a chance to release a little steam when he took the witness stand on February 10th—and blamed the murders on Amaral.

"He did it," Dickens testified. "He pulled the trigger. It was his idea."

The former youth counselor claimed he was headed toward an area known as Half Dome on the night of the killings when he got lost and turned into the rest stop. He said that once they were there, Amaral grew angry and accused him of being uncaring. Amaral then jumped out of the pickup and ran across the interstate.

Suddenly, Dickens said, he heard a shot. "I pretty much froze when I heard the shot," he said. Moments later he saw the muzzle flash of a second shot. "I've never been so scared in all my life."

Dickens said he started out of the rest stop and headed east, but he changed his mind, made a U-turn across the median, and headed back to Yuma. He saw Amaral running along the side of the interstate and stopped.

"I didn't know about the killings until he told me," Dickens said.

Asked why he didn't turn Amaral in, Dickens said he was worried he would be charged as an accessory. His probation would be revoked, he feared, and he would go to prison. Dickens said he was also afraid of Amaral. At 6 feet, 4 inches and 260 pounds, Dickens was 10 inches taller and 100 pounds heavier than Amaral. Dickens was also 10 years older. But Dickens said that didn't matter. He said Amaral was a black belt in karate, dealt drugs, and played with handguns.

"He never went anywhere without a gun," Dickens claimed. "He was a tough cookie."

The case went to the jury on February 22nd. Two days later, jurors convicted the one-time juvenile counselor of two counts of first-degree murder, two of armed robbery, and one of conspiracy to commit armed robbery. Jurors did, however, find him not guilty of two counts of premeditated first-degree murder and conspiracy to commit first-degree murder, which was seen as a partial victory for the defense. It still meant that Dickens would very likely spend the rest of his life behind bars.

Dickens' former pal, Travis Amaral, didn't fare much better. On Friday, March 5, 1993, the 16-year-old confessed killer was sentenced to 65 years in state prison for his part in the double murder.

Before sentencing, Amaral took a parting shot at his old friend and mentor. Dickens, in testimony at his trial, described his relationship with Amaral as "intense." But in a psychiatric exam before his sentencing, Amaral claimed that Dickens was a homosexual predator who had seduced him when they met at the Temecula treatment center.

"At first he would give me back rubs," Amaral said. "I was lying on my bed and took my shift off." He said the back rubs escalated to fondling and then to sexual intercourse. Amaral said he tried to resist Dickens's sexual advances but felt powerless to do so.

"I was just a kid," Amaral whined.

"STRIPPED AND STRANGLED IN A LIMO!"

by Michael Sasser

The naked body of the white woman was sprawled out in front of a green trash bin. Officer Robert McCann of Florida's Davie Police Department watched as a team of paramedics examined her and confirmed that the young woman was dead.

It was just before noon on Sunday, January 3, 1988. South Florida was still recovering from the New Year's celebration. But in Davie, the new year brought only misery to the victim of an obvious crime—and a rare homicide to the community. Situated north and west of Miami and Hollywood, Davie is a rural suburb of farms where shoppers can pick their own vegetables and fruits, and country good manners. The Dumpster was behind a plant nursery on University Drive, a main drag for the western part of Broward County. Yet even on this grim morning, the trees beyond the nursery waved in a pleasant, cooling sea breeze.

"I was here to work on a car for a guy who works around here," the man who discovered the body told Officer McCann. "I couldn't find the guy's van, so I was driving around, looking. I happened to drive back here and I saw that body. At first I thought it was a mannequin or something. Then I realized it was real. I was sure she had to be dead, so I went in and told the manager. He came out with me, we saw her there, dead. Then we called the police."

"Did you touch the body at all?" McCann asked.

"No—nothing," the man said. "But we knew she was dead."

The dead woman had brown hair and no clothes on at all. She appeared to be in her early or mid-20s. The victim was lying on her back, and her mouth was covered with silver tape. The same kind of tape was on both arms. The left arm was under the body, the right arm was partially extended. Both feet were fully extended outward and pointed southwest.

Officer McCann noted that the woman had several gold rings on her fingers. A white pullover blouse or tank top lay near the left side of the body.

Detectives, crime scene specialists, and a medical examiner's team arrived shortly after 1:00 P.M. Among the new arrivals was then-Detective Dennis Mocarski. Mocarski was assigned to be the lead investigator on the case.

After the crime scene was secured to preserve its integrity, the technicians started the long process of looking for clues in the grisly crime.

A medical examiner did a preliminary examination of the body. He alerted detectives to a piece of jewelry on the victim's hand.

"We've got a high school ring on the victim," the M.E. said. "From Coconut Creek High. The name on the ring is Deborah Herdmann."

The victim's body was removed from where it lay and transported to the morgue for a complete autopsy. At 2:30 that afternoon, the M.E. reported his findings to Detective Mocarski.

"The victim's neck is kind of loose, but does not appear to be broken," the pathologist said. "There is some trauma to the back of the neck. My belief now is that the cause of death was asphyxiation."

Now Mocarski knew the cause of death, but he still did not have a positive identification of the victim. All he had was the name on the ring.

Back at the Davie police station, the detective obtained a 1982 Coconut Creek high school yearbook. A photo of Deborah Lynn Herdmann verified that Deborah was indeed the deceased victim.

It was 9:30 that night before detectives were able to locate Herdmann's family. Detective Mocarski confirmed their relationship to the victim and met with them an hour later.

One member of the family positively identified Deborah from a photograph. Distraught though they were, the relatives were able to provide considerable information.

"We were worried about Deborah," the relative told the detectives. "Deborah's roommate said that Deborah was going out with a guy named Vince yesterday."

"Why did that worry you," Mocarski asked.

"Because Deborah supposedly said that this Vince guy had a violent temper, and that she was frightened of him," the relative said. "In fact, Deborah supposedly left word that if she wasn't home by three-thirty, then her roommate should be worried."

The relative told the sleuth that she personally paged "Vince" earlier in the day.

"I asked if he went out with Deborah yesterday," the relative said.

"Did he?" Mocarski asked.

"He said that he didn't," the relative replied. "He said that he called her at noon yesterday and canceled."

The relative gave the detective Deborah's address and phone number, where the deceased girl's roommates could also be reached.

Just before midnight, Detective Mocarski traveled to Deborah Herdmann's home, which was on the 4000 block of Northwest 87th Avenue in rural Davie. There, he and his colleagues met with two male roommates of the victim's—Drew Hall and Dusty Cairn.

"Both of us were getting ready to move out," Cairn told the investigators. "Deborah was supposed to take over the apartment herself."

Detective Mocarski started to tell the roommates about Deborah's death. The two men stopped him.

"We heard about it from a relative of Deborah's who lives up in north Fort Lauderdale," Hall said. "She called about an hour ago."

Mocarski asked the men when they had last seen the young woman.

"I saw her about twelve-thirty yesterday afternoon," Cairn offered. "She said that she was leaving to meet a date."

"Did you see her leave?" Mocarski asked.

"No," Cairn replied. "I left for work before she left the house. But that is the last time I saw her."

Hall made a similar statement. Neither man knew much more about the victim's plans—where she was going or what her time frame of activity was.

Detective Mocarski told Hall and Cairn that he needed them to go to the police station in the next few days to give a complete statement. Both men readily agreed to do so.

The investigators then examined Deborah's belongings in an attempt to learn whatever else they could about the crime. The search turned up nothing. Her possessions included the normal things a young woman would own, but no clues to her killer.

It was well after midnight when Detective Mocarski left the victim's residence. He had little to work on—no eyewitnesses and few, if any, physical clues. He had a second-hand statement about a man the victim may have been seeing. He had the cause of death. And, Mocarski knew one other thing: Whoever killed Deborah Herdmann had not done so in a robbery or any other well-planned crime.

No, this crime was messy and ill-conceived. The body was not well hidden, and the victim's valuable jewelry was left untouched. Then there was the significant fact that Deborah Herdmann was found naked.

The Florida winter night was breezy and cool. Every gust of wind whispered, as though it had secrets to tell. When Detective Mocarski finished for the evening, the darkest secret of all had not yet revealed itself to him.

That secret still to be unearthed was, who killed Deborah Herdmann? And why?

The next morning, Monday, January 4th, dawned sunny and full of promise. Detective Mocarski traveled to north Fort Lauderdale, just miles away, to meet with another relative of Deborah's. This relative was the individual who had informed the victim's roommates about the slaying. Also, according to the relatives who had already been interviewed, this relative was close to Deborah and would surely know something about her recent activities.

Those family members proved to be right.

"I last spoke to Deborah about ten-thirty in the morning on the second," the relative said. "She said that this guy, Vince, was supposed to pick her up for a date. She was getting dressed and ready while I was talking to her."

"Did she got out with Vince often?" Mocarski asked.

"I know he called her a lot," the relative replied. "I think they actually set this date a couple of weeks ago.

"Later, I spoke to Dusty, her roommate," the relative continued. "He said that the last thing he heard Deborah say was that if she wasn't back by three P.M., to start worrying."

"When did you start to worry?"

"Not until I didn't hear from her all day on Sunday, the third."

"Do you know Vince's last name or his whereabouts?"

"I believe his last name is Walsh—Vincent Walsh," the relative said. She didn't have much other information that could help the budding investigation, but she did agree to give a formal statement.

At 2:00 P.M., Detective Mocarski reinterviewed Deborah's roommates for formal, recorded statements. Dusty Cairn provided the same information as before, and also recalled the conversation he had last had with the victim—which was also recounted by Deborah's relative. Cairn confirmed that the victim had said she was worried about the date with Vincent Walsh.

"Vince was supposed to be planning a surprise for Deborah," Cairn told the sleuth. "Deborah heard from a friend of Vince's, named Mike, that Vince was planning a special trip for the two of them."

Cairn agreed to allow police to search his vehicle. Technicians removed and tagged a number of items, but they found nothing obviously relevant inside.

Later that evening, Detective Mocarski took a statement from Drew Hall. Hall provided the same information that Dusty Cairn had. However, Hall said that he personally hadn't thought much of the victim's statement about being worried and he didn't know whom Deborah was going out with.

Just before 11:00 P.M., Detective Mocarski reached Vincent Walsh on the telephone. Walsh agreed to meet with the detectives at 2:00 P.M. the next day—Tuesday, January 5th.

Up to this point, an alleged date with Vincent Walsh was the only lead the detectives had to go on. So far, forensics hadn't turned up anything else.

Meanwhile, the story of the crime and the investigation

had made the local news. As a result, a single witness called the police with possibly relevant information.

"I knew Deborah Herdmann," the witness said. "She lived at my place for a short time. I also know that she and my girlfriend both lived with a guy named Vincent Walsh once for a couple of weeks."

The witness had met Walsh.

"He was known to have a pretty violent temper," the man said about Walsh. He led the detectives to a neighbor's home where some of Deborah's belongings had been stored. The victim's possessions included some photo albums and shoes, but nothing obviously significant to the probe.

At 7:00 P.M., the detective finally sat down with 26-year-old Vincent Walsh at the Davie police department. Walsh agreed to give a taped, sworn statement about his relationship with Deborah Herdmann.

"I first met Deborah in October of last year," Walsh began. "We went out three or four times in the next month or so. We were close for a while."

"When was the last time you saw her?" one of the detectives asked.

"She helped me move into my current apartment," Walsh said. "That's the last time I saw her."

"But you've spoken to her since then? You called her?"

"Well, I have spoken to her, but really only when she called me."

"You never made dates with her?"

"Actually, I did," Walsh said. "But I always broke them."

Walsh told the detectives that he did make a date with Herdmann for January 2nd. "But I called to break it," he said. He also told the probers that he drove a limousine for a living.

"Did you ever take Deborah for a ride in your limousine?" one of the detectives asked.

"No," Walsh replied. Nonetheless, he agreed to allow the police to inspect the interior of his limo.

The detectives conducted a search of the car. The limousine was a gray, four-door Lincoln. Inside, the technicians removed some small carpet fibers from the floors and mats. Walsh readily agreed to help the police in whatever way he could.

A woman had accompanied Walsh to the police station. She identified herself as Pam Donner, a friend of Walsh's. Detective Mocarski spoke to her briefly in private.

"I need to speak to you," Donner told the investigator. "But I don't want Vince to know about it."

Mocarski asked her why the secrecy was necessary.

"I'm afraid of Vincent," Pam said. It crossed Mocarski's mind that a lot of people seemed to feel that way about Walsh.

Pam was not able to return that evening to speak to the sleuth, but she said she would try the next day.

When Vince Walsh and Pam Donner left that evening, the investigators felt no closer to finding out what had really happened to Deborah Herdmann. Walsh was their only suspect so far. But, despite plenty of statements that the man had a violent temper, there were no eyewitnesses to link him to the crime, and Walsh himself had been a cooperative witness, so far.

Was Walsh hiding something? If so, did Pam Donner know what Walsh's carefully guarded secret was?

There were plenty of questions, but still no breakthrough answers.

At 10:45 A.M. on Wednesday, January 6th, Detective Mocarski responded to a summons from the crime laboratory.

"We've got some news that you guys will want," a technician told Mocarski. "We found some fabric fibers on the victim's body. We tried them against the evidence fibers you brought in. We got a match. Same carpet."

The evidence fibers were those that had been collected from the inside of Vincent Walsh's limousine.

The situation was becoming clearer. But, at this point, Pam Donner was the only person who could further illuminate the strange happenings.

Detective Mocarski spent the rest of the day trying to locate Pam. Several of his phone calls went unanswered, and a visit to the woman's home turned up no one there.

At 5:00 P.M., the detective returned to the police station. There, another investigator told Mocarski that he'd been visited by a relative of Pam Donner's.

"She was very worried about Pam," the other detective said. "Vincent took her for a ride last night after they left here."

The relative said she knew the details of a conversation that took place during that ride.

"Pam said that Vince wanted her to change her recollection of what happened on the second and third," the relative had said. "I'm worried because Vince has a violent temper."

The relative alleged that Vincent had been violent to Pam—he had assaulted her before.

Although the relative had no information pertaining to Deborah Herdmann's slaying, she did have something to offer to the investigation. She gave the police a statement which Detective Mocarski himself reviewed on his arrival at headquarters.

At 9:00 P.M., Mocarski returned to Pam Donner's home and found her there. Pam agreed to give the detectives a statement. She began by saying that Vince did take her for a drive on the previous evening.

"He wanted me to change my story about the chain of events on the night of January second, and the next morning," Pam said.

"What *did* happen?" Detective Mocarski asked her.

"On the morning of the third," Pam said, "Vince went

to the local grocery store and rented a steam machine to clean the interior of the limousine." She also told the probers that Walsh had a violent temper and had struck her before.

The detectives scrambled to the grocery store. Records there verified Walsh's rental of the steam cleaner. The records and the machine itself were taken in for evidence. Technicians were assigned to search the contents of the cleaner's storage tank for possible evidence from the limousine.

Except for the carpet fibers, all the evidence the sleuths had so far was strictly circumstantial. But it was still important, and it was rapidly convincing the detectives that they were on the right track.

The next morning—Thursday, January 7th—Detective Mocarski and other sleuths went to where Vincent Walsh was employed. They called Walsh out and asked him to return to the station. Walsh agreed to go along.

In the police car, the sleuths read Vincent Walsh his Miranda rights, and he indicated that he understood them.

At the police station, the detectives questioned Walsh about Deborah Herdmann and about the day of the crime. Walsh repeated the same statement he'd made before.

"Would you be willing to take a polygraph test?" one of the detectives asked.

Walsh agreed to the test.

Unfortunately for Walsh, the polygraph was not kind to him. According to the attending technician, Vincent Walsh was not telling the truth, or all he knew about the murder of Deborah Herdmann.

"How about, I give you another statement," Walsh said, "and actually tell you what happened."

The detectives thought that would be a refreshing change.

"I was involved with what happened," Walsh said. "But I didn't kill her."

The way Walsh started his story, the detectives initially doubted the truth of what he was saying. But, surprisingly, the rest of his statement rang true.

"This other guy—Mike—and I were getting sick and tired of Deborah," Walsh said. He claimed that the woman had been calling and harassing both men.

Tired of some perceived wrongdoing, Walsh said, he and Mike hatched a plan. Two and a half weeks earlier, Walsh had made a date with Deborah for Saturday, January 2nd.

"The plan was just to teach her a lesson," Walsh told the sleuths.

As part of that plan, Walsh abducted Deborah in his limousine, then stripped and tied her up with electrical tape. Shortly afterward, he met Mike. Their plan was to drive the woman around and eventually drop her off somewhere in the Everglades."

But the so-called plan went very wrong.

While they were driving on the west side of town, Deborah, obviously terrified, started screaming and struggling against her bonds. That was when Mike, in trying to quiet the girl, did silence her—for good.

"I was driving her," Walsh told the sleuths, apparently offering an excuse. A very weak excuse, the investigators thought.

Finally, Walsh detailed how the victim's possessions were tossed in another Dumpster at an area gas station. Later, he rented the steam-cleaning machine and cleaned the limousine, hoping to get rid of any evidence.

The investigators recorded Walsh's new statement. Then several detectives were dispatched to pick up "Mike," who was identified as 35-year-old Michael Bedford. They found Bedford, and he voluntarily accompanied them back to the station.

Initially, Bedford denied any knowledge of, or participation in, the murder of Deborah Herdmann. What he didn't know was that the detectives knew plenty already.

"Why don't you let us tell you a little about what we already know," one of the sleuths said. The investigators proceeded to inform Bedford of some of the things they'd heard Vincent Walsh admitting.

Michael Bedford broke down. "Okay! Okay!" he said. "Nobody was meant to really get hurt."

Bedford gave a statement that was very similar to Walsh's. He, too, said that the victim supposedly wronged them and that it was the abductors' intention to drive Deborah around for a while before dropping her off.

Detective Mocarski asked about the moments leading up to Deborah Herdmann's death.

"She started resisting me and fighting," Bedford said. "I tried to control her and I heard a snap. I told Vince that I thought I broke her neck."

According to Bedford, Walsh continued driving around while the victim's face changed colors and she stopped breathing.

"We were going to drop her off in the Everglades," Bedford said. "But we were running low on gas, and Vincent got nervous when a couple of police cars drove by us."

That was when the two men saw the Dumpster behind the nursery and decided that was where they would get rid of Deborah's body.

"We threw her stuff in a Dumpster at a gas station on University Drive," Bedford said.

Listening to both accounts of what happened was a chilling experience for the sleuths. Bedford's statement read like a third-person account of a television program. He coolly stated that, in trying to quiet the victim, her neck "just snapped"—as if he himself had nothing to do with it.

Both men said that their actions were a response to somehow being bothered by the victim. As far as the crimefighters were concerned, it was a poor, pitiful excuse for taking the life of a 23-year-old woman.

Detective Mocarski and his team arrested Vincent Walsh and Michael Bedford on charges of first-degree murder.

Both subjects' admissions were powerful evidence against them.

Still, the veteran detectives knew that under certain circumstances, almost any evidence can be suppressed. Mocarski and his colleagues spread out to find corroborative evidence.

Vincent Walsh's limousine was impounded for evidence. The matching fibers placed the victim inside the limo.

The homes of both suspects were searched. In Bedford's house, they found two interesting items. Number one was a message on his answering machine from Vincent Walsh—a message which was obviously faked for a phony alibi. Also in Bedford's home were 40 thirty-five-millimeter photographs and 10 Polaroid pictures of nude women and dead bodies.

It was clear to the probers that neither suspect was a choirboy before the murder.

Michael Bedford stood trial and was found guilty of first-degree murder. He was sentenced to die in Florida's electric chair. An appeal court, however, eventually reduced his sentence to life in prison.

Vincent Walsh was convicted and sentenced to life in prison, to run concurrently with a 12-year sentence for the kidnapping.

Victim Kathy Fogleman, 28, wearing dress found near her at the crime scene.

Cabbie Keith Allen Brown, 33, ran over Fogleman after raping her.

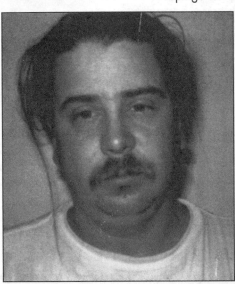

Fogleman's body was found a few feet from an old barn.

Tire tracks ran across Fogleman's chest and arm.

Victim Walter Burnett, 21, fell prey to carjackers.

Gregory Sean Fray, 25, claimed he did not know his partner planned to kill Burnett.

Victim Jessica Guzman, 10, was the object of a massive search in October 1990.

After cabdriver Alejandro Henriquez, 29, was arrested for killing Guzman, police were able to tie him to other murders.

Henriquez murdered Shamira Bello, 14, in July 1988.

Coed Lisa Ann Rodriguez, 21, was killed by Henriquez two years after Bello.

The Young Circle bus stop where Joseph
Besaraba opened fire, killing two.

Drifter Joseph Besaraba with his attorneys Dennis Bailey and
Jane Fishman.

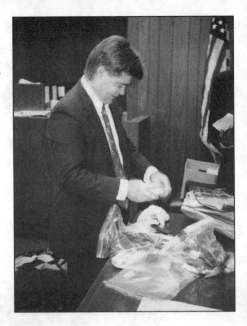

Bailey examining some of the prosecution's evidence against Besaraba.

Graduate student Bryan Bernstein, 22, was found gunned down in his car at an Arizona rest stop.

Bernstein's wife Laura, 22, was dead in the passenger seat beside him.

Sixteen-year-old runaway Travis Wade Amaral told police he had killed the Bernsteins for money with former youth counselor Gregory Dickens.

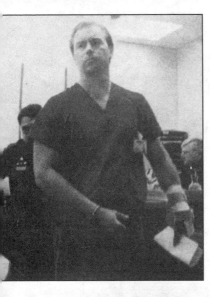

Amaral claimed that Gregory Dickens, 26, was a homosexual predator.

Prosecutor Conrad Mallek shows jury Amaral's gun.

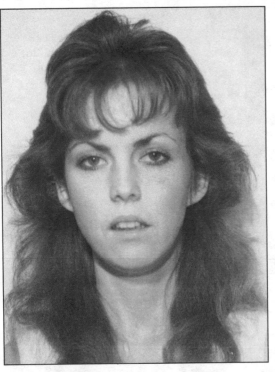

Victim Deborah Herdmann, 23.

Herdmann's nude body was found near
a plant nursery's Dumpster.

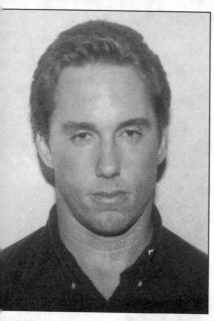

Vincent Walsh, 26, planned to teach Herdmann a lesson by leaving her naked and bound in the Everglades.

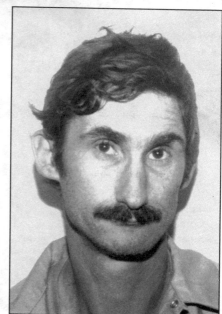

While subduing the struggling Herdmann, Michael Bedford, 35, claimed her neck just snapped.

Donnie Dwight Kay, 37, was sentenced to 20 years for killing a sixteen-year-old prostitute in Portland, Oregon.

Police in Texas, North Carolina, and Virginia sought Randolph Greer, 18, for a string of violent crimes ranging from robbery to rape to murder.

Detectives Jay F. Whitt (*top*) and Dwight Rooker of the Greensboro Police Department sought Greer for the armed robbery of a jewelry store that left one dead and several severely injured.

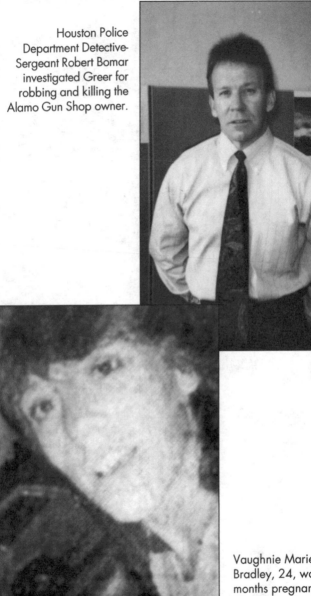

Houston Police Department Detective-Sergeant Robert Bomar investigated Greer for robbing and killing the Alamo Gun Shop owner.

Vaughnie Marie Bradley, 24, was five months pregnant at the time of her death.

adley's body was found in the road ditch
r days before a child support hearing with
her ex-lover Gaylon Franklin.

From California to Oklahoma, ex-con Gaylon
Ronald Franklin Jr. left a trail of ex-wives,
ex-lovers, and young children he refused
to support.

On his first homicide, the Bradley case, Det. Matt Palmer (*top*) was teamed with 15-year veteran lawman Det. Gary Ross.

"HOMICIDAL TRUCKER!"

by John Griggs

The sun climbed lazily over the secluded upstate South Carolina lake, its yellow morning rays slowly revealing the grisly secret shrouded by the previous night. By 7:10 A.M. on Sunday, August 27, 1989, when the sun had been up for an hour, two fishermen were casting their lines in Lake Bowen. Water spiders skated across the glimmering surface, and thousands of cicadas whined in unison from the wooded shore. Now and then, a fish broke the water's surface.

Suddenly, the fishermen spotted a figure floating near the South Carolina Highway 9 bridge. A careful look revealed that it was a human body.

The fishermen rushed to the nearest phone and called for help. Within a short time, emergency workers and deputies with the Spartanburg County Sheriff's Department arrived on the scene.

A team of deputies headed out in a boat and pulled the body back to shore. The emergency workers who examined the female floater pronounced her dead. To the officers, this didn't look like any accidental drowning during an adventurous Saturday night dip.

The woman was fully clothed, and she appeared to be

in her late 30s to mid-40s. Her appearance made it apparent that she had been beaten about the face. Her hands were tied behind her back with shoelaces.

She was still wearing jewelry, suggesting that robbery had not been her killer's motive.

There was no identification on the corpse.

The deputies worked the crime scene by the book, inspecting the area in what proved to be a vain hunt for evidence. They sketched the body and crime scene, and shot photos. But they just didn't have much to work with.

Captain Mike Ennis, working under Sheriff Bill Coffey, drew the assignment as the chief investigator on the case. He and his fellow deputies would work with investigators from the State Law Enforcement Division (SLED). The case promised to be a tough one to crack.

On Sunday afternoon, the officers cleared the lake area and had the body sent for autopsy. Back at headquarters in Spartanburg, the county seat, they scanned missing-person reports, looking for a match to their body, but none of the individuals listed in the reports on file matched the description of the unidentified victim.

The pathologists came up with a preliminary autopsy report early on Monday. According to that report, the woman had died of asphyxiation—either from strangulation or drowning; it hadn't been possible to specify. Nonetheless, the injuries on her neck suggested that someone had throttled her.

In addition, the bruises on her face, back, shoulders, upper arms, hands, wrists, and feet made it evident that she'd been beaten.

Even if the woman had drowned, she'd apparently been beaten beforehand, and someone had tied her hands behind her back. Any way the detectives looked at it, they had a murder case on their hands. What they didn't have was an identification on the victim.

That all changed on Monday.

An area man who'd heard news reports about the discovery of the body wondered if it wasn't a relative of his. The detectives soon found out that the victim was indeed the man's relative—42-year-old Velma Faye Gray of nearby Traveler's Rest, South Carolina.

Her relatives positively identified the body on Monday. The victim's kinsman told the sleuths that he played in a traveling band with Velma Gray, who also had a day job as a typesetter. On Saturday night, they'd played a club in Asheville, North Carolina, about a two-hour drive from the lake. He and Velma left the western North Carolina club in two separate cars early on Sunday, heading home to South Carolina.

Along the way, the man said, their cars had gotten separated, and he never saw Velma again. She'd been driving a red 1985 Mazda RX-7.

Where was the car now? There was a strong possibility that it could tell the sleuths plenty about what had happened to her. In any event, it was a vital but missing piece of this frustrating homicide puzzle.

Late on Monday, three women who'd heard the news reports about the victim came forward with a tantalizing tidbit of information: They'd seen a woman fitting Velma Gray's description standing by a wrecked Mazda on U.S. Highway 25 early on Sunday. They reported that the woman had been talking to a mysterious trucker.

The car was gone from the spot where the women had seen it. The investigators checked out the site for any leftover evidence, but they found nothing. The spot was at the intersection of U.S. 25 and the White Horse Road extension, not far from Lake Bowen. It was in Greenville County, which neighbors Spartanburg County to the west.

The Greenville County sheriff's deputies would soon lend a hand in the probe.

The three women said they had stopped their car briefly. They'd seen that the woman matching Velma

Gray's description was crying, and they heard her saying, "I wrecked my car! I wrecked my car . . ."

The witnesses saw the trucker stop his rig and walk toward Gray, so they drove off, assuming that the man was going to help her.

The witnesses helped the lab specialists develop a composite sketch of the driver. With copies of the composite in hand, the detectives began scouring truck stops and trucking firms throughout the area, hunting the mystery trucker.

The investigators considered the driver only as an important witness who might provide valuable information about events preceding the woman's death. They did not regard him as a suspect in Gray's murder.

By Tuesday, August 29th—the day after the three witnesses had come forward—teams of deputies were hunting the car in their vehicles, on foot, and from the air. On Tuesday afternoon, deputies in a plane finally spotted the missing car. The Mazda, apparently damaged, was parked in a field in northern Greenville County.

The parking spot was an obscure point off U.S. 25, hidden among some trees. As the officers began going over the car, they quickly turned up a large number of fingerprints. Those prints soon led the sleuths to a local resident, who happened to have his prints on file.

Before daybreak on Wednesday, the individual, 21-year-old Neal Vernon, was giving Greenville Detective Larry N. Belew a statement. He said he'd found the car abandoned beside U.S. 25, and had it towed to a place where he got it running.

But by the time he got the Mazda going, Vernon said, he heard the news reports and realized that he'd stumbled into a homicide case. He admitted to taking some jewelry from inside the car; detectives later found that jewelry at his residence.

Vernon stressed that all he did was take the abandoned car and the jewelry—he didn't kill anybody.

The sleuths checked out Vernon and his story. They quickly determined that he was telling the truth. After charging him with auto larceny, they continued their hunt for Velma Gray's killer.

(Vernon later pleaded guilty to a reduced charge of using the car without the owner's consent. He was sentenced to five years in prison.)

Later, deputies using metal detectors combed the site where the Mazda had apparently been wrecked. They found nothing of evidential value.

The frustrating probe dragged on as the detectives continued their hunt for the mystery trucker. The days since the slaying occurred turned into weeks, the weeks into months. In December, Gray's family and friends offered a $3,000 reward for information leading to the arrest and conviction of her killer. By February 1990, the reward had climbed to $5,000.

Despite the growing reward purse, solid tips were just not coming in.

But in the late spring of 1990, the probe suddenly got red-hot.

When sleuths with North Carolina's Asheville Police Department called the Spartanburg deputies to run a background check on 22-year-old Leslie Eugene Warren, a murder suspect in another case, Warren soon became a suspect in Gray's slaying.

Velma Gray had played with the band in Asheville, a Blue Ridge Mountain town, on the last night of her life. Warren was from Candler, a small town near Asheville. Detectives Don Babb and Ted Lambert of the Asheville PD were among those investigating Warren.

And, as the Asheville police told their counterparts in South Carolina, Warren had worked for a trucking company based near Spartanburg. That's why the Tarheel

State sleuths had called Spartanburg for background information.

Ironically, the South Carolina sleuths had obtained a photo of Warren while they'd been methodically collecting photos of numerous South Carolina truckers shortly after the discovery of the slaying. But when shown the array of photos, including Warren's, the three women who had seen Velma Gray by the highway on the last night of her life had not picked Warren out as the trucker who stopped to help her.

In fact, the sleuths had interviewed Warren even as they'd routinely interviewed numerous other truckers. They remembered that he hadn't been nervous when he said he wasn't the trucker from Gray's wreck scene.

Given the new information from North Carolina, the South Carolina sleuths fixed a collective hard eye on Mr. Leslie Warren. Was he in fact the mysterious trucker from the wreck scene? Who was he, anyway?

Besides being an ex-trucker, the sleuths learned, Warren was also a former soldier with the U.S. Army, he had worked factory and construction jobs, and he was a high school dropout. Having grown up in the Asheville area, he'd had relatively minor troubles with the law since his juvenile years. The incidents included charges of burglary and assault.

Warren's counselor at the Juvenile Evaluation Center in Swannanoa, North Carolina—near Asheville—had been 39-year-old Jayme Denise Hurley. Now, Hurley was missing and foul play was suspected.

The Asheville police outlined their case for the South Carolina cops. A relative of Hurley's had reported her missing on May 25, 1990. She'd last been seen at an Asheville Grocery. The detectives checking into Hurley's past had found reason enough to begin looking at Warren as a possible suspect. Within four days of Hurley's disappearance, the investigators had come up with enough evidence to link Warren to Hurley's purse, and to charge him with stealing it.

But their interview of Warren failed to produce enough evidence to charge him in connection with Hurley's disappearance. So the detectives charged him with stealing the purse. Warren was placed in the Asheville jail, and his bond was set at $25,000.

A judge later reduced that bond to $1,000, and Warren made it and walked out on June 7, 1990.

Asheville Police Chief Gerald "Jerry" Beavers later told a reporter, "Our system of jurisprudence says that on minor charges, a person has a right to have a bond. We did not have a body and we did not have a murder charge at that time."

As the detectives from both Carolinas began finding out all they could about Warren and how he might be connected to their prospective cases, the North Carolina lawmen began a massive hunt for Hurley's body. For five days, 400 officers from the Asheville police, the Buncombe County Sheriff's Department, and other police agencies combed the Asheville area in a grueling search. It proved to be fruitless.

The South Carolina detectives came to Asheville, where they joined their North Carolina colleagues and continued their background check on Warren with regard to the Gray and Hurley cases. Upon checking his Army background, the sleuths soon learned that he was also a suspect in a New York murder.

Lieutenant Ed Grant of the New York State Police supplied the Dixie officers with the background on his case, which involved a 20-year-old woman.

Patsy Diane Vineyard had been reported missing by her husband in April 1987. Her husband was an Army infantry soldier at Fort Drum. He and Patsy lived off base at Sackett's Harbor, a military suburb.

The investigation showed that Warren had served in

a unit with Vineyard's husband, and he'd known the couple.

Several weeks after her disappearance, Patsy Vineyard's body was found floating in Lake Ontario. She had died of strangulation.

Lieutenant Grant and his colleagues worked the case from their headquarters in Watertown, New York. Dozens of sleuths worked the probe, conducting hundreds of interviews.

The detectives eventually came to believe that an acquaintance had to have killed Vineyard. It was a preconceived slaying, the sleuths felt, planned well by a killer who was confident that he would not be tagged as a suspect in the case.

In their methodical probe, the New York investigators determined that Warren was one of the few soldiers excused from a two-week duty tour that Patsy Vineyard's husband had been required to take. Thus, the investigators figured, Warren would have known that Patsy would be alone. She disappeared during that two-week duty tour.

The New York detectives had questioned Warren at length, but they'd failed to crack him. In fact, they remembered, he hadn't even been even slightly nervous when he told them that he knew nothing of Patsy Vineyard's death.

Leslie Warren left New York with a bad-conduct discharge from the military in March 1989, after a court-martial in which he was convicted of larceny and unauthorized absence.

Now, as the South and North Carolina sleuths focused on Warren, the New York probers dusted off their own files. Soon, the New York officers joined the Carolina sleuths at the Asheville police headquarters.

Lieutenant Grant was especially qualified to work on this case: he specializes in probes of serial killers. He later said of these crimes: "This kind of homicide is considered to be a motiveless murder. He [the perpetrator] has a mind-set that causes him to be compelled to commit this kind of [crime]. This is the kind of individual who gets up in the morning and feels he has to kill somebody. They'll go and do whatever they have to do to get through the day."

By mid-July, the investigators hadn't seen Leslie Warren in over a month. They came to believe that he was on the run.

The detectives from the three states went over their evidence and decided that it was time to pick up Mr. Warren and have a talk with him.

On the morning of Tuesday, July 17, 1990, they entered Warren's name and description into the National Crime Information Center (NCIC) computer network. He was described as a white male, 5 feet 11 inches tall, weighing 194 pounds, born October 15, 1967. The description included his Social Security number, his North Carolina driver's license number, and information about a falsified South Carolina driver's license he was alleged to have.

The computer alert noted that Warren might be armed and driving a gray Kawasaki Vulcan motorcycle, and that he was known to frequent campsites, and might have a sleeping bag and tent with him. The network dispatch also specified that he had a "punk-type" hairstyle, long in back and short on the sides and top, and he had recently dyed his hair and goatee an orange-blond.

The next day, with Warren still missing, Jayme Hurley's body was found in a shallow grave in a remote section of the Pisgah National Forest, off the scenic Blue Ridge Parkway. The site was not far from Warren's hometown, Candler. Hurley's car was found on Friday, July 20th, in a nearby wooded area.

An autopsy later determined that Hurley, too, had been strangled.

That same Friday, the three-state investigative team

sought help from the press and the public in apprehending Warren. At a 10:00 A.M. press conference in Asheville, they designated Warren as a serial-murder suspect, and distributed brief chronologies of each of the three cases. Spartanburg Sheriff Coffey, Asheville Police Chief Beavers, and New York Lieutenant Grant conducted the conference.

The South Carolina detectives said they had drawn up a warrant charging Leslie Warren with the first-degree murder of Velma Gray. The New York and North Carolina officers had not yet sworn out any warrants.

That Friday afternoon, a tipster informed the officers that Warren was staying at a house in High Point, North Carolina, and gave them the address. High Point is about three hours east of Asheville, in the state's rolling Piedmont region.

The sleuths alerted the High Point police, who moved in on the modest wood-frame house in the 300 block of Phillips Avenue in the city's northwestern section. Just before 3:00 P.M. on Friday, the High Point police arrested Warren without incident on the South Carolina murder warrant.

Late that day, officers brought Warren to the Asheville headquarters. Under interrogation, he broke and confessed to killing Velma Gray. Warren made his statement to Captain Ennis of the Spartanburg County Sheriff's Department. Warren said that he picked up Gray after her car had run off the road. She asked him for a ride to a phone where she could call for help. In his tractor-trailer, Warren drove Gray to a convenience store a short distance away.

"Before she could get out of the truck," Warren told Captain Ennis, "I grabbed her and choked her."

Then, he said, he drove her body to the lake. There, he tied the dead woman's hands behind her back with shoestrings. He said he intended to tie something heavy to the corpse so it would stay at the bottom, but "I couldn't find anything to weight her with."

The suspect said he couldn't recall exactly what he was thinking as he committed the act, but he did know that he was killing the woman.

That was it. The months of frustrating sleuthing and mystery, all to solve what seemed to be a motiveless crime. Why Warren committed murder may never be known. The answer, as far as the experts are concerned, is hidden somewhere in the dark recesses of his mind.

As he continued to talk into early Saturday, Warren also allegedly confessed to the slayings of Patsy Vineyard and Jayme Hurley. The Asheville officers charged Warren with the murder of Hurley. The New York officers, while morally satisfied that Warren had killed Vineyard, held off on charging him.

Then, Warren laid a bombshell on the task force gathered in Asheville: he allegedly said he'd killed a fourth woman in High Point. He allegedly told the sleuths where they could find the body of 21-year-old Katherine Noel "Kat" Johnson.

The investigators quickly telephoned High Point police. Within the hour, on the second floor of a downtown parking deck beside the Radisson hotel, a team of High Point officers found the nude body of Johnson in the trunk of her Renault—just where Warren had allegedly said the body would be.

A preliminary autopsy report soon showed that Johnson, a part-time student at the University of North Carolina at Chapel Hill and former restaurant worker at the hotel, had been strangled. Strangled, just as Jayme Hurley and Patsy Vineyard had been. The pathologists, it should be recalled, had ruled that Velma Gray died of asphyxiation, either from strangling or drowning.

The High Point authorities, who had thought that the cases were somebody else's nightmare, now had a bad dream of their own. Early on the Saturday morning of Warren's arrest, High Point sleuths drove to Asheville and charged Warren with Katherine Johnson's murder.

From witnesses, the investigators soon learned a number of things about Warren's stay in High Point. Warren cruised into High Point on his motorcycle a week before—on Friday the 13th. He looked up a relative of a friend of his from the mountains. The relative, Rita Small, was a bartender at the High Point Radisson.

Small was also a young mother who rented the Phillips Avenue house where Warren was arrested. She had put up Warren on her couch after he'd told her that he was in High Point to visit for a while. Warren seemed nice, friendly, and talkative. He partied with Small and her friends—among them, Katherine Johnson.

On Sunday, July 15th, Johnson met Warren at a party. Later, back at Small's house, Johnson took a ride with Warren on his motorcycle. She was riding behind him, and it turned out to be the last time she was seen alive.

Johnson and Warren had had drinks, some witnesses told reporters, but the couple weren't drunk.

Warren drove back to Small's house alone on his motorcycle early on Monday. He left his motorcycle, got into Johnson's Renault, and drove off.

By midmorning on Monday, he was back at Small's place, asleep on the couch. When he arose, he seemed hung over, but otherwise normal. He said that he'd spent Sunday night with Johnson at her motel room, and then she had left early on Monday to get back to summer school in Chapel Hill. The Renault was gone.

Warren's arrest and the revelations that followed shook Small. "What freaks me out is, I could have been next," she told a reporter about her houseguest. "It's so hard to believe. He was so normal."

Clearly, Warren was a paradox to the people he'd had contact with, as well as the investigators.

"We think that Warren is an intelligent person," Sheriff Coffey said. "We think that he is resourceful, but certainly is a very dangerous individual. He can be unpredictable.

"We think that the kidnapping and murder of Velma Faye Gray was a crime of opportunity. We think he saw her on the side of the road and saw that as an opportunity to do what he did."

The sheriff said he felt that the slayings of Jayme Hurley and Patsy Vineyard were carefully planned.

In the weeks after his arrest, Leslie Warren was held in the Asheville jail without privilege of bond. The Asheville sleuths fielded a steady stream of inquiries from other law enforcement agencies which were checking into possibilities that Warren might have committed some criminal act in their jurisdictions.

Asheville police spokesman Alan Hyder, commenting on the steady stream of inquiries to reporters, noted that the trucking company Warren worked for had routes from Florida to Canada.

As for the crimes Warren had been charged with, the prosecutor in charge of the Johnson case made a statement to the press in late July 1989. "It might be a while before he's debriefed and set for trial anywhere. We'll just try to figure out a way that everybody can get their case resolved in the most efficient manner," said North Carolina's Guilford County District Attorney Jim Kimel.

At a conference in August 1991, the prosecutors from the three states decided that the South Carolina authorities would have the first crack at Warren. His trial for the murder of Velma Gray began in September 1993 in Greenville, South Carolina. Even though the fishermen had found Gray's body in Spartanburg County, the evidence determined that she was killed within Greenville

County. That's why the trial was held in Greenville, the county seat.

Prosecutor Warren Mowry did not seek the death penalty against Warren in his trial at the Greenville County Courthouse. The case did not include an aggravating factor, which is required by state law to warrant the ultimate punishment. Although Gray's death was brutal enough, it wasn't committed during another felony, such as robbery, it wasn't committed for financial gain, and it appeared that the victim hadn't suffered unduly. Hence, no death penalty.

In his opening statement, Prosecutor Mowry told the jury that he had no eyewitness to Gray's slaying, but he promised to create a "full and complex" jigsaw puzzle with the testimony of other witnesses.

In his opening, Greenville County Public Defender John Mauldin suggested that some of the pieces in the state's puzzle might be missing, and he urged the jury to view Warren as being innocent until and unless proven otherwise beyond a reasonable doubt.

The state's case started off with the testimony of one of the three women who saw Velma Gray with a trucker on the last night of her life. The witness admitted under cross-examination that she hadn't been able to pick Warren out of the photo lineup soon after the slaying occurred. She testified that the trucker was Warren, but admitted that she'd seen his photos on TV news programs after his arrest.

Defense Attorney Mauldin moved for a mistrial, basing his request on the woman's testimony. Judge Henry F. Floyd denied the motion, but said he might reconsider. Floyd did instruct the jury to disregard Drake's identification of Warren as the trucker.

The state's case gained strength as Captain Ennis took the witness stand and testified about Warren's confession.

In his closing argument, Prosecutor Mowry told the

jury that no promises were made, nor was any force used to get Warren's confession, and that it did include details about the slaying known only to the police. The prosecutor conceded that he was unable to establish a motive for the killing, but he advised the jury to focus on the killer's identity, not his reason for killing.

The jurors deliberated just under three hours on Wednesday, September 15, 1993, before returning with their verdict. They found Leslie Warren guilty of first-degree murder. He immediately received a life sentence.

After Judge Floyd recessed court, dozens of Velma Gray's family members hugged and cried outside the courtroom.

Prosecutor Mowry said he believed that Warren's confession played a key role in the conviction.

By late October 1993, Warren was still awaiting trial in the two North Carolina slayings, and he had yet to be charged in the New York killing. The prosecutors planned to pursue the Asheville case after the South Carolina conviction.

He has not been charged in any more slayings. In accordance with his constitutional guarantees, Leslie Eugene Warren must be presumed innocent in the deaths of Patsy Diane Vineyard, Jayme Denise Hurley, and Katherine Noel "Kat" Johnson until and unless proven otherwise by due process in a court of law.

"HITCHHIKING TEEN HOOKER'S HORROR ORDEAL!"

by Gary C. King

Saturday, August 2, 1986, proved to be a grueling day for Evelyne Clampett, a maid who worked at a small motel in the 14800 block of Northeast Sandy Boulevard on Portland, Oregon's east side. While the summer sun bore down on the city, Evelyne sweated profusely as she pushed her utility cart along the narrow outdoor walkway in front of the rooms where prostitutes normally brought their johns, and where all-night parties and one-night stands were the norm on weekends. Evelyne looked at her watch as she stopped in front of another room, a unit where a "stay over" was registered.

The guest had been there for several days already, according to the room assignment sheet, and Evelyne figured that the room needed to be stripped by now. Being a small operation, daily service wasn't provided to the longer term guests, unless someone specifically requested something. It was 11:30 A.M., Evelyne had noticed, nearly lunchtime. Despite the fact that her stomach was growling from hunger, Evelyne decided to clean this one last room before stopping to eat her sandwich, which she carried with her in a brown paper bag atop her utility cart.

After assembling fresh sheets and towels and other items that she would need, Evelyne knocked on the door three times. Using her passkey, she opened the door several inches and dutifully called out, "Maid." Receiving no response and assuming that the guest was out of the room for a while, she pushed open the door the rest of the way.

Evelyne had barely taken two steps into the room when she suddenly realized why no one had answered her. Across the room directly in front of her lay the motionless body of a woman, sprawled on the bed. Evelyne called out several more times, asking whether the guest needed any maid service, but still received no reply. When the realization that the woman might be dead finally struck her, Evelyne gasped and let out a shriek. Her whole body tightened as she backed stiffly out of the room, still unsure of the condition of the lifeless figure. She had recognized the person as the guest who had checked in earlier in the week, but didn't recall seeing her anytime during her shift. Nauseous and scared, the maid ran to the front office.

"Call the police!" Evelyne yelled at an idle desk clerk, startling him to attention. "I think I just found a dead woman!" Evelyne was out of breath and her heart thumped hard against her rib cage as the clerk, reaching for the phone, looked at her with wide eyes.

Moments after the 911 call was received at Portland's emergency communications center, an officer out on routine patrol near the motel heard the sketchy dispatch (about a possible dead body) as it crackled over his radio. Paramedics were already on the way, he heard, and since he was in the vicinity, he broadcast that he would take the call and proceeded to the motel.

When the officer arrived, two paramedics were already notifying their supervisor that no lifesaving efforts were needed. The partially clad woman was dead. The Portland

Police Bureau officer, not seeing any signs of respiration and noting that the victim's face had a bluish cast to it, quickly reached the same conclusion. He notified his dispatcher that he needed additional police department personnel at the scene, preferably a homicide unit, to investigate what he termed "a suspicious death."

While waiting for additional help to arrive, the officer secured the area and sealed off the room. He noted the names of the paramedics, and added as a footnote to his handwritten preliminary report that nothing, as far as he could tell, had been touched or moved by anyone prior to his arrival.

Portland Detectives William Law and Thomas Nelson were assigned to investigate the suspicious death, which became Case Number 86-77325, the city's 33rd homicide of the year. They arrived at the motel a short time later, and were soon joined by a deputy medical examiner and a representative from the Multnomah County District Attorney's Office.

The corpse, they noted, was that of a young woman. Her body was cool to the touch, likely at or near room temperature. She was blond and slender, and they guessed that she was in her mid-20s. It looked like she had been slapped or punched prior to her death. Because of the bluish color of her face and the markings on her throat, they theorized that she had been strangled manually. Although they found several items of personal effects in the room, there was no identification of the victim. Because of the victim's tawdry appearance, her garish makeup and wild hair, and because of the skimpy outfits found in the room and the fact that the motel was a known haven for hookers, Detectives Law and Nelson strongly suspected that the victim was a prostitute. They also reasoned that the name on the registration card was an alias.

* * *

After viewing and photographing the body exactly as it had been found, the investigators called in a crime scene unit to process the room for clues. One of the technician's trained eyes focused quickly on an ashtray, which he recognized as having a smooth bottom surface that made it a good source for possible fingerprints. The technicians also focused their attention on tabletops, water glasses, and other items that held potential as evidence, which they seized, bagged, and marked after the items were photographed and their locations noted. They also seized the bedsheets, pillowcases, and towels, which they hoped might contain trace evidence such as hair, clothing fiber, even semen if it turned out that the case was of a sexual nature.

As they bagged evidence, the investigators found a pair of size 54 men's underpants in the room. Could they belong to their suspect? they wondered. If so, he was a very large man who would likely be capable of easily overpowering a woman the size of the victim. Or did the underwear belong to another man who had previously visited the room, such as a john, but who had not had anything to do with the victim's death? Detectives Law and Nelson quietly pondered the possibilities, but came up with only more questions, not answers.

When the two sleuths interviewed Evelyne Clampett, she said there wasn't much to tell. Still upset, the mild-mannered maid nervously said that she hadn't seen anybody whom she could particularly characterize as a suspect or who was otherwise associated with the body. There were a lot of suspicious characters who frequented the motel, like drug dealers and prostitutes, but no one whom she could single out for the detectives. She hadn't noticed anyone loitering around during her shift, and hadn't heard any screams or commotion during the morning.

Although the detectives had little doubt that the victim's death had been caused by an act of violence, they found no signs of forced entry to the room and only a few signs of what they could construe as a struggle. There were no broken windows, and the door and door frame were intact.

Had the young woman been killed in an attempt to cover up a sexual assault or rape, to prevent her from going to the police? they wondered. Or had robbery been the motive? If she was a hooker, had she brought a trick to her room who had suddenly become violent?

Because drug dealers often conducted business out of the motel, Detectives Law and Nelson considered the possibility that the victim had been involved in a drug deal that had gone awry. They also thought it was possible that she might have simply opened the door to someone she knew, who then killed her for any number of reasons. It was even possible that her assailant had somehow obtained a passkey and had been lying in wait when she returned to her room. She also might have opened the door to someone who used a ruse, such as a motel employee, who simply pushed his way into her room. The detectives reasoned that any one of those scenarios could have occurred, but there was no way they could know for certain until they had more information or a suspect in custody who was willing to talk.

As they spent the day interviewing motel employees and long-term guests, Law and Nelson eventually learned that a white man in his early 30s had been seen in the vicinity of the victim's motel room during the early morning hours. Witnesses described the man as taller than 6 feet, and said that he was wearing a white swimsuit. Because no one who worked at the motel fit that general description, the lawmen all but ruled out that a motel employee had been involved.

The man was seen driving a sharp-looking, late-70s model AMC Jeep Renegade that had a significant amount of custom work, the detective were told. Witnesses said that it had a four-to-five-inch red stripe running down the side, and had orange pinstripes around the doors and wheel wells. The vehicle had a black undercarriage, and chrome around the outer frame wheel wells. The differential housing covers were also made of chrome. The Jeep had a soft top, was equipped with a roll bar, and had a red five-gallon gasoline can on the back and a winch attached to the front. "Renegade" was written on both sides of the hood, and inside a pair of red dice with white dots hung from the rearview mirror. Also, the vehicle was equipped with oversize mud tires and deep-dish type mag wheels.

The detectives felt very lucky that they had obtained such a detailed description of the vehicle, but they were also disappointed that nobody had obtained its license plate number or the state in which it was registered. Nonetheless, they took down the description of the Jeep and the possible suspect and sent out a regional APB, hoping they would get lucky.

When they returned to their offices at the Portland Justice Center, Law and Nelson mulled over the case and tossed ideas off one another. Both agreed that what they had learned so far amounted to pretty slim pickings. The more they thought about the case the less hopeful they were that it could be solved quickly. If they could only identify the victim, the cornerstone in any homicide investigation, they figured the case might move forward a little more quickly. Because they believed that the victim had been a prostitute, the detectives brought in several patrol officers who normally worked the city's prostitution hot spots in the hope that one of them might recognize the victim. Little did they know that the move would be their ace in the hole, at least with regard to making the identification.

Jim Ferraris is a Portland policeman who works the

82nd Avenue strip that runs between Portland and Oregon City, where prostitution is rampant. He was on patrol when he heard the call on his police radio about the possible hooker who had been killed. Ferraris immediately got in touch with Detectives Law and Nelson, and agreed to meet them at the morgue to see if he could recognize the victim. Perhaps, he reasoned, she had been someone with whom he'd been in contact along his beat.

After the body was pulled out of the refrigerated storage unit, Ferraris took one look at the dead female and recognized her immediately as Tina Jo Sutton, a prostitute who often went by the handle "T.J." on the street. She wasn't in her mid-20s as the detectives had believed, Ferraris said, but was only 16, aged beyond her teenage years by her rough life-style. She had only just become eligible for her driver's license, they learned.

"She was a pretty tough cookie," said Ferraris, "a very tough street kid. She had a lot of hostility inside of her. She'd be hooking and I'd stop her, and she would get very angry and deny it and threaten to report me to the Internal Affairs Unit." Even though Tina wasn't the first teen hooker he'd seen succumb to life on the streets and knew that she wouldn't be the last, Ferraris was saddened over her untimely death.

Detectives Law and Nelson seemed surprised when they learned that Tina was only 16. Like Patrolman Ferraris, they were sorrowful that a girl as young as Tina was now lying dead on a cold slab in the morgue because of her life-style. She looked much older, they observed, and had track marks on her arms from injecting illicit drugs.

"Anytime someone dies it's a tragedy," said Nelson. "But the tragedy here is that this girl was only sixteen years old. It's a waste of life. Sure, she was hooking and doing drugs, but she didn't belong out there. Somewhere along the line she got messed up, and you wonder what this sweet thing was doing out in this mess."

During the autopsy conducted by the state medical examiner, Dr. Larry Lewman, it was determined that Tina had died from strangulation, just as the detectives had suspected. Someone with powerful hands, they believed, had killed her. But who?

The two detectives began checking into Tina's background, standard procedure in any homicide, and reasoned that by doing so they might get lucky and find the person who killed her. He was out there somewhere, they knew. In many cases, it's a sure bet that the perpetrator can be found somewhere in the victim's background. But because Tina was most likely a victim of opportunity because of her hooking activities, the detectives felt like they were grasping into thin air for the clues they needed. Both lawmen knew that a lot of luck would be needed to catch her killer.

Tina, they learned, came from a middle-class Portland family. Her parents had divorced when she was 10. According to family members, Tina was an only child who possessed a lively imagination. Although she liked to play by herself a lot, she also made friends easily. Slumber parties were common in her home while she was growing up, and she seemed to lead a normal childhood. But somewhere along the way, everyone agreed, something went wrong. At the time of her death, the sleuths learned, Tina was supporting a $75-a-day drug habit the only way she knew how, by selling her body on the streets of Portland. It was something that she had been doing for a long time, and she had become proficient at it until her number came up.

According to the detectives, after her parents' divorce, Tina took to the streets. She began skipping school, and cut off many of her friendships with classmates. Instead of doing the things that most teenage girls do, Tina began hanging out beneath a Portland railroad bridge with other street urchins, often smoking marijuana and drinking alcohol while listening to hard-rock music on the radio. It soon became a way of life for Tina, and, in the seventh grade, at age 13, school officials discovered marijuana in her locker during a routine drug search.

Detectives Law and Nelson were told that Tina had been reported as a runaway numerous times in her short life. A search of police files turned up at least 30 such reports. Each time Tina would run away, the police would track her down and bring her home, according to a Multnomah County Juvenile Court counselor. Before she turned 14, Tina was using LSD, amphetamines, hallucinogenic mushrooms such as liberty caps, downers, cocaine, and codeine.

"Tina's story shows what can happen to anyone's child," said the court counselor who supervised Tina's case. "There was such a sadness about her. She wanted to be a normal sixteen-year-old, but the street was her identity. That's foreign to a lot of people, but it was powerful. She was good at it, and on the street she was in control of her life."

Shortly after school officials found the marijuana in her locker, Tina was admitted to an inpatient treatment program in Spokane, Washington. While there, Tina told the doctors that she drank alcohol often, as much as four times a week, which they considered a lot for a 13-year-old who shouldn't have been drinking at all, and she said that she smoked marijuana daily. It was while in the Spokane treatment center that doctors also found out about Tina's frequent use of other drugs.

After about two months, Tina was sent home. She soon began skipping school again, however, because her classmates taunted her about having been sent to a drug treatment center. She again returned to the sordid life on 82nd Avenue, where no one cared about her life-style and drug use. She began staying in seedy motels with other street kids and prostitutes who provided cheap sex to older men for $20, sometimes less.

When the detectives hit the pavement on 82nd Avenue and talked to some of the other street kids who, like Tina, made the asphalt their home, they pieced together a profile of a hot-looking blond girl who dressed provocatively and often partied all night. That was what Tina had been doing on the last night of her life, they finally determined. Friends and acquaintances told the detectives that Tina was hanging out near Southeast 82nd Avenue and Schiller Street on August 1st, where she was last seen at 3:00 A.M., waiting for a john whom she could proposition.

The detectives discovered that some of the other street kids had looked up to Tina. They located at least two teenage girls whom Tina had taught the ways of the street, particularly how to become prostitutes and to watch out for the police.

"She was beautiful," one of her friends told the detectives. "But she hit the road hard. She was a runner, and she didn't like to be told what to do. On Eighty-second Avenue no one is better than anybody else. Tina didn't have a lot of friends in her straight life. Out here she had friends. She liked the high. She was a junkie, a crankster."

The friend explained that Tina used crank, a powerful methamphetamine, which she injected, or "mainlined," into her veins, sometimes several times a day. The meth injections kept her awake for several days at a time, the friend said. Tina once contracted hepatitis, presumably from using dirty needles, but nonetheless continued to work as a hooker no matter how sick she felt.

"I was impressed with her aside from her looks," said a teenage boy who had known Tina. "At thirteen, she was doing it for herself. She didn't have no pimp. She taught me about the streets. She taught me how to con and she taught me how to survive. She wasn't real open, but there was a real person under there. I ain't cried about her [death] yet, but when I sober up I probably will . . . Tina was the first person to shoot me up with crank . . . I've been hooked ever since."

At age 15, the detectives learned, Tina and a boy traveled to Los Angeles, where they stayed with the boy's relatives. Tina, however, became even more heavily involved in drugs and was soon working as a nude dancer and a hooker. She was arrested at a motel across the street from Disneyland after she came on to an undercover policeman. Authorities sent Tina home and barred her from returning to California until she turned 18, an age that many people felt she would never see. Upon Tina's return to Portland, she was enrolled in a county program that teaches street kids how to return to a normal life.

For the first time in her young life, Tina had a place she could call her own, an apartment that she shared with another girl who was also enrolled in the program. At first it looked like Tina might turn over a new leaf and straighten out her life. She had plenty of food to eat; she studied and earned money legally. But it just wasn't enough. The street continued to beckon her, and when Tina's probation from the California offense officially ended and authorities had no further legal hold on her, Tina left the program and returned to her life on the streets.

"When she came to us, she was a stereotyped prostitute," said one of the program's counselors. "Lots of makeup, wild. Tina couldn't open up. There was a lot of loneliness in her. She had so much anger inside, but she wouldn't open up and talk about it. It was easier for her to talk about the past than the here and now. . . . She wanted to be normal, but kids like her have the street life-style ingrained in them. It becomes their identity. There was a part of her that wanted to leave the street and a part of her that didn't. It was a tug of war."

"Tina had no business being in the situation she was in," said another counselor. "The key to Tina's tragedy is that she got too deeply into drugs and could not find a way out. That happens to hundreds of kids. It can happen to anyone's child, but almost every parent will deny that. It happens to the best of families and to the worst of families."

The detectives were inclined to agree, particularly about the tragedy of Tina's addiction to drugs. Because of Tina's extensive drug use, Detectives Law and Nelson began to speculate that the girl might have been killed by drug dealers. It was possible, they reasoned, that Tina had owed money to them and was unable to pay up. After additional work on the streets, the sleuths began to focus on two dealers in particular who were known to draw kids into their lair, then use them by getting them addicted to drugs so that they would have to sell their bodies to support their habits. They also used the kids, particularly girls, to act as "bag bitches," transporting drugs and money for them. The dealers also required them to provide new drug customers or face the consequences of beatings or, worse, at least in the kids' minds, risk being cut off from their supply of drugs.

"They had the motive and the opportunity," said Detective Nelson of the two dealers whom he and Law were focusing on. After considerable additional work, however, including undercover operations, the detectives soon realized that their theory about Tina's death had been incorrect.

"We could never prove anything, and there was a shadow of a doubt," said Nelson. "We kept the case open, but eventually figured that it would never be solved."

To make matters worse, results of the tests that were performed on the crime scene evidence turned out to be largely inconclusive. With little else to go on, the detectives resumed their search for a suspect the hard, old-fashioned way—legwork.

At one point, the detectives became hopeful that they would solve the case when they talked to another prostitute who worked 82nd Avenue and had known Tina. The hooker said she and several other people had seen a guy who they knew only by the name of "Tom" talking to Tina just before she was believed to have died. Tom, she said, drove a white Jeep with "either a blue or green stripe around it." He had also picked up several other hookers on a number of other occasions.

The description that the hooker provided of the vehicle sounded like the Jeep that had been seen at the motel where Tina was killed, but the description was too vague to bring the sleuths any closer to identifying and collaring the killer. Even the name, they reasoned, wasn't much to go on. It could have been, and likely was, an alias since johns often used fictitious names in their dealings with hookers.

As time went on, the leads in Tina Sutton's case petered out. The detectives occasionally received a tip, but they had other cases to work on and little came of the leads that filtered in on Tina's case. Even though they followed up each and every clue, there simply wasn't much to go on.

By the summer of 1987, however, the sleuths' interest in Tina's case was renewed when a rash of unexplained prostitute disappearances struck Portland. They wondered, in the back of their minds, whether the disappearances could be related to Tina's death. Several of the missing hookers had worked on 82nd Avenue, and the detectives went out and pounded the pavement again to see what they could learn. Ultimately, though, the probers were again disappointed with the results of their efforts. Although Portland's hookers were tense and upset over the disappearances, they simply did not know anything that could help Detectives Law and Nelson.

Before the summer was over, however, a Canby, Oregon, businessman was arrested for the brutal murders of eight Portland-area hookers and the detectives again felt a glimmer of hope in Tina's case. Dayton Leroy Rogers, 34, was taken into custody after witnesses at a Denny's restaurant watched him chase, tackle, and then stab to death a naked woman, later determined to have been a prostitute, in the eatery's parking lot in August 1987. Less than a month later, a hunter unwittingly stumbled across the nude remains of seven other women in the Molalla forest just outside Portland, all of whom would be identified as some of Portland's missing prostitutes. Naturally, Detectives Law and Nelson wondered if Rogers had been involved in Tina's death.

Although intrigued by Rogers's case, Law and Nelson were also disappointed when they got together with the detectives working that investigation. Rogers's victims, they learned, all bore stabbing wounds to their bodies, and one victim had been eviscerated from her vagina to her sternum with what authorities suspected was a machete. Several others had had their feet sawed from their bodies, just about the ankle. Because Rogers's M.O. did not fit into Tina Sutton's case, and because there was no physical evidence linking Rogers to Tina's murder, the Portland sleuths gave up that avenue of the probe. Rogers, who became known as Oregon's worst serial killer to date, was later convicted and sentenced to death. But Tina Sutton's killer was still out there.

Two additional years passed, and no new leads surfaced in Tina's case. Case Number 86-77325, although still officially active, was virtually at a standstill, and the detectives now had little or no hope of ever solving it. It wasn't until Sunday, March 5, 1989, that the case finally broke, taking the sleuths completely by surprise. At about 2:30

P.M., a large man walked into the Multnomah County Sheriff's Office, his face bearing a quizzical, almost puzzled look.

"I'd like to speak to a detective," said the man calmly. "I want to confess to a killing." The man, who identified himself as Donnie Dwight Kay, 37 years old, was taken into an interrogation room. As a formality in such cases, he was advised of his rights under Miranda before being questioned.

Meanwhile, Detective Nelson was working in his office that same afternoon, catching up on an endless stream of paperwork that all cops have to deal with, when his telephone rang. The caller identified himself as a Multnomah County sheriff's deputy.

"Is there anyone in the homicide unit who can fill me in on a killing that occurred inside a motel room in 1986?" he asked, explaining that the motel was located at Northeast Sandy Boulevard and 148th Street. Nelson, recognizing the location and the motel, was suddenly very interested.

"That's my case," replied Nelson. "The girl who was killed there was Tina Sutton. Why do you want to know about it?"

"Some guy just walked into our office and said that he killed the girl," the deputy responded. Nelson nearly dropped the telephone as his anticipation soared.

"What does the man look like?" asked Nelson.

"He's about six foot three, and looks like he weighs around three hundred and thirty pounds."

"Do you know what kind of car he was driving when the crime occurred?"

"Yeah," the deputy replied. "He said he was driving a white four-wheel drive then."

Bells went off inside Nelson's head as memories of the witnesses' statements, who told of seeing a white Jeep in the motel's parking lot, came flooding back. He also recalled how he and his partner had found a pair of size 54 men's underpants inside the room where Tina was killed. Nelson instructed the deputy to hold Kay, then called Detective Law, who had the day off. Law readily agreed to go out and interview Kay along with Nelson.

When the detectives arrived, they took Kay into an interrogation room. They read him his rights again, but Kay waived them, saying that what he had done had been eating away at him for years and that he had to get it off his chest. Kay explained that he had come close to confessing several times in the past, but had always backed out. He said that he drove to Portland from Milton, Washington, a small town near Tacoma, on Tuesday, March 31st, to confess to Tina Sutton's slaying, but just couldn't bring himself to the point of coming in. So he took a room at a motel and brooded about it for several days until, finally, that Sunday, he awoke and decided it was time to come clean. He explained that he didn't know which agency was investigating the crime, but decided to drive to the sheriff's department.

As Donnie Kay related his story, he explained that causing the girl's death had turned his whole life around. He'd never been in trouble before, and dealing with the guilt of what he had done became unbearable. He said that he had turned to drugs and alcohol in his desperation to forget, and had been treated in mental hospitals for depression. Despite the psychiatric help, he was never able to tell anyone what was really troubling him. Kay explained that he either had to turn himself in, or commit suicide.

Kay said that he had been living in Eugene, Oregon, at the time of the homicide, but had later moved to Milton, Washington, where he worked at a truck parts store. He had been in Portland visiting relatives, and at one point had seen Tina hitchhiking. He picked her up and they drove to her motel room. He paid her $50 to have sex with him.

Kay explained that he caught Tina at one point trying to take money from his wallet, despite the fact that he had already paid her. They hadn't had sex yet, and Kay became enraged and demanded his money back. Tina refused to return the money and kicked him, which only served to enrage him further. Kay said he remembered hitting Tina once, then he blacked out. He said that the next thing he knew he had his hands around the girl's neck, her face had turned blue, and she had died.

After more than six hours of grueling interrogation, Detectives Law and Nelson charged Donnie Kay with murder. He was held without bail in Portland's downtown Justice Center Jail.

"It was a chance encounter," Law said of Kay's meeting up with Tina Jo Sutton. "He and Tina were together maybe all of twenty minutes. We never identified him as a potential suspect. The chances of him going undetected were great. He was extremely remorseful. He felt extremely guilty and said that regardless of what happened to him he had to get it out in the open."

"It's like reading a good book and getting to the end and finding it missing," said Nelson. "Then, years later, someone hands you the ending." Nelson added that he was relieved the case had finally been cleared.

A background check showed that Kay had been telling the truth when he said he'd never been in trouble before. He had no criminal record. Instead, he was a decorated Vietnam veteran, and many who knew him described him as a hardworking person who never displayed signs that he could be violent. However, a court-appointed psychologist who evaluated Kay for the prosecution found that he had a propensity toward "explosive behavior" under stressful situations or when he'd been drinking or using drugs, but was otherwise "basically a person who wouldn't hurt anyone."

After negotiations with the Multnomah County District Attorney's Office, Kay's lawyer, David Wagner, made it known that he would put on a defense of extreme emotional disturbance if the case went to trial. Wagner contended that Kay had committed first-degree manslaughter, not murder.

After thoroughly reviewing the case, Deputy D.A. Marilyn Curry tended to agree. Curry indicated she was "persuaded that a jury would come back" with a manslaughter verdict after finding that Kay's actions were "an intentional killing under extreme emotional disturbance." As a result, Donnie Kay was allowed to plead guilty to first-degree manslaughter in Tina Sutton's death. Although law enforcement officials were satisfied that the case had been tidily wrapped up and that justice had been served, others, particularly Tina's family, weren't happy about the way it ended. For them, it would never be over.

"The feeling I get from the district attorney and everyone was that because [Tina] was a prostitute her life made less difference," said one of Tina's relatives, angry over the plea-bargain arrangement. "They said a jury would look at things like that. But what you do . . . doesn't make someone [killing] you all right."

"Those thirty minutes of my life [with Tina] cost me the rest of my life," said Kay at his sentencing on Tuesday, June 6, 1989. "I came forward because I thought it was the right thing to do."

Multnomah County Circuit Judge William McLennon sentenced Donnie Dwight Kay to 20 years in prison, the maximum sentence for first-degree manslaughter. However, the actual time served will be determined by the state parole board.

"WHY DID THE BUDDIES BEHEAD THEIR REDHEADED FRIEND?"

by Barbara Geehr

The two young hunters had always loved the stretch of woods bordering Highway 16A in Orangedale, Florida, an unincorporated and virtually unpopulated community about 23 miles from St. Augustine. They had been there many times—sometimes to hunt the deer that roamed the wild and untamed woodland and other times simply to hunt relief from the pressures of their everyday world.

In the midafternoon of Monday, November 11, 1991, the youths, who had been hunting deer since early morning, decided to call it a day. They hadn't sighted a single buck or doe; only squirrels, snakes, and chipmunks had crossed their paths. However, as the youths started heading out of the woods, they came to a clearing where they found something they had never seen before—and hoped never to come upon again. It was the skeletonized remains of a human body, partially concealed under a cover of leafy branches. Among the bones and on the surrounding ground lay several pieces of rotted female clothing:

a jacket, a shirt, dungarees, underwear, and a single small black boot.

Not daring to explore the area further, the two youths ran all the way out of the woods to the convenience store on 16A, where they called the St. Johns County Sheriff's Office and explained that they had chanced upon some apparently human remains.

"We can wait for someone to meet us here at the convenience store," the youths offered. "Then we can lead them to the clearing where we found the remains."

"Good!" said the dispatcher on the other end of the line. "Officers will be there within the next half-hour."

It was nearly six o'clock by the time Sergeant Charles West, two deputies, and the watch commander reached the convenience store. With daylight already slipping away, West and his accompanying officers followed the two youths across Highway 16A to a dirt road that cut a path through the heart of the woods. They walked about a quarter-mile south along the narrow road, turned sharply east to enter the forest, and then made their way through the dense underbrush and towering pines for a few hundred yards to a small clearing.

There, with the early November dark about to encompass them, they could little more than briefly view the burial site and note the rotted female clothing. Sergeant West had the area roped off as a crime scene and posted the accompanying deputies to stand watch throughout the long, chilly autumn night.

At nine o'clock the following morning, November 12th, West returned to the crime scene accompanied by the entire crimes-against-persons unit of the St. Johns Sheriff's Office, as well as investigators from the Florida Department of Law Enforcement (FDLE) and the county medical examiner, Dr. Terrence Steiner. They searched for evidence and had the remains of what had once been a human female removed to Dr. Steiner's office.

The main piece of evidence the team collected, besides the victim's rotted clothing, was a bright orange key holder with car ignition and trunk keys attached by an equally bright orange bungee cord. Otherwise, the only other items found were such generic trash as an empty cigarette pack and a piece of cellophane.

At autopsy, Dr. Steiner determined that a nick in the victim's left rib indicated she had been stabbed in the heart with a small dagger, commonly called a Bowie knife. He also stated that someone had tried to chop off the victim's head with a second, much larger knife.

Dr. William Maples, a world-famous forensic expert from the University of Florida in Gainesville, was called in on the autopsy and was able to put together a general description of the victim. He said she was probably an adult white female between 20 and 25 years of age, approximately 5 feet 4 inches tall, weighing somewhere between 135 and 148 pounds and with medium-length light-brown hair. "There was also evidence she was getting orthodontic treatment," he added.

In routine fashion, St. Johns County sheriff's investigators searched through missing-person reports already on file but found no descriptions of missing women that matched the description of the victim found in the Orangedale woods. Sergeant West next released to law enforcement agencies and news media throughout the state information about the slaying, a description of the victim as put together by Dr. Maples, and a plea for help in making an identification.

Response in the first few days was nil. Then the sergeant received an interesting phone call from a reporter from the *Florida Times-Union,* a daily newspaper in Jacksonville.

"I don't know if what I am about to tell you is important," the man said, "but after receiving your press release, I got to remembering a telephone call I received some five months ago from a woman residing in Wilmington, North Carolina. To be more specific, the actual date of the call was July first, a Monday. I happened to note it, along with the woman's name and telephone number, on the calendar I keep on my desk."

"What was the call about?" West asked.

"The woman identified herself as a relative of twenty-two-year-old Stacy Ann Willetts. She said that Stacy's family had become greatly concerned about her welfare. Stacy and two male companions had left Wilmington in Stacy's 1981 Mustang on June twenty-second. She said they were headed for St. Augustine.

"On June twenty-fifth," the reporter continued, "Stacy telephoned the relative to say that she and the men had reached St. Augustine safely and were going to try to find a reasonable motel where they could stay while looking for jobs. She also promised to phone again as soon as the three found suitable lodging. The woman said not a single family member had heard from Stacy since that telephone call."

"What you're telling me sounds like the beginning of a missing-person report," Sergeant West commented. "Why would this woman be phoning you? Did you happen to know her or Stacy Willetts by chance?"

"No," the reporter said, "but I got the call by chance. When the woman phoned the paper, she simply asked for the news department, and I happened to be the one who answered."

"Okay, so this woman telephone the newspaper, apparently believing the paper would run a missing-person story about Stacy Willetts, and you happened to field the call?"

"That's the way it went," the reporter said. "I told her we only ran such stories when they originated in a law enforcement agency. I suggested she contact either the St. Augustine Police Department or the St. Johns County

Sheriff's Office and file a missing-person report. None-theless, she insisted upon giving me a detailed description of Stacy Willetts.

"I didn't hear from this woman again, so I assumed Stacy Willetts had eventually got around to letting her family know where she was or, possibly, had even returned home. In fact, I completely forgot about the call from the Wilmington woman. Until this morning, that is, when I received your press release about the young woman in the Orangedale woods.

"When I read the description of the woman, it rang a bell," the man went on. "I remembered the telephone call from the woman in Wilmington and the description she'd given of Stacy Willetts. They seemed to be pretty much the same."

"Now you're getting interesting," West commented.

"I flipped through the pages of my desk calendar until I got to the notations I made about the call. Fortunately, I'd written down the woman's name and telephone number. I just called her. She said no one in the family had heard from Stacy since that telephone call of June twenty-fifth. The woman also mentioned that she had filed a missing-person report—not there in St. Augustine as I had suggested, but with the New Hanover County Sheriff's Department there in Wilmington."

The sergeant took down the North Carolina woman's name and telephone number and thanked the reporter for his information. West immediately assigned homicide Investigators Patricia Greenhalgh and Frank Welborn to follow up on the lead. West gave them the number of the North Carolina woman that the reporter had given him.

"Get a good description of this Stacy Willetts," he told them, and if you agree it generally matches the description of the victim found in the Orangedale woods, find out if you can get the missing girl's dental records. Also find out about the two male companions the Willetts girl left with and the tag number on the 1981 Mustang they were traveling in."

Investigator Greenhalgh immediately telephoned the Wilmington woman. After relating the events that led up to the call, Greenhalgh explained, "The only way we can determine whether or not the remains are Stacy's is through a comparison of the victim's dental work with Stacy's dental records."

"I understand," the Willetts relative said, "and one of us will phone Stacy's dentist right away to tell him it's okay to release her records.

"I should let you know, though, that we did file a missing-person report on Stacy with Detective Tom Landry of the New Hanover County Sheriff's Office right here in Wilmington over four months ago," the relative continued. "There have been some developments on the case—even reports that Stacy is alive and well—but we don't believe them. If Stacy *were* alive, she would be in touch with her family, and no one in the family has heard from her since June twenty-fifth, the day she arrived in St. Augustine. I believe you should probably get in touch with Detective Landry."

"We'll do that," Greenhalgh said.

Putting down the phone, Detective Greenhalgh related the information the Wilmington woman told her to Frank Welborn, her teammate on this investigation, as he had been on many other homicide investigations in the past.

"Let's break the ice by asking this Detective Landry to pick up and forward the dental records," Welborn said. "There's no point in getting further involved in a New Hanover County case unless we get positive identification that our remains are actually those of the missing Wilmington woman."

Detective Tom Landry readily agreed to pick up and forward the needed dental records. When they arrived,

Greenhalgh and Welborn turned them over to Medical Examiner Steiner, who found a match between them and the dental work of the human remains discovered on November 11, 1991.

Investigators Greenhalgh and Welborn then checked back with Detective Landry in North Carolina on the progress he had made during the four months that he had been investigating Stacy Ann Willetts's disappearance.

Through a series of phone calls, the Florida sleuths learned that Stacy had left Wilmington with 25-year-old John Marquard and his bosom buddy, 26-year-old Michael Abshire, on June 22nd. "Stacy had previously lived with Marquard for a short time," Detective Landry explained, "but at this particular time, she had been back living with relatives for about a year, during which time she had neither seen nor talked to him.

"Then she just happened to run into him and Abshire at a bar. The meeting was purely accidental. Nonetheless, for Stacy, it rekindled the old flame. Marquard, who had once visited St. Augustine and fallen in love with its beaches, spent the evening painting a romantic picture of what it would be like for all three of them—Stacy, Abshire and himself—to drive there, find jobs and live happily ever after. He said the only problem was, neither he nor Abshire had the car necessary to make the trip.

"Stacy not only bought Marquard's picture but also offered her car, a 1981 Mustang, which needed some repairs. For Marquard and Abshire, that was a problem they could solve easily. They fixed the Mustang, moved Stacy's belongings to the home of a friend on June twenty-first and, on the twenty-second, headed for St. Augustine. Her telephone call to relatives to let them know the three had arrived safely is the last contact she had with anyone in her family."

Landry said he had managed to locate the motel in St. Augustine where Stacy, Marquard, and Abshire had stayed for three days. "The motel records show the three checked out on the morning of June twenty-eighth. The trail went cold after that, despite our having issued a missing-person report on Stacy and a BOLO [Be On the Lookout] on her Mustang."

"One of Stacy's relatives indicated there had been some recent developments in the case," Greenhalgh said. "What can you tell us about that?"

The Wilmington detective recounted an incident in Pinellas County, Florida, in which a sheriff's deputy pulled over a 1981 Mustang for running a stop sign at five o'clock in the morning on September 14th. "The officer vaguely remembered a BOLO on an old-model Mustang, which had been received at the Pinellas County Sheriff's Office three or four months before. So when the driver could not come up with a registration for the vehicle, the deputy pulled both him and the car in. In checking the BOLO, he found the pulled-in vehicle and its tag matched the description of Stacy Ann Willetts's Mustang and its tag number."

"And who was the driver?" Greenhalgh asked.

"Abshire."

Somewhat surprised, the St. Johns County investigator said, "Okay, let me get this straight. Abshire isn't the one Stacy Willetts lived with for a short time. He was simply the bosom buddy of Marquard, who *did* have a relationship with Stacy. But it was *Abshire* who was driving Stacy's car?"

"Right."

"How did Abshire explain that?"

"He said he and Marquard had bought the vehicle from Willetts for two hundred dollars at a bar in St. Augustine where she had become involved with a truck driver who had apparently picked her up. According to Abshire's story, Willetts was going to take off with this truck driver so she didn't need her car. But she *did* need money. He and Marquard came up with a hundred dollars apiece."

Greenhalgh wanted to know what happened to Willetts.

"According to Abshire," Landry said, "the last he and Marquard saw of her, she and the truck driver were pulling away from the bar in a green pickup truck. I asked him if he knew there was a missing-person report out on Stacy Willetts. He said he did not and that the last time he and John Marquard had seen her—which, he repeated, was when she and the truck driver drove away in the green pickup—she was very much alive and well."

"Where is Marquard?"

"Abshire gave us an address where his buddy could be located, a city address," Landry explained. "We called the police department, and a detective from there located and interviewed Marquard. He told the same story as Abshire told the county investigators: the two had bought the Mustang from Willetts for two hundred dollars, had last seen her drive off in a green pickup with a truck driver she had met at the bar, and was alive and well at that time. There was no cause to arrest Marquard.

"But Abshire turned out to be a different story," the Hanover County detective explained. "A check on Abshire by the Pinellas County officer who had picked him up revealed that Abshire was wanted back in North Carolina for violation of probation. The officer arrested him on that charge and had him transported back to Wilmington. He is presently being held at the state prison in Raleigh."

"What about the Mustang? What happened to it?"

"A couple of Stacy's relatives drove down to Pinellas County, picked the vehicle up, and drove it back to Wilmington. I assume it's still there."

Detective Greenhalgh obtained the name, address, and telephone number of the Wilmington relative who had picked up the Mustang. She thanked Detective Landry for his tremendous help in setting the stage upon which the investigation into the slaying of Stacy Willetts was about to begin.

A check on the evidence recovered at the crime scene became one of the first steps in that investigation. Sergeant West wanted to know for sure that the car keys found at the crime scene were keys to the ignition and trunk of Stacy Willetts's 1981 Mustang. He called the male relative who had picked up the Mustang in Pinellas County and driven it back to Wilmington. In response to the sergeant's request, the relative faxed a photo of the keys to the St. Johns County Sheriff's Office. When placed alongside a photo of the keys found at the crime scene, there seemed to be a match. But seeming to be a match was not sufficient for the sergeant. He asked the relative to drive Stacy's Mustang to the sheriff's office in St. Augustine, so that the keys that had been taken into evidence could be tried in the ignition of the car.

When the relative arrived, the evidence keys started the car with no problem.

Meanwhile, Investigator Greenhalgh had been following a similar course of action in checking on the one small black woman's boot that had been recovered at the crime scene. She mailed a photo of the boot to the female relative with whom Stacy Willetts had been living prior to the St. Augustine trip, then interviewed her by phone.

The relative readily identified the boot as Stacy's. "I was with Stacy when she bought those little black boots," the relative said. "I hated them. I didn't want her to take them with her on the trip to St. Augustine, but she loved them and wouldn't leave them behind."

With the body found in the Orangedale woods positively identified as Stacy Ann Willetts and the evidence collected at the crime scene identified as belonging to her, it was now time to interview the last-known persons to have seen the young woman alive—Michael Abshire and John Marquard. Sergeant West assigned Investigators Greenhalgh and Mary Levek to interview Abshire at the state prison in Raleigh, North Carolina. Investigators Welborn and Jennifer Strickland took on the task of locating and interviewing John Marquard in Pinellas County.

Greenhalgh and Levek arranged to meet with Detective Landry in Wilmington so he could accompany them to Raleigh to witness the Abshire interview. Welborn and Strickland made similar arrangements to meet with the police officer in Pinellas County who had located and interviewed John Marquard.

It was the Saturday afternoon of November 16, 1991, when Investigators Greenhalgh and Levek began their interview with Michael Abshire at the state prison. With tape rolling, Abshire readily waived his right to have an attorney present and agreed to answer whatever questions the investigators asked.

He talked freely about how the trip from Wilmington originated, how he, Marquard, and Willetts had stayed at a motel for three days after their arrival in St. Augustine, how they filled out applications for work at several places, and how Stacy had been the only one offered a job. "She was supposed to go to work as a waitress at a cafe-type restaurant, but she decided not to take the job. She didn't want to do that kind of work," he said.

"Meantime, me and John weren't having any luck landing anything, our cash was getting low, and we couldn't decide whether to head back home or go to another city where jobs might be more plentiful. Then Stacy and this truck driver got together at a bar in St. Augustine and she decided to take off with him.

"We bought the Mustang from her for two hundred bucks so we would at least have a set of wheels. The last we saw of Stacy was when she and the truck driver pulled away from the bar in a green pickup."

"Let's take a break, go off the record for a while," Investigator Greenhalgh said, as she switched the tape recorder off. "I believe your story up to the point of the bar incident," she explained, "but the bar incident doesn't hold water for any of us. You know and we know that Stacy Willetts never got out of St. Augustine, that there was never a truck driver with a green pickup.

"The only people who could have possibly killed Stacy Willetts are you and John Marquard. For your information, while we are here questioning you, two other investigators from the St. Johns County Sheriff's Office are in Pinellas County, questioning John Marquard. Are you going to let him pin this murder on you or are you going to tell the truth about what really happened? Have a cup of coffee and think about it."

Abshire downed three cups of coffee before making up his mind to talk. "I don't really know where to begin," he said.

"The beginning is always a pretty good place," Greenhalgh said, as she switched the tape recorder back on.

"That would be back in Wilmington when John got Stacy to offer using her Mustang for making the trip to St. Augustine," Abshire said. "Before we even left town, John told me he was thinking about getting rid of Stacy. She bothered him a lot; they did a lot of bickering.

"When we stopped at a convenience store in South Carolina on the way down, they got into a big argument; and when him and me were together in the men's room, he said, 'We're going to take her down a dirt road and kill her and just leave her there. I've had enough of this.' I was doing the driving at the time, and I told John there was no way I would let this happen.

"I guess the final straw broke for him after all three of us filled out applications for work and Stacy was the only one who got a job. Then she didn't take it. John kept telling her she wasn't pulling her weight. He was getting kind of frayed around the edges between looking for a job in the days and looking for girls at night."

Abshire next recounted how, after two nights at the motel the three had checked into upon their arrival in St. Augustine, he and Marquard went out and found an apartment. "The landlady explained the apartment was strictly for two persons and would not be ready for occupancy for a week," Abshire said. "We gave her a hundred dollar deposit; and when we left there, I knew John had definitely made up his mind that Stacy had to be killed."

"How did you figure to get away with murder?"

"We happened, at that very time, to cross a bridge over a river which was bordered by deep woods on both sides. Then when we got a little farther along the road, we saw this narrow dirt road that cut a path right through the heart of the woods. John said we'll get her into the woods on some ruse, kill her there, and throw her body into the river where the alligators will eat it and she'll never be found. It was when we were on our way back to the motel from there that we concocted the story about Stacy taking up with a truck driver and taking off with him in a green pickup."

Asked what ruse they used to get Stacy into the woods, Abshire answered, "We told her we'd run into a couple of guys who had a cabin in the woods, that they were throwing a party, that we'd been invited and could bring her along."

"And she believed you?"

"Yeah. She knew John and me played survival games and Dungeons and Dragons in the woods lots of times."

"So she went with you willingly, completely unaware of what was going to happen," Greenhalgh stated. "So what did happen when you got to the woods?"

"John and me geared up—put on the camouflage attire, then the suspenders where we hooked the knives, weapons, flashlights, and other portable stuff. We even brought along some fireworks. We left the Mustang on the dirt road and then walked single file into the woods.

"I led the way, Stacy was behind me, and John was behind her. When we got to the point where the river we crossed on the road should have been, there was no river. It didn't come down that far. Our whole way was blocked with the density of the trees and the underbrush. We couldn't go no farther. We had to turn around and head back."

"Did you still lead the way?"

"Yeah. It was me, then Stacy, then John."

"Okay, go on," Greenhalgh urged.

"When we reached a small clearing is when John grabbed Stacy and put his hand over her mouth, and I heard a muffled scream. I turned around, saw John slit Stacy's throat and stab her in the heart with his dagger, and then throw her on the ground. He then handed me the dagger, and I stabbed her in the side.

"After that, John took his big knife from his pocket and started to decapitate Stacy. He then handed me his big knife and told me to do the same thing. Which I did."

"What happened after that?"

"We tried to dig in the ground to bury her, but the ground was too hard, had too many roots. So we covered her body with branches and then left the area."

"Where did you and Marquard go after the killing?"

"We drove to Orlando, got a couple of piddly jobs there, and then decided we might do better in Pinellas County."

Investigator Greenhalgh said, "You have made this confession of your own free will? You have not been offered any deal to make this confession?"

Abshire replied, "There has been no deal. I confessed because I want to show the judge that I regret what happened; I want to be halfway decent."

While St. Johns County Sheriff's Investigators Pat Greenhalgh and Mary Levek were getting a confession from Michael Abshire at the jail in Raleigh, two other St. Johns County Sheriff's Investigators—Frank Welborn and Jennifer Strickland—were getting a similar confession from John Marquard in Pinellas County.

In separate trials, jurors found both men guilty of first-degree murder and of armed robbery in the stealing of Stacy's Mustang. In both cases, the jurors recommended a penalty of death in the electric chair.

On Friday, February 5, 1993, Circuit Judge Richard Watson sentenced Michael Abshire and John Marquard to death. Both men are currently awaiting execution of their sentences.

"HANGING IN A CLOSET!"

by Charles W. Sasser

Keystone Lake lies large-fingered among wooded green hills some 20 miles west of Tulsa, Oklahoma. Storms sweep across that portion of "Tornado Alley" during the spring and summer, damaging many of the lovely lake homes and cottages that ring the lake. On the north side of the lake, in the tiny resort community of Westport, a split-level waterfront house abandoned because of storm damage concealed a dreadful secret during the waning days of August 1991.

In Tulsa on the evening of August 28, 1991, a man who identified himself as the husband of a housewife named Laura Launhardt telephoned police to report her missing. The man said he last saw his wife that morning as he prepared for a business trip to the Oklahoma capital, about two hours southwest of Tulsa. He was supposed to return to Tulsa in the afternoon to accompany Laura on an appointment with her psychologist.

Laura, as he later explained it, had been "real stressed out . . . [her father's death] was hard on her. She began taking stress-related medication around the time her father died."

The husband discovered that his business in Oklahoma

City took longer than expected. At around 2:30 P.M., he telephoned home to explain to Laura that he could not return in time for her appointment. No one answered his call. He left a message on the answering machine.

When he arrived in Tulsa later that afternoon, he found his wife still not home. She had not picked up her son from school. A neighbor had driven the 10-year-old boy home. Incoming messages remained on the answering machine. There was no note, no missing clothing, nothing to indicate where Laura might be.

"There was no way in hell she was just going to blow it off and not pick [her son up after school]," Laura's husband insisted. "I realize she's been under stress, but this is highly unlike her. Something must have happened."

He signed a missing-person report on 34-year-old Laura Launhardt, described as an attractive white female brunette of medium height and build who was last seen wearing a multicolored blouse and matching skirt of a flower motif. Also missing was her two-tone tan-and-brown 1986 Chevrolet Astro minivan.

After receiving reports like this, police commonly broadcast a routine APB (all points bulletin) and maintain communications with the missing person's relatives. Most missing persons are not really missing; they merely either leave home after a spat or disagreement or neglect to let someone know where they are going. They almost always show up again after a short while.

However, suspected foul play in the Launhardt case prompted police to go a step or two farther and launch a major crime investigation.

Police have several ways of tracing people. One of the most common in an era of plastic and paper money is to pick up on a person's use of credit cards and checks. This method is relatively slow at first, as it takes a few days for the paper trail to lay itself out.

From Wednesday, August 28th, until Saturday, August 31st, nothing surfaced to illuminate Laura Launhardt's mysterious disappearance. She seemed to have vanished into the thick air of that Oklahoma August. Her husband hounded his banks and credit card companies trying to pick up a clue to aid police.

On Saturday, August 31st, veteran Tulsa Homicide Detective Gary Meek was catching up on some paperwork when he received a telephone call from Muskogee, a town about 50 miles southeast of Tulsa. Muskogee Police Detective Kelly Veach informed Meek that two white males had just entered a Git 'N Go convenience store in his town and attempted to obtain cash by using a bank's automatic teller machine (ATM) card bearing Laura Launhardt's name.

"There was apparently a female with the subjects," Veach went on. "Could she be your missing person?"

Detective Meek didn't know.

Within the hour, however, Meek and Homicide Sergeant Wayne Allen were en route to Muskogee. They questioned the clerk at the Git 'N Go on 32nd Street, who informed them that the two males entered the store around 3:40 P.M. that Saturday afternoon. It was now almost 5:30 P.M. The customers had purchased food and attempted to use the ATM card at the store's teller machine.

"The card belongs to my wife," the elder of the two males asserted. "We're staying next door at the motel. Can I sign for her?"

"The owner of the card has to sign," the clerk responded.

"All right. We'll run next door to the motel and get her signature."

The customers never returned.

The clerk described the males as a rawboned, hollow-cheeked man in his mid-20s with longish brown hair, and "a kid" of about 16 or 17 with light brown hair and a pouty baby face.

"Better than that," the clerk added, "the store's security camera has them on film."

Detective Meek requested a copy of the film. Sleuths then crossed over to the Catalina Motel on the opposite street corner. The Catalina had a double row of rooms back-to-back with doors opening in opposite directions. Under questioning, the motel clerk recalled two young men checking into the motel around 7:00 P.M. on Wednesday, August 28th. That happened to be the same day Laura Launhardt turned up missing.

"They drove a brown van," the clerk continued. "It seems they might have had a woman with them, but she didn't stay here at the motel."

Meek said he assumed the name used on the motel check-in register was false, but he ran it through police Records-and-Wanteds anyway. Sure enough, Records had nothing on it, not even so much as a traffic ticket.

The two males left the motel almost immediately after returning from the Git 'N Go. However, they were paid up through the night. A maid said that they left personal property in their room, including packages of new clothing from the local Dillard's department store.

Expecting the occupants to return, Meek and Sergeant Allen set up surveillance on the motel. After several hours, however, other duties called them back to Tulsa. Muskogee police took over the watch.

The suspects did not return to their motel room.

Sunday, September 1st, was looking like a busy day for Tulsa investigators. After the first clue in a case falls into place, others seem to follow like dominos in a line.

Police learned that there had been considerable activity on Laura Launhardt's ATM card since her disappearance, starting with a $500 withdrawal from an ATM at a grocery store in Sand Springs, a Tulsa suburb, on the afternoon of August 28th. That was followed the next day by an ATM withdrawal of $230 in Muskogee.

A man and a teenage boy had also used the missing woman's Dillard's credit card on a shopping spree in Muskogee on August 29th. Dillard's employees recalled that two white males—an older rawboned man and "a kid"—purchased clothing, including a man's expensive leather coat, at the department store.

"They were really very quiet," a salesman said. "I tried to start a conversation with them, but they really didn't respond. The older guy did all the talking. The kid stood in the background."

The quiet customers had also bought a $52 bottle of Red by Georgio perfume. That purchase once again thrust important questions into the probe.

Who was this female for whom the perfume was intended? Could she be Laura Launhardt? Had Laura run away from home with these men? If not, where was she now?

Muskogee Detective Kelly Veach, who was keeping tabs on the Catalina Motel and the suspects' room, called Detective Meek near noon on Sunday with important news. One of the room's occupants—the desk clerk said it sounded like the boy—had telephoned, saying, "We didn't use the room last night after all. But I'll come out at about five this afternoon to pick up our stuff."

Meek would be waiting for him.

Meek, Sergeant Allen, and Detective Roy Heim sped to Muskogee. There, using the probable cause of Laura's Dillard's card having been fraudulently used, coupled with the presence of Dillard's purchases inside the Catalina Motel room, the probers obtained a search warrant. The search of the room reportedly uncovered credit card receipts bearing Laura's name and her signature, obviously forged.

By this time, police believed that whoever the female

was with the mystery man and boy, they didn't think it was Laura Launhardt.

Laura Launhardt, they said, was . . . well, things weren't looking up for her well-being.

Prompt, if nothing else, described the boy who cruised into the motel parking lot at almost exactly 5:00 P.M. in a beat-up sedan accompanied by two other teenagers. Detective Meek recognized the youth who got out of the vehicle as the one who was filmed on the security camera at the Git 'N Go trying to use Laura's ATM card. The teenager jumped back in surprise as authorities quickly surrounded him.

"We need some answers," Meek snapped.

The boy identified himself as Daniel Paul Waller Jr., 16. Records indicated the high school dropout had been in and out of trouble for much of his teenage years. Most recently, in May, he had been charged with auto theft and released to his family's custody. He ran away from home. On July 29th, police arrested him on additional charges, including breaking and entering. He plea-bargained to being delinquent and was again released to his family. That was less than a week before Laura Launhardt disappeared.

The law has strict requirements on police interrogations of juvenile suspects. However, juveniles may be questioned as witnesses against other suspects—and police are not required to gag a juvenile to keep him from talking.

Waller, Detective Meek said, "couldn't keep quiet."

"Where's your friend?" detectives asked the boy.

"He and his girlfriend left for Louisiana yesterday," came the recorded reply.

"What's his name?"

"Lonnie Richie, I guess. I only met him last Wednesday."

The two, Waller said, met by chance at an east Tulsa recreation hall—"a hangout for kids on the way to trouble," said Tulsa County Assistant District Attorney Tom Gillert.

"Thieves and no-goods have some kind of radar which attracts them to each other," commented one police officer.

Only hours after Waller and Richie became acquainted, they were on their way to trouble. A.D.A. Gillert asserted that the pair went to the Kmart department store on East 21st Street, intent on selecting a victim to rob. Waller said they were just "hanging out."

Shortly after noon, a young woman left Kmart and, according to Waller, voluntarily offered him a ride home. Richie suddenly whipped out a gun, Waller said, and pointed it at both the woman and Waller.

"You're both going with me!" he barked.

"He kidnapped you, too?" Detective Meek asked to clarify.

"Yes," Waller replied.

The youth's statement then described how Richie forced the woman, now identified as Laura Launhardt, to drive west out of Tulsa to the Lake Keystone region. They drove around Pawnee County for some time, looking for Richie's relative. Finally giving up on that, Richie selected a road off SH-51 that led into the lakeside settlement of Westport. A narrow gravel road wound through thick scrub timber to an isolated house at the end of a cul-de-sac overlooking Keystone. The house had been abandoned because of storm damage.

Richie forced his victim and Waller to enter the vacant house, where he bound Launhardt hand and foot and took her purse. The man and the boy then left together in the commandeered minivan.

"Did he kill her?" Meek asked.

Waller evaded the direct question. Meek reworded it: "Was she still breathing when you last saw her?"

"She was trying to," Waller responded.

That was nearly five days ago. It was unlikely that the bound woman could have survived that long without food and water. Nevertheless, Detectives Meek and Heim set out immediately on the 90-mile journey to Lake Keystone on a rescue attempt. They had to try. They took Waller with them to show them the way.

Police records revealed that Lonnie Wright Richie, 24, had, like his younger companion, been crime-prone for most of his life. In 1988, Los Angeles County, California, sentenced him to serve four years in Avenal State Prison for burglary and forgery. He was paroled in July 1990.

In May 1991, police in Claremore, Oklahoma, a Tulsa suburb, nabbed Richie for the burglary of a fast-food restaurant. Arrested and convicted under a different name, Richie served three months in the Rogers County Jail before being released again on July 15th, this time on probation.

In a strange twist of irony, Richie's cellmate in Rogers County was Gary Alan Walker, a "mad-dog killer" convicted for abducting Tulsa newswoman Valerie Shaw-Hartzell from another shopping center parking lot and slaying her. Walker demanded that Richie be removed from his cell.

"He's crazy," Walker complained. "I don't want him in with me."

Could Richie nonetheless have picked up some tips from Walker on abducting women from parking lots?

On August 28th, the day of Laura Launhardt's disappearance, Lonnie Richie would have been on parole from California and on probation in Oklahoma. It also turned out that he was suspected of a July 18th extortion attempt and was a prime suspect in the robbery of the SW Airport Hotel in Tulsa.

"We just cannot seem to keep our known criminals behind bars," groused a disgruntled police detective. "They keep getting 'rehabilitated.' "

While Detectives Meek and Heim sped through the darkness of Sunday night toward Keystone Lake, Tulsa Sergeant Wayne Allen and Muskogee Detective Kelly Veach coordinated other ends of the investigation and led the manhunt for Lonnie Richie. Waller had provided them with valuable information about the kidnapping— and, now, perhaps murder—suspect.

Later testimony would disclose that Richie had met a girl in California named Maudie Dean. Maudie migrated with Richie to Oklahoma, where she lived with him at various places, including the Lake Keystone area, until the ex-convict's apprehension in Claremore. While Richie languished in jail for three months, Maudie played house with another man, John Cotter of Muskogee.

After his release, Richie pursued Maudie afresh. That explained the $52 bottle of perfume. It was Maudie Dean who had accompanied Richie when he fled Oklahoma. Police said John Cotter was angry over the loss of his girlfriend and eagerly cooperated with the investigation.

"Richie arrived in Muskogee around sundown on Wednesday," Cotter told authorities. "Some kid was with him. Richie said he paid seventeen hundred dollars for the minivan he was driving. He tried to sell it to me."

Detectives entered descriptions of Lonnie Richie and Maudie Dean, along with Laura Launhardt's van, into the NCIC (National Crime Information Center) computer and broadcast hot sheets on the missing woman's credit and ATM cards. The nationwide dragnet for the fleeing fugitive had been cast wide by the time detectives escorting Daniel Waller reached the storm-damaged abandoned house on Lake Keystone. It was 11:00 P.M. of a near-moonless night.

Also by this time, Waller had added considerable embellishment to his first story. No, the teenager amended, he had not been exactly kidnapped. Richie and he together selected Laura Launhardt as their victim. They kidnapped her at gunpoint in front of Kmart and drove around aimlessly for a while in Pawnee County, trying to figure out what to do with her, before Richie remembered the abandoned house. It lay not far from where he and Maudie Dean lived when they first arrived from California.

Richie and Waller took Launhardt's purse containing credit cards and cash and left her tied up while they drove to a local convenience store to buy a Dr. Pepper and some cigarettes.

"She can identify us to the cops," Richie mused. "I should have killed her."

The robbers returned to the house. According to Waller, Richie warned the youth to stay back so he wouldn't have to watch the ex-convict "take care" of their hapless victim. Waller said he heard a commotion. He stepped forward and saw the victim tied by her neck to a clothing rod inside a closet. Richie was lifting her feet off the floor so that she would strangle to death.

"You could not have imagined worse than this," Chief Prosecutor Tom Gillert would remark later. "You can't make sense out of taking a woman and hanging her."

Now, on that lonely dark road near the lake, 16-year-old Daniel Waller huddled subdued in the unmarked police car with Detective Meek while Detective Heim entered the house to take a look. He returned a moment later. The house had revealed its dreadful secret.

"She's in there," Heim said.

Laura Launhardt's badly decomposing body hung by the neck from a clothing rod inside a small closet off the bathroom. Her bound feet trailed on the floor, knees bent. It could have taken as much as five minutes for the black webbing strap around her neck to cut off all air to her lungs and stop her heart from beating.

Crime scene experts spent the rest of the night scouring the house for trace and physical evidence. By daylight, they reported finding little physical evidence to link suspects to the scene. About the only thing they learned was that the victim had apparently not been raped. Sacks from Kmart containing tea candles and medications lay nearby. Kmart sales slips indicated the purchases had been made on August 28 at 12:30 P.M.

Apparently, Laura Launhardt had walked from Kmart where she encountered, in broad daylight in a busy city parking lot, two thugs ready to murder her for whatever cash her purse might contain.

"I want this guy in prison," exclaimed a grim-faced Sergeant Allen.

Lonnie Richie had a two-day headstart. With Daniel Waller behind bars and the national manhunt for Richie launched, Detective Meek utilized the next few days in sweeping Tulsa, Pawnee, and Muskogee Counties for additional witnesses to corroborate Waller's statements. Richie had managed to thwart justice at least twice during the past two years. This time, authorities vowed, the ex-convict would end up on death row where such heartless fiends belonged.

"Some crimes are so enormous," said A.D.A. Gillert, "that the symmetry of justice is not right unless the ultimate punishment is imposed."

Meek soon added other witnesses to a list that included John Cotter of Muskogee, the Catalina Motel desk clerk, the Git 'N Go attendants and their security tape, and Dillard's department store salespeople who together already contributed a vast amount of evidence against ex-convict Lonnie Richie.

After Richie's photograph appeared on the news as part of the manhunt effort, a Kmart shopper recalled having seen two males she identified as Richie and Waller hanging out at the store's parking lot on that fateful day. She said the two approached her as her daughter played on a little carousel.

"It sure would be nice to be able to be that happy again," Richie had commented to the woman.

"I remembered him because of that," the shopper told police. "It was unusual under the circumstances. Ordinarily, strangers don't say that."

A Pawnee County man named Mel Climber also provided valuable information. He subsequently testified that at about 3:00 P.M. or so on the afternoon of Laura's abduction, he saw the two suspected killers and their victim on a secluded and heavily timbered oil lease less than two miles from where police recovered the woman's body. He said a pair resembling Richie and Waller stood near a brown van while a woman attended to bodily functions in a nearby weed patch. As Climber approached, the man police identified as Richie reached into the van and "stuck something in his back pants."

"This is rugged country," Climber assured police. "Most generally I'm the only one that goes up there."

"We came up here to relieve ourselves," the older man explained.

Climber said the woman lowered her voice "and said something I didn't hear. She repeated it. I still didn't hear. Then she said, 'Well, nothing,' and turned and walked off."

"She probably saved the guy's life by not making a ruckus," a police officer surmised. "It was a very brave and caring thing she did."

On Wednesday, September 4th, Tulsa County's Chief Prosecutor Gillert charged the fugitive Lonnie Richie and his former teenage sidekick Daniel Waller with the crime of first-degree murder, kidnapping, and robbery with a firearm. An Oklahoma racketeering law permitted any county in which a series of crimes occurred to take jurisdiction. Gillert contended that since the crime spree had started in Tulsa, the trials should be held in Tulsa.

As the week slowly passed, authorities tracked Lonnie

Richie and Maudie Dean through Oklahoma, Arkansas, and Louisiana. Still driving Launhardt's Astro minivan and using her credit cards, the couple left a paper trail "a blind man could have followed."

They used Laura's Texaco credit card in all three states. On Monday, September 2nd, a man subsequently identified as Richie attempted to use the victim's credit card to pay for meals at a restaurant in Baton Rouge, Louisiana. Since the card bore a woman's name—first name Laura, last name beginning with L—the waitress jokingly asked if the card was stolen.

Richie apparently became flustered. He stammered that he had the wrong card and would go out to the car and get the right one from his wife.

He hurried outside, jumped into a brown van, and sped away without paying. Restaurant employees obtained the Oklahoma license plate number and notified Baton Rouge police. The number proved to be a "hit." Oklahoma authorities wanted the van and occupants in connection with a murder.

New Orleans police were notified.

"It looks like he's still heading south," Detective Meek guessed. Meek bided his time.

Three days after the recovery of the kidnapped woman's body, four days after Richie began his flight, authorities received their first solid lead on the fugitive's whereabouts. According to accounts of that period's events, the fickle Maudie Dean proved to be her lover's downfall.

On Wednesday night, September 4th, she reportedly telephoned her ex-lover John Cotter in Muskogee and confided to him that she was tired of Richie. She asked if Cotter would send her a bus ticket to New Orleans to come home to Muskogee. Cotter agreed—and then he telephoned Detective Meek with the news.

The elated sleuth quickly coordinated with New Orleans investigators to have plainclothesmen staked out at the bus station when Dean arrived to claim her ticket. Perhaps Richie would be with her. Then Meek settled back to wait.

Sure enough, at approximately 4:35 A.M. on Thursday, detectives led by Sergeant Bob Young of the New Orleans Police Department observed a scraggly young man and an equally scraggly young woman cautiously enter the bus station. The station was almost empty at that hour. The couple approached the ticket counter. The woman identified herself as Maudie Dean.

That was the cue. Pistols appeared in the fists of grim policemen who had been warned that Lonnie Richie should be considered armed and extremely dangerous. Surrounded, the fugitive paled visibly and surrendered.

"The arrest was without incident," announced Sergeant Young.

Parked outside at the curb sat Laura Launhardt's van. Inside it were Laura's credit cards and a receipt where Richie under his own name had pawned a .380 semiautomatic pistol, presumably the one used in Laura's abduction.

"I didn't do it," Lonnie Richie asserted as he was taken into custody for the murder. "I bought the van from Daniel Waller."

That was reportedly the only comment the ex-convict made about the brutal slaying. He then asked for an attorney.

"There are murders to gain an inheritance, to remove a witness, to eliminate an enemy, or just to get a fistful of dollars," concluded a *Tulsa World* editorial. "But the taking of a terrified mother, a total stranger, and her long ride to a horrible death is no ordinary murder. This is why the death penalty stays on the books."

Murder charges against defendants Richie and Waller bounced around in state and appellate courts for over two years. Although his murder trial was delayed, Richie went to trial in 1992 for robbing the SW Airport Hotel in Tulsa, six days before he kidnapped and murdered Laura Launhardt. Found guilty on November 4, 1992, he was sentenced to 29 years in the state penitentiary.

On September 27, 1993, a Tulsa jury finally found the ex-convict guilty of first-degree murder, armed robbery, and kidnapping and sentenced him to the death penalty, plus additional prison time totaling 209 years.

"The guy deserves to die," exclaimed Laura's widower. "There is no doubt in my mind. He showed no feeling whatsoever."

On October 16, 1993, after having testified against his cohort in crime, Waller, now 18, pleaded guilty to the same sequence of crimes. In arguing for a stiff sentence, A.D.A. Gillert contended there was a "good possibility" it took two people to "hoist [Laura's] body" against the clothing rod in the closet to complete her strangulation.

Waller received a sentence of life in prison plus 15 years.

Daniel Paul Waller Jr. is presently incarcerated in the Oklahoma State Penitentiary. Lonnie Richie waits out endless appeals on death row to determine his ultimate fate. Police point out that Laura Launhardt, like most victims of murder, had no such appeals process at the time Richie callously hanged her on Lake Keystone over three years earlier.

"TRIO BLAZED A 3-STATE TRAIL OF BLOOD!"

by Charles W. Sasser

It made no sense, police said. Father and son—both ex-convicts—gunned down in their ramshackle hull of a house near Montrose, Missouri.

The dead men wouldn't have won any good-housekeeping awards, detectives observed as they swarmed to the crime scene on that cold winter's Monday of January 8, 1990. The house resembled the centerpiece of some huge junkyard.

"Both victims had police rap sheets," said Thomas Van Zandt, sheriff of Lafayette County, Missouri, and spokesman for the Missouri Rural Crime Squad. The squad was composed of crack lawmen from throughout the state who banded together into a task force to investigate particularly difficult or heinous crimes. The Montrose murders fell under both categories.

A relative of the victims had discovered the grisly setting. She told officers led by Henry County Sheriff Jerome Wareham, as well as Highway Patrol Investigators Harvey Oberweather and Larry Plunkett, that she and her boyfriend drove from Independence, Missouri, to borrow a trailer from the deceased. There was no snow, but the lowering clouds bespoke an imminent storm. The couple arrived at the rural Montrose residence around 3:00 in the afternoon.

"We knocked and nobody came to the door," she told the officer. "The door wasn't locked, so we looked inside. We first saw the body on the floor in the kitchen. We looked up, and there another one was, lying on the floor in the middle of the living room."

Detectives arrived, sealed off the isolated murder scene, and launched into the first phase of the homicide probe by identifying the dead men.

The corpse in the kitchen, they learned, belonged to Roy E. Donahue, 40, son of Frankie T. Merrifield, 59, who lay dead a few feet away in the living room. Police said both men had been arrested for crimes such as writing bad checks, weapons violations, and assault. Donahue had served hard time in the state penitentiary starting in 1985 for killing another man, a murder charge subsequently reduced to manslaughter.

"Frankie and Roy have had a checkered past with the law," a friend of the pair later commented. "But they're not that way anymore. They've been living quietly out here, not associating with shady people or anything. Frankie and Roy were going straight."

Nonetheless, detectives had no option but to take into consideration the victims' records as they searched for evidence. The two ex-cons lying dead from bullet wounds mutely raised the question, whom might they have crossed enough to want them dead? Were the killers friends or relatives of the man Donahue was convicted of killing in 1985?

The nearest neighbors were far enough away that they probably wouldn't have heard gunshots. Frustrated, police despaired of finding witnesses within the immediate area. At least initially, they had to depend upon trace and latent evidence from the crime scene.

"And it was scarce," said Sheriff Van Zandt, *"real scarce."*

Crime scene sketches showed Roy Donahue's body lying fully clothed face up in the kitchen with a single bullet wound to his chest. Reports indicated that the bullet that ended his life was a .38-caliber. There was little blood. His leather wallet lay next to him; there was no money in it. Near one outstretched hand lay a partly smoked cigarette.

The older man, Frankie Merrifield, lay sprawled on the carpet in the living room. He rested on his right side, one hand reaching toward his dead son in the kitchen. He was also fully clothed, with bloodstains on his shirt from a single small-caliber bullet hole in the sternum. Next to him, police found a cigarette lighter and another emptied-out wallet.

In the kitchen doorway between the two corpses, a detective pointed to a single spent .22-caliber cartridge casing lying on the floor. Such evidence indicated that the men had died from two separate weapons. Did that also mean at least two assailants? police wondered.

At the beginning of any homicide investigation, and sometimes for a long time afterward, there were more questions than answers.

Lights left burning in the kitchen, plus the condition of lividity and rigor mortis in the corpses, provided an approximate time of death. "It seems they died after dark, probably sometime early last night," a detective mused.

That meant the shooting occurred Sunday evening, January 7th, less than 24 hours before the discovery of the bodies.

Detectives also wondered aloud if the victims might not have known their killers. For one thing, there were no signs of forced entry to the residence, probably meaning the gunmen had been voluntarily admitted. For another,

Donahue died smoking a cigarette, as though he were at ease with whomever he'd let into his house.

It wasn't much to go on. Faced with the prospect of no witnesses, no suspects, and little evidence, Sheriff Jerome Wareham requested the assistance of a task force from the Missouri Rural Crime Squad.

"Empty billfolds next to the bodies meant the motive was probably, but not necessarily, robbery," said Sheriff Van Zandt. "We had a feeling that more than robbery was involved. We began questioning dozens of people who knew the victims. We couldn't find anyone who might want revenge or who had something to gain from the deaths."

The house had not been ransacked. The only things obviously missing were a .22-caliber pistol and a .38-caliber revolver.

"Frankie and Roy had the guns the last time I was here," said the relative who discovered the slayings. "They're gone now."

From this fact, another question arose: Had the victims been greased with their own weapons?

"For all we know right now," admitted one frustrated lawman, "these two guys could have been wasted by green Martians driving a pink flying saucer."

Crimes never occur in a vacuum. The veteran sleuths working the case understood in theory that one crime can be tied to others by a single thread. The only problem lay in finding and recognizing that thread and following it to its source.

For example, on Sunday afternoon, January 7th, police in nearby Kansas City investigated the theft of a white 1985 Ford utility van stolen from the City Wide Chemical Company. It was one of a score of vehicles reported stolen within the same time period.

And on Sunday night, January 7th, apparently a few hours after the Montrose double slaying, a woman in

Sand Springs, Oklahoma, a Tulsa suburb, told police that she was leaving an all-night restaurant when a man jumped out of a dirty white van and charged toward her across the parking lot. She ran back inside the restaurant. The man, she said, was tall, with gray hair and a full gray beard. There were "two or three other people" in the van with him.

And on Monday afternoon, January 8th, only about three hours after the discovery of the Montrose murders, Deputy Jack Branson of the Noble County Sheriff's Department in central Oklahoma received a trouble call to check out an abandoned vehicle. The location was just north of the junction of U.S. 77 and State 156, what was known locally as the Marland Y. The deputy turned left along a skinny dirt road flanked by cornfields on either side. He was about 90 miles from Sand Springs, Oklahoma, and about 300 miles from where Sheriff Thomas Van Zandt and the Missouri Rural Crime Squad were puzzling over the Merrifield-Donahue slayings.

The abandoned vehicle, a white 1985 Ford utility van, sat partially blocking the country road.

"It wasn't there at five-thirty P.M.," said a farmer at the end of the road. "But when I started out of here about six, there it was."

"Did you see the people who left it?" Deputy Branson asked.

The farmer hadn't.

A check of the vehicle's license plate through the FBI's National Crime Information Center (NCIC) revealed that the van was reported stolen in Kansas City on Sunday. No suspects were listed. The van simply disappeared from where it had been left parked.

"Odd," said Deputy Branson. "The van wasn't stripped or anything. The thief had to have had another car and someone else to pick him up. Or they stole another car.

Something's going to come up missing from around here."

Noble County authorities dusted the stolen van for fingerprints, but it seemed to have been wiped clean. The officials marked the case "Pending."

Apparently, the thread had not yet been broken.

On Tuesday, January 9th, just before noon, Oklahoma's Kay County Sheriff Glenn Guinn received a phone call from Sheriff Billy Bowen of Hemphill County in the northern Texas panhandle.

"We've stopped a yellow 1975 Chevrolet pickup here in Canadian, Texas," Sheriff Bowen reportedly relayed to his Oklahoma counterpart. "Something's hinky about it. Could you check it for us? The tag is registered to a Richard Denney, Route One, Tonkawa, Oklahoma, in Kay County."

A routine trace through the post office led Sheriff Guinn and D.A.'s Investigator Raymond Hamm to a modest little farmhouse about a mile and a quarter north of the Marland Y. It was about 1:00 P.M. on a sunny winter's afternoon. A wide unfenced lawn wrapped around the front of the house to the back, where fences contained milk goats and guinea fowl.

No one answered the knock at the front door. The officers tried the back door. It was unlocked, but again no one answered their knocking. The officers ventured into the house, calling out, "Mr. Denney? Mrs. Denney? Is anyone home?"

The lawmen froze in midstride. A macabre scene met their eyes.

Someone's frail little grandmother sat slumped in a chair at the kitchen table, her head lolled back, eyes staring frozen open in horror. Lying facedown on the floor near her was a short, husky old man dressed in work clothing. A pool of drying blood surrounded him.

Quickly checking for signs of life, the officers discovered that both elderly people were dead of gunshot wounds. The woman had a large-caliber wound in the chest. Because she was sitting, she had bled little. The old man had two similar bullet holes in him—one in the upper chest, the other lower down. His blood had drained out onto the floor.

After securing the scene, Sheriff Guinn notified Noble County Sheriff Jerry Cook. The white farmhouse was just inside the Noble County line. Cook assumed jurisdiction over the investigation.

A tall athletic man of 46, Sheriff Cook had devoted more than 20 years of his life to law enforcement, starting as a trooper with the Oklahoma Highway Patrol. After a six-year tour as undersheriff in Noble County, he became sheriff in 1988. Experienced, articulate, and aggressive, the sheriff quickly organized a major crime probe. The team started with identifying the bodies and processing the crime scene for evidence.

The victims were readily identified as Richard Denney, 61, and his wife Virginia, 60. Relatives notified of the tragedy promptly discovered that a yellow 1975 Chevrolet pickup owned by the retired welder and his wife were missing, along with the dead woman's purse and a few other items.

"Whoever [the killers] were got about sixty-one dollars, a pocketknife, cigarettes, a cigarette lighter, and the pickup truck," said Noble County D.A. Joe Wideman.

"It looks like someone came up to the house and was admitted," added Sheriff Cook. "Whoever it was robbed the old people, gunned them down execution-style at close range, then fled in the pickup. They must have been in a hurry. The house was not ransacked. They took whatever was in sight and ran."

State medical examiners later determined that the Denneys were shot at extremely close range by a .38-caliber weapon. They estimated the time of death at between 4:00 and 6:00 P.M. on Monday, January 8th.

Deputy Jack Branson had recovered the stolen utility van at 6:00 P.M. on Monday about a mile south of the Denney residence. At that time the Denneys may have been dead only minutes.

"We immediately assumed a connection between the stolen van and the murders," said Sheriff Cook.

Rural neighbors expressed shock and outrage over the senseless slaughter. That night they left lights burning and made sure their doors were locked.

"The Denneys wouldn't hurt anybody," exclaimed a relative. "They lived off the land. They were poor people who didn't ask anyone for anything."

According to news accounts, both Denneys were battling cancer. Richard, a U.S. Army veteran who fought in both World War II and Korea, was undergoing treatment for skin cancer at the Veterans Hospital in Oklahoma City. Virginia Denney was recovering from a more serious form of cancer. The couple rented the farm by the month. They raised guinea fowl to sell and the goats for milk because Virginia's high blood pressure wouldn't allow her to drink other milk.

"As far as being happy, they've had a lot of problems over the years," recalled a neighbor. "They were just barely making it. They were just hanging on. They were quiet and hardworking. Most people in town didn't know about them or their illnesses until this happened."

Sheriff Cook's sleuths found that the bullet that killed Virginia Denney had pierced her thin body and continued out through a kitchen window behind her. Sighting through the bullet hole in the window, Cook estimated the bullet's trajectory. Miraculously, his deputies searching a short-grass pasture behind the house found the .38-caliber death bullet, stained with blood, lying in the grass. It was to prove a valuable piece of evidence.

The recovery of the stolen vehicle so near the Oklahoma slaying site soon revealed a possible thread linking it to the double slaying in Montrose, Missouri. Detectives in the two states checked off points of similarity between their cases:

✔The van was stolen in Kansas City on Sunday, January 7th, less than 100 miles from Montrose.

✔Merrifield and Donahue were gunned down Sunday night, January 7th; one of the weapons used was a .38-caliber.

✔The Denneys were slain on Monday night, January 8th, with a .38-caliber handgun.

✔Police found the stolen Missouri van about a mile from the crime scene in Oklahoma.

✔The victims in both states lived in isolated rural areas.

✔All victims were shot in the chest at extremely close range, execution-style.

✔Neither house had been ransacked; the suspect or suspects took whatever was immediately available and fled with it.

✔The common thread seemed to lead to Canadian, Texas, another 250 miles west of the Denney slaying site, where police had apparently recovered the Denneys' stolen yellow pickup.

Detectives in both Oklahoma and Missouri announced they were heading for Texas as fast as they could get there to confer with Hemphill County Sheriff Bill Bowen. By Tuesday night, January 9th, more than a dozen out-of-state lawmen converged on the Hemphill County Sheriff's Office in Canadian, Texas, where they learned details of the yellow pickup recovery.

The Missouri and Oklahoma cops were told that Tuesday morning, January 9th, had dawned cold and icy in the Texas panhandle. In the small town of Canadian, the attention of Mrs. Rosie Green, a member of the Neighborhood Crime Watch, was drawn to a yellow pickup that cruised slowly once, then twice, then a third time around her block. She telephone the sheriff's department to report the suspicious vehicle.

Deputy Douglas Tennate responded to the call. Minutes later, he spotted the slow-moving pickup occupied by what appeared to be two men and a woman. The driver seemed tall with gray hair and a gray beard; the passengers were a much younger couple. Tennate radioed in his contact, then switched on his flashing lights. He was just outside Canadian city limits.

Sheriff Bowen overheard the radio traffic. Operating on good instinct, he jumped into his own car and raced to provide backup for his young deputy. Later, lawmen would comment that an officer alone stopping the trio might have found himself in deadly serious trouble. As it happened, however, Bowen arrived almost immediately.

Suspicious that the people in the pickup might be burglars, the two officers worked together to extract the strangers one at a time from the truck. In short order, two men and a woman found themselves lined up outside on the ice with their palms planted flat on the hood of the pickup. They were, police said, as scroungy and mangy a trio as ever traveled through Texas.

Although none of the three could produce a driver's license, the sheriff found enough documents on each to identify them. The driver, 6 feet tall and running to a paunch, was Robert Wesley Knighton, 48. His pallor beneath the gray beard could have been that of a mortician or an ex-convict too long isolated from the sun.

The second man, short and slender with longish dark hair and soft, almost girlish features, was Lawrence Lingle Brittain, 17.

The woman, Ruth Renee Williams, was short, with reddish hair and a face that looked hard and dull. She said she was Knighton's girlfriend.

A cursory inventory search of the yellow pickup produced two handguns, one a .22-caliber pistol, the other a .38-caliber revolver. Powder residue in the barrels and around the muzzles indicated that both had been fired recently.

The guns told the Texas officers that they had stumbled upon something far darker than mere prowlers casing for an easy burglary. A computer check disclosed that the strangers were all ex-convicts from Missouri. In addition, the men were wanted by Missouri police for escaping from a nonsecurity prerelease center.

At the time of his escape, records revealed, Knighton was serving a 40-year sentence for a 1974 manslaughter-kidnapping conviction. "The details I've got are sketchy," said Cranston Mitchell, chairman of the Missouri Board of Probation and Parole, "but there was a shooting of some guy he knew, which led to the kidnapping of a family of three."

Although Knighton received conditional parole on November 15, 1989, he was supposed to remain at a Kansas City prerelease center until January 15th. Instead, he and another prerelease inmate, Lawrence Brittain, slipped away from the house on Sunday, January 7th. That was the same day the white utility van turned up stolen.

Brittain was serving time at the center for auto theft.

Reports further disclosed that Ruth Williams was a self-admitted former prostitute and drug addict who met Knighton and Brittain at the prerelease center where she was undergoing drug treatment.

Allegedly, the three took off together after authorities proposed to transfer Brittain to another facility in another city.

"We didn't want to be separated," the woman allegedly explained.

Sheriff Bowen recalled that Brittain's eyes darted nervously and Williams fidgeted as police escorted them to jail. Once behind bars, Knighton reportedly made several comments to Texas Ranger Gary Henderson that increased police suspicions about the trio's activities since they left Kansas City three days before.

"Yeah, I stole the pickup from an old man and woman in Oklahoma," he muttered. Then he said, "I know they're going to kill me over this deal. I just don't want the kids to take the heat for it. I told them in Missouri they should never have let me out. I can't make it on the outside."

Knighton allegedly fell morosely silent after that, speaking to police only to request an attorney.

In the meantime, police laboratories in three states worked overtime in ballistics comparing the death bullets in four homicides to the firearms recovered by Sheriff Bowen and Deputy Tennate in Texas. Detectives in Missouri identified the recovered guns as having belonged to the dead men in Montrose. More important, experts reported that the bullet that passed through Virginia Denney and fell in the pasture outside had been fired by the .38-caliber revolver that was in the possession of Knighton, Brittain, and Williams when they were arrested.

The trio were no longer considered mere prowlers. Possession of the weapons and possession of a dead couple's pickup truck elevated the travelers to the status of prime murder suspects. Police focused on them in an attempt to unravel a bloody thread that had apparently started in Kansas City and hopefully ended in Canadian, Texas.

"I hope [Knighton] tells them he shot those people," Williams said to Brittain in the presence of Noble County Police Officer Tom Duroy. "Bob won't let us hang. He'll take care of us."

As surely as spring followed winter, cops knew there

was no such thing as honor among criminals. The trio readily snitched on each other if they thought they saw a personal advantage in it. It was obvious to all detectives, said Sheriff Jerry Cook, that the weak links in the little group of suspected killers were Brittain and Williams.

Police went to work on the two, grilling them about their three-day odyssey that left four dead people in its wake. The woman, Ruth Williams, broke first. She began by saying that she thought she was emotionally disturbed because she was unable to feel sorrow and cry over the tragic events she was party to. She then callously laid out a bizarre story of cold-blooded murder that covered more than 300 miles and 72 hours.

According to subsequent testimony, Williams related how she and the two escapees fled Kansas City in the stolen van. In Springfield, Missouri, they ran low on money and needed a vehicle to replace the stolen van. They headed north to the house of Frankie Merrifield and Roy Donahue, whom Brittain knew and with whom the fugitives had visited briefly on Sunday after leaving Kansas City. They were going to rob the men.

Knighton smiled, Williams said, as he gunned down the two men with their own guns.

"I was kind of laughing because I was scared," Williams noted, adding that they robbed the dead men of a small amount of cash, some beer, and the two firearms. She and Knighton then had sex in the van because they were so exhilarated by the action.

"After the shootings," Williams continued, "[Brittain] said he wanted to be like Bob, that he looked up to him. Bob kept referring to [Brittain] as 'the pup.' He said you don't become a dog unless you kill someone."

The trio then headed west to Oklahoma.

Through some chance, several Oklahomans likely escaped a fate similar to that of the Missouri men.

In the Tulsa suburb of Sand Springs, Williams continued, they spotted a woman coming out of a restaurant. Knighton "was going to take her money and her car and she was going to be shot." Apparently, the woman "got scared" when she saw Knighton and ran back into the restaurant.

At Hallet in nearby Pawnee County, the fleeing killers stopped at a small country store clerked by a woman. "I'll rob her," Knighton decided, but about that time, the woman's husband and son drove up. Knighton cursed their bad luck.

The next afternoon, farther west in Oklahoma, Knighton picked out a farmhouse.

"Bob was talking about going in there and getting money and I said no because there's children there. Bob was going to shoot them and take their money."

Shortly thereafter, they came upon a small white farmhouse where there were milk goats and guinea fowl. They stopped the van and looked the house over. Knighton observed that it was Brittain's turn to become a dog by shooting the homeowners and robbing them.

Knighton pulled the van into the driveway. He waved and smiled at a short, pudgy old man who greeted them. Then he drew his deadly dark revolver. Williams watched Knighton march the old man into the house at gunpoint, followed by Brittain.

Brittain later told Williams about an old woman who was also in the house. Knighton handed the .38 revolver to Brittain and told him to become a dog. Brittain then allegedly told Williams, "I froze up and couldn't do it."

Williams heard a single gunshot. Brittain ran out the front door with his fingers in his ears. He stopped. He turned. He went back inside. There were two more gunshots.

"Brittain said Bob shot the old man and stood there a few minutes, then shot the old lady as she pleaded for her life."

"At least these people got to say their prayers," Brittain remarked later.

Knighton, Williams said, was drunk at the time. Afterward, "he freaked out, was crying, twitching. He said he hated having to shoot the old woman."

With the death toll now at four, the Missouri trio abandoned the white van on a side road a mile away and fled west in the farmer's yellow Chevrolet pickup. At least one other Oklahoman avoided death by the luck of the draw.

After having an argument with a mechanic at a gas station, Williams said, "Bob reached in his pocket to reach for his gun. . . . I told him, 'No, you promised you wouldn't.' We took off."

In Canadian, Texas, the trio cased another house "to take over. . . . The plan was to go up to the door, go inside and hold them at gunpoint and shoot them and stay there for a while."

Instead, the cooperation of an alert neighbor, a quick-acting deputy, and a wily sheriff propelled the suspected murderers into the nearest Texas jail cell where, with the cooperation of lawmen in two other states, they soon compiled an impressive amount of evidence. Prosecutors began filing an array of charges against the three fugitives—including auto theft, interstate transportation, armed robbery, illegal possession of firearms, and four counts of first-degree murder.

"[The case] certainly qualifies for the death penalty," said Noble County D.A. Joe Wideman. "From the evidence we've been able to put together, it was a premeditated, execution-style murder."

Governor John Ashcroft of Missouri and Governor Henry Bellmon of Oklahoma worked out an agreement to try all four murders conjointly—"For both states' benefit," explained D.A. Wideman.

Prior to trial, Ruth Renee Williams pleaded guilty to accessory to murder and was sentenced on February 22,

1990, to 15 years in the Missouri State Penitentiary. The following month, in March, Lawrence Lingle Brittain pleaded guilty to first-degree murder in the four deaths and received a life sentence in the Missouri penitentiary.

Plea bargainings placed both young accomplices on the witness stand to testify against Robert Wesley Knighton when his case came to trial in Noble County, Oklahoma, in November. On November 7, 1990, his jury deliberated three-and-a-half hours before finding him guilty of all murders. Judge Neal Beekman sentenced him to death.

Brittain, the "pup" who failed to become a "dog," and Knighton's girlfriend Williams are presently serving their sentences in Missouri. Knighton, the self-described "dog," is awaiting execution of his sentence in the Oklahoma State Penitentiary.

"SADISTIC HANDYMAN DEFILED & STRANGLED THE PRETTY HOUSEWIFE!"

by Barry Benedict

In May 1991, two detectives with the San Diego Metro Task Force hunched over a table at the windowless downtown headquarters, searching through evidence in a four-year-old unsolved murder case.

The victim was a 22-year-old Orange County housewife and former high school valedictorian. Her strangled, half-naked body was discovered in a federally protected wildlife lagoon, north of San Diego.

The murder, which had initially caused a sensation in the local press, had long since dropped from the headlines. And like most old unsolved murders, this one didn't look promising.

It was August 28, 1986, when a worried man with plenty on his mind called the San Diego Sheriff's Office to say that he wanted to make out a missing-person report on his wife, Nancy Allison White.

The husband, a marine sergeant temporarily assigned to El Centro, California, said Nancy joined him on August

25th to celebrate their wedding anniversary. The next day, she returned to their home in Orange County, California.

He related that at three o'clock, he got a call from Nancy. She told him that her 1974 Volvo sedan had over-heated, and she was stranded at a rest stop east of El Cajon, near San Diego. The husband told Nancy he couldn't get away, so he advised her to contact Warren and Jackie Grummett, family friends who were baby-sitting their infant son.

Nancy did call the Grummetts. Warren told Nancy he would be right there and advised her to wait for him by the car. When Warren arrived at the rest stop, he found Nancy's Volvo with the windows rolled down. A woman's overnight bag containing a purse was sitting on the driver's seat next to a hairbrush. There was no sign of Nancy.

Warren removed the overnight bag from the front seat and left a note for Nancy under the windshield blade, asking her to call the Grummetts if she returned.

Later that evening, Nancy's husband drove to the rest stop. He searched the car but, like Warren Grummett, found nothing to indicate that Nancy had met with foul play.

Nancy's husband checked local hospitals and called everyone he knew, but no one had seen Nancy or had any idea where she might be.

A sheriff's deputy took the missing-person report and checked the car at the rest stop.

Two days later, the missing woman's husband and Warren Grummett returned to the rest stop and passed out fliers bearing a photograph of Nancy's face and a description of her. A story on the search for the missing woman made the evening news and the next day's newspaper.

The search ended on September 2nd, when two motorcyclists detected a foul odor coming from the wildlife sanctuary near Carlsbad, California. They followed their noses to a clump of waist-high brush and saw the body of a half-naked woman lying facedown in a reed bank. The bikers quickly called the police.

The Carlsbad Police Department briefly handled the case, before turning it over to the San Diego Sheriff's Office, with Sergeant Tom Streed as the lead investigator.

Nancy White had been brutally and sadistically murdered. According to the autopsy report, the former high school valedictorian, on her way home from her wedding anniversary celebration, had been beaten with blunt force, which had flattened her lips against her bottom teeth, broken her nose, and blackened both eyes. She had been manually strangled. She had also been sexually assaulted, and her panties and bra had been forced into her rectum.

Investigators were shocked and repulsed by the brutal crime and were determined to find Nancy White's killer.

Warren Grummett, the Whites' friend and baby-sitter, told Sergeant Streed that he had spotted two other vehicles when he pulled into the rest stop shortly after eight o'clock—a white-and-blue Volkswagen van and a blue pickup truck with a camper shell on the back.

A Cal Trans crew that was at the rest stop restriping the parking lot spotted a third vehicle, an 18-wheel furniture truck, on the day Nancy White disappeared.

Streed questioned the owner of the Volkswagen van, a homeless man who lived in the van with his hippie girlfriend. He also questioned the driver of the 18-wheel truck. Those two men were not immediately ruled out, but the probe focused on the owner of the blue pickup with the camper shell on the back, a 57-year-old itinerant gardener name Elmer Lee Nance.

Nancy's husband told police that he'd spotted the camper when he arrived at the rest stop to search for his wife. He had talked to the driver, but the driver refused to say anything to him.

Nance listed an El Cajon address on his car registration. But Nance wasn't living there at the moment. Apparently, he had been living out of his blue camper.

A bulletin was issued on the vehicle.

On September 4th, Highway Patrolman Wayne Simmons spotted the pickup at a rest stop and pulled in behind it. Nance poked his head out the window and drove over the sidewalk to get away. Simmons followed the camper to a trailer park where he saw the driver disappear into one of the trailers.

Simmons confronted Nance and told him that he was under arrest. Nance responded with a string of profanities and punched Simmons in the stomach. Simmons threw Nance to the ground and handcuffed him.

Nance was cursing and screaming as he arrived at the county jail. "That son of a bitch had no right to do that," he snapped.

Nance was arrested and taken to an interrogation room. In a two-hour interrogation, the grizzled handyman admitted he was parked at the interstate rest stop on the afternoon of August 27, 1986. He said he left about five o'clock and went to his friend's home at the trailer park, where he took a shower and changed his clothes. He returned to the rest stop about nine o'clock and saw a 1974 Volvo parked two or four spaces from the one where he usually parked. He said he couldn't remember the color of the vehicle but recalled the windows were down and that no one was present.

He said a man later approached him that evening— Nancy White's husband—and asked if he had seen the driver of the car, but he ignored him because, he said, "I just didn't want to get involved. I didn't know him from nothing and besides I never saw no girl."

Nance said repeatedly that he "didn't know nothing about the girl, who she was or whatever happened to her other than what you just told me." He said he was unaware that she had been murdered or that the police were looking for him until the highway patrol officer pulled up behind his car.

Asked why he fled from the rest stop and then punched the officer who came after him, Nance replied simply, "He pissed me off."

Nance said that two days earlier, deputies opened his camper shell and shined a light in his face. "I didn't like that one bit. It wasn't right."

He explained that he took off from the highway patrol officer because he wanted to get to his friend's house and that when the patrol officer knocked on the door, he "saw red."

Nance was arrested in connection with the assault on the patrol officer. While in jail, investigators gave Nance a polygraph examination and searched his camper.

The polygraph exam was inconclusive, and the search did not turn up physical evidence connecting the 57-year-old handyman to Nancy White's murder. Two days later, Nance was released.

The investigation changed its focus to other avenues, none of which proved productive. Although no arrests had been made, Sergeant Streed believed that they had already fingered the right suspect—Elmer Nance. Witnesses had put Nance at the rest stop after Nancy White reported that her car had broken down and before Warren Grummett had arrived to help her. Nance also apparently had a hair-trigger temper, and had punched a highway patrol officer, even though the officer was armed.

Investigators also observed that when arrested, the 57-year-old handyman had scratches on one hand. Nance had told detectives that he had gotten the scratches while "working on my truck and getting tools and things out of the back end of my camper."

Investigators were struck by something else—that

Nance had a prison record, and had been diagnosed as "MDSO"—mentally disordered sex offender.

Elmer Lee Nance was a good suspect—a damn good suspect. But without physical evidence, an eyewitness, or a detailed confession, investigators had nothing but their own suspicions.

"You know, Lee, either one of two things is happening," Sergeant Streed told Nance at his interrogation. "Either you're a hell of a lot stupider than I think you are, or you're a hell of a lot smarter than I think you are. And I'm not sure which."

Two days after his arrest, Elmer Lee Nance left the county jail a free man.

Nance was still free in August 1990 when San Diego Detectives Dan Hatfield and Ron Thill were assigned to the Metro Police Task Force, a multiagency task force assigned to investigate a string of 45 murders of women, mostly prostitutes and drifters, whose bodies had been found in rural parts of San Diego County. Sergeant Hank Olais was their supervisor.

As a Metro investigator, Hatfield had investigated the "Trash Bin Murders," a string of slayings of women whose bodies had been set on fire and dumped in trash bins. He was also instrumental in the arrest of a 41-year-old ex-marine charged with the sexual assaults and murders of female hitchhikers.

Now Hatfield and his partner, Detective Ron Thill, wanted to make it "three for three."

The Nancy White file was the size of several telephone books and packed with crime scene photos, autopsy reports, audiocassettes, hurriedly written memos, and scraps of paper with license-plate and telephone numbers. The detectives listened to the interrogation tapes, made a time chart, and searched for witnesses in the case that was now five years old.

The homeless couple who had spotted Nancy White at

the rest stop were no longer homeless. Investigators located them in a small town in Iowa. And the truck driver, who had been taking a nap on the day Nancy White pulled into the rest stop, was still a truck driver, only he no longer worked for the San Diego furniture company that employed him four years earlier. When Detective Hatfield located him, he was out of work and living in a rundown home in Ocean Beach.

But most of the time, detectives focused their investigation on Elmer Lee Nance.

Nance was born in San Diego. According to county records, Nance's parents separated when he was 13. His father died, according to Nance, when a "doctor killed him. I know that. They gave him an overdose of medicine."

Nance described his father as "a good person. We'd go everywhere. Even church every Sunday. Oh, he'd drink a little bit, but then everyone did."

Nance's mother had died in October 1984. Again he blamed the doctors, saying, "It was their fault. She didn't die a natural death. I got mighty mad, and it was only [a relative] who stopped me from killing the doctor."

In a probation report, Nance recalled a quirky homelife punctuated by arrests. At age five, he remembered his father came home from working on a trash pickup and had a Coca-Cola bottle filled with wine. "I drank of that. I thought it was Coke. I stumbled out of the house but couldn't get back in."

At age 13, Nance was placed in Seeman Ranch School in El Monte, an institution for troubled juveniles. "They said I was running wild in the neighborhood," Nance told a psychologist.

In 1951, Nance, tired of San Diego, jumped a freight train heading east. He got off in Longview, Texas, struggled to make ends meet, and was ultimately convicted of burglary. "Got me four years and eight months in a cotton field," Nance said. "Hard labor." After his release, he went to Odessa, got arrested for burglary again, and served four years in prison.

When he returned to San Diego, Nance married a woman 15 years his junior. His mom and dad signed the papers. "I didn't marry her, she married me," Nance said. "I don't know. I thought I'd try it and see what it was like."

Nance said he worked nights and weekends to support his family, hauling trash and later working in a quarry cutting boulders into slabs with a rock saw.

Nance prided himself on his work ethic. "I was always working," he told one probation officer. "I took money from welfare to go to Oregon, but when I got there, I worked mowing lawns at a golf course. After that I went to Casper, Wyoming. Didn't think I would make it in that old car of mine, but I did. When I got there, I found work as a tar man and part-time mechanic. Made good money."

Nance's handyman existence held little more than a tabloid curiosity for the detectives. What perked their interest was Nance's arrest in 1974 for child molestation. The victim was a teenage girl.

Typically, Nance asserted that the police were wrong and that he was the victim.

"They said I took a kid's clothes off of them," he told his probation officer. "I didn't take no clothes off of anybody. I don't know who accused me. I never did find out. There was a trial, and they had this kid up on the stand. I don't know if she knew what she was talking about. I got convicted and sentenced to Patton."

At Patton State Hospital, Nance was diagnosed as a mentally disordered sex offender. He spent two years behind bars. Nance claimed the girl who put him behind bars was confused and didn't know what she was talking about.

The girl said differently, however. Traced to San Ysidro, California, through a trial witness whose name appeared in court records, she told detectives that Nance had forced her to orally copulate him several times a week over several years.

A teenage boy said he was also assaulted regularly. Reached at the Texas State Correctional Facility at Huntsville, the youth remembered Nance as a sadistic child molester who "bent me over a table and did me like a woman." The youth claimed the sexual assaults had ruined his life and were responsible for putting him behind bars. He said he wasn't surprised that Nance was a suspect in a rape-murder case.

After reading Nance's criminal record and talking to his victims, neither were Detectives Hatfield and Thill.

Their next step was to find Nance. The now 61-year-old handyman had long since left San Diego, but investigators turned up an address for him at the Downtown Hotel in Barstow.

In May 1991, Hatfield contacted the Barstow police and spoke to Detective Andy Espinoza, who checked out the hotel, only to learn that Nance was gone.

Detectives traced Nance to Casper, Wyoming, where he was living out of a fleabag hotel and working part-time jobs.

Hatfield and Thill contacted the Natrona County Sheriff's Office, then flew to Casper. Hatfield found Nance and told him they were detectives working on the Nancy White murder and that they wanted to question him because he was a witness.

"What we are doing is going back to talking to everybody who was somewhere connected, such as yourself, as a witness."

Not overjoyed to see the sleuths, Nance agreed to talk, but said, "I sure don't know much. It was a long time ago."

The detectives questioned Nance at the Natrona County Sheriff's Office. Afterward, Nance sat for a polygraph examination. When the exam was completed, they drove him back to the fleabag hotel where he was living.

In his statement, Nance said he "didn't remember much," said repeatedly, "She is dead, isn't she?" and expressed surprise when told that the victim had a young son. "I'll be darned," he said.

The polygraph examiner told a different story, though. He said Nance had given numerous deceptive answers to the test questions.

Investigators returned to San Diego. In August, however, they decided to take another crack at the convicted sex offender and suspected rapist-murderer.

Nance had left Casper, Wyoming, and was traced to Barstow. Detective Andy Espinoza swung by the Downtown Hotel but was unable to find the suspect or his vehicle. Surveillance of the hotel didn't turn Nance up, either.

On September 27th, Detective Espinoza spotted Nance's camper pickup at the Downtown Hotel. He watched Nance get into the truck and followed him to a nearby market, where he arrested Nance for failure to register as a convicted sex offender.

Detectives Thill and Hatfield arrived in Barstow on September 27th, and made a beeline for the Barstow police station. Both sleuths were convinced that Nance was Nancy White's killer. Nance had failed polygraph exams given at different times by two different examiners. And everything the detectives had learned about Nance since reopening the White file a year earlier pointed to him. But detectives had little more than a hunch—no eyewitnesses and no physical evidence linking Nance to the murder.

With little to lose, Hatfield and Thill decided to go for broke. Five years earlier, sheriff's detectives had handled

Nance gently. Now the sleuths were going to take the gloves off.

Nance was brought into an interrogation room. Hatfield and Thill identified themselves. There were no smiles. They gave the impression that they didn't give a damn if Nance talked or not. They were going to put him away; if he wanted to tell his side of the story, well, they would take the time to listen.

There were three confessions. Halfway through the first, as Nance began to deny that he ever saw Nancy White, Detective Thill cut him off.

"Mr. Nance, shut up and listen, goddamn it! Shut up! Now listen to me! We have talked to an awful lot of people here, and all through your life, all you've been doing is saying other people lie. Well, you, friend, are a goddamn liar. You know, you tell us a bunch of bull. You're a child molester. You've been [messing] around with kids. You're saying everybody else is [screwed] up. Bull! You're the most [screwed] up person I've seen in a long time!"

"All right," Nance mumbled.

The aging handyman then changed his story. Under sharp questioning, he told detectives that he had seen Nancy White on the day she disappeared. He said he was at the rest stop when she drove up in her late model Volvo. She was pretty and she was alone. He said he went over to her car and tried to start a conversation with her.

But when he asked her if she wanted to have sex and she responded by calling him a "dirty bastard," he said he got mad. Nance said he cursed the "uppity bitch" and hit her with the back of his hand across her face.

"Did you have sex with her?" he was asked.

Nance shook his head.

"Let me make it a little easier for you," Detective Thill said. "Did you have oral sex with her?"

"No."

"Did she call you names?"

"Yeah, a bunch of them."

"Is that how you got the scratches on your hand?"

"I don't remember."

At one point, Nance said, "I didn't kill that woman. I didn't go out killing nobody. I had no gun. I had no kind of weapon, no knives. Just throw me in f___ jail and get it over with. I am sick and tired of this."

Leaning forward, Detective Hatfield told Nance, "I'm looking at your eyes. Man, I mean you're about ready to break. I mean, I feel bad for you."

Nance laughed.

"I really mean it. I mean you got tears in your eyes right now."

After more grilling, Nance admitted that he hit Nancy White with the back of his hand, took her to the back of his camper truck, and raped her. The action took place on the floorboard.

"She asked me to stop, but I didn't," Nance said. He said during the rape he might have placed his hands on her throat or pressed his forearm against her throat, because after he was finished, she was dead. He then wrapped her body in a blanket and left her in the camper trunk. She was there inside when White's husband spoke to him at the rest stop.

For the next few days, Nance drove around, wondering what to do with the body in his camper. He finally turned off the highway and drove to a place where "there was no water and no people.

"I pulled her out of the back and just dumped her off," he said. "I don't know where. In California somewhere."

When asked if it was possible that he had stuffed her panties and bra into one of her orifices, Nance asked, "What's an orifice?"

When given an explanation, Nance said, "I don't

know if I could have done such a thing. It probably could happen."

After the confession, Nance admitted to police that he would probably go to the gas chamber if a jury found him guilty for his crime. He said he had initially lied about his noninvolvement because he did not want to go to jail. Even so, he said that he felt better now having told the truth.

He even admitted that Detectives Hatfield and Thill had treated him nice. He then told them, "I'm going to be sixty-three tomorrow, and they have a free dinner down at Denny's Restaurant. You think I can go?"

Elmer Lee Nance was booked into the county jail and charged with murder. On June 8, 1992, he was found guilty of raping and murdering Nancy White.

The now 63-year-old handyman did not get the death sentence as he had suspected. But he was sentenced to a maximum sentence of 38 years to life in prison.

Elmer Nance will be approximately 93 years old before he is considered eligible for parole.

"THE DESPERATE TEEN CROSS-DRESSED TO KILL!"

by Det. Nelson Andreu

In the early afternoon hours of Thursday, January 2, 1992, the manager of a local coin laundry was walking from his business to his nearby home along one of Miami's residential streets in a neighborhood plagued by crime. On the fringes of Liberty City, the area is predominantly residential, with the exception of numerous small businesses on the main streets.

As the laundry manager walked south from the laundry, he suddenly spotted what appeared to be a considerable amount of blood on the street. It had rained the night before and the blood had apparently been thinned by the downpour, but enough remained to pique the manager's interest. At first, he thought that maybe a dog or a pedestrian had been struck there by a car. Despite his curiosity, though, he had to get home. Later, after completing whatever tasks he had to do home, he headed back to the landry. When he reached the site where he had seen the blood, this time he decided to check it out.

As the laundry manager stood back and followed the blood pattern with his eyes, his gaze was drawn to an adjacent vacant field. The lot, overgrown with grass and some large trees, was filled with mounds of debris and rubble. Walking towards the lot, the man noticed that near the street was a heap of leaves and debris that seemed out of place. As he drew closer, he saw what looked like a human arm protruding from beneath the debris.

Believing that there were human parts hidden within the mound, the manager backed away, turned, and ran to the coin laundry to call the police.

The first lawman to arrive was Officer Ted Carracciola, a uniformed cop with many years of street experience. He met the manager at the laundry and together they walked over to the site of the grisly discovery. Officer Carracciola cautiously picked his way through the field, being careful not to disturb any potential evidence. The laundry manager pointed out the suspicious mound, and Officer Carracciola continued walking the last few steps alone. Avoiding sharp twigs and large spiderwebs, the lawman verified that what the manager had seen was indeed a human body, or at least parts of a body, buried in the debris.

The officer slowly backed out of the lot, got on his police radio, and reported his gruesome find to the police dispatcher. Carracciola requested that the on-call homicide detectives and crime scene technicians be sent to the site.

Detective Jon Spear and I were part of the on-call homicide team that day, and we were soon both on the scene. When we arrived, Officer Carracciola and Sergeant Tony Rodriguez met us and briefed us on the laundry manager's discovery. Detective Spear and I walked over to the rubbish pile. All that we were able to see was a portion of a shoulder and what looked like a right arm. It was partly covered by what appeared to be a man's white or light-colored short-sleeved shirt. The shape of the mound led us to believe that hidden under the layers of leaves and garbage was an entire body.

Before anything could be disturbed, before the first leaf could be moved, the entire area had to be photographed and documented by the crime scene technicians. That job was delegated to technician Willard Delancy. Technician Delancy had worked many murder scenes with Detective Spear and me. We pointed out a few areas of special interest, but we knew that Delancy could handle the toughest of crime scenes without our directions. While Delancy was preparing his equipment, Spear and I inspected the area for additional clues. We were able to see a very faint pattern to the blood, which led from about the middle of the street to the vacant lot.

Between where the blood pattern ended on the street and the area inside the lot where the remains were, we observed drag marks, leading us to believe that the victim had been either killed or dumped on the street, then dragged through the field. While Detective Spear continued to hunt for clues and to assist technician Delancy, I went out to try to find other possible witnesses. I went door to door, asking all the neighbors if they'd heard or seen anything strange the night before. What I kept getting, however, was the often-heard answer: "I was sleeping and I don't know nothing."

As I continued walking through the neighborhood, I ran across a group of kids. They were between 8 and 12 years old, both boys and girls, and were curiously watching the police activity. I inquired if any of them had seen or heard anything. Without the hesitation shown by the local adults, some of the kids told me they'd heard a couple of shots around midnight. Although they hadn't seen anything, the fact that they heard the shots at least told us that the crime probably took place right where we were, not somewhere else. It also told us that we were probably not dealing with an automobile accident, in which a hit-and-run driver might have panicked and concealed the body. We now felt that we had a murder on our hands, probably caused by gunshot. For the moment, we had nothing else to go on.

The victim was still covered with debris at 2:06 P.M., when Dr. Emma Lew, a medical examiner, and Assistant State Attorney David Waksman arrived. We apprised them both of the limited facts we had been able to gather thus far, and then they began their own part of the investigation. Dr. Lew took her own set of photographs, and A.S.A. Waksman took notes on what we told him.

A short time after Dr. Lew's arrival, I was assigned the task of helping her uncover the body to examine it. I rolled up my sleeves, tucked my tie into my shirt, and slipped on a pair of rubber gloves. Dr. Lew, Technician Delancy, and I tracked our way through the trees to the pile of rubbish. As I began excavating the leaves and the debris, Dr. Lew and Technician Delancy shot photos to document the uncovering of the makeshift grave.

Once all the debris was removed, we saw the body of a white male, facedown and fully clothed. With rigor mortis having set in, the rigid corpse was difficult to turn over, but the medical examiner and I finally managed the task. The victim's flesh was partially covered with red ants and dried blood, but we were able to estimate his age to be around 60.

We turned the dead man's pants pockets inside out and saw that they contained only loose change. He had no wallet on him, nor any identification, and he had sustained what appeared to be at least three gunshot wounds—one to the chest and one to the back. His left elbow had a fresh abrasion, probably caused by being dragged across the asphalt to the field. When Dr. Lew finished her preliminary examination, we had the corpse removed from the field and transported to the Dade County Medical Examiner's Office.

With the scene work out of the way, the area thoroughly canvassed, and the body on its way to the morgue, Detective Spear and I headed for the medical examiner's office. Since we'd found no identification on the victim, we needed to get copies of his fingerprints and a Polaroid photograph—after the bugs and blood had been washed from his face. Before we could fingerprint the victim, though, we needed to get scrapings from under his fingernails. Technician Delancy had already placed plastic bags over the victim's hands to prevent any traces of evidence under the fingernails from being lost during the removal and transportation of the corpse.

At the medical examiner's office, we met with technician Hector Infante, who removed the bags, collected the fingernail scraping evidence, and took a set of the victim's fingerprints. Then the morgue attendant cleaned off the victim's face, and we were able to take a Polaroid photograph. That done, Dr. Lew began the laborious task of photographing, measuring, and carefully examining all of the wounds, abrasions, and other minor injuries on the corpse. When the doctor had completed her external examination, she took her scalpel and began the internal postmortem.

In every murder prosecution, the medical examiner's testimony is of great importance. Defense attorneys always try to show that their clients were not responsible for the killings they have been accused of, and medical testimony can usually defeat a defense attempt at putting the blame on someone else. All the medical examiners take great pride in their work and are always very precise in their documentation for later court presentations. Dr. Lew was no exception. She worked for hours, making sure that everything was done perfectly, from a forensic point of view.

Detective Spear and I returned to where the body was found and showed the photograph of the victim's cleaned-up face to the people in the area. Unfortunately, no one seemed to know the victim. After a couple of hours of running into dead ends, Detective Spear and I returned to the homicide office to complete the initial paperwork on the murder case. It was now 7:00 P.M., and Detective Spear and I had been working for 12 hours. Having run out of leads, we decided to call it a day.

Spear and I were at our respective homes only about an hour, when Spear got a call from the homicide office. Sergeant Mike Colombo had received a call from a Latin female who'd seen the six o'clock news reports about the police discovery of an unidentified body. The caller told Sergeant Colombo that a relative of hers was missing and she feared that the unidentified body might be her relative. Spear then called me at home, told me about the caller, and we agreed to meet back at the homicide office as soon as possible. That call might be our first break in this whodunit.

A short time later, we were knocking on the door of the female caller's apartment. The crime scene and the caller's home were on opposite ends of the county. It was about a 15-mile drive from one locale to the other. We found it a little odd that the "John Doe" might have been killed so far from home.

Before we showed the woman the victim's morgue photograph, we needed to get some background information on her relative. She told us that she had not seen or heard from her relative, whose name was Horacio Gonzalez, since around midnight on January 1st. The physical description she gave us matched our dead man. She added that he always carried a wallet with identification and should have had at least $20 on him. Even before we showed her the photo, we were nearly convinced that her missing relative was indeed our dead victim. One important factor was that when her kinsman left their home, on January 1st, he was driving his car.

We had to get all the information we could before showing the woman the photograph, because our experience has shown that once the relatives learn that their loved one is dead, they get understandably hysterical, and we wind up being unable to continue interviewing them. Once we felt we had all the information, including the description and tag number of Gonzalez's car, we showed the photo to the woman and her other relatives who had by now gathered at the apartment. All of the family members positively identified the individual in the photo as their relative—Horacio Gonzalez.

From what we heard, Gonzalez had been drinking and then had some type of an argument at home. He became upset and left the apartment near midnight. That was the last time anyone in the family saw or heard of him. Before we left the relative's apartment, Detective Spear called the homicide office and relayed all the information on Gonzalez's car, so that it could be entered into the computers as a stolen vehicle.

Spear and I left the apartment at 9:30 P.M. We returned to the area where the body had been found, hoping to turn up the missing car. We searched in a wide radius around the murder scene—in alleys, backyards, and parking lots—but we found nothing. Once again, we returned to the homicide office and knocked off at about midnight.

For the next several days, Detective Spear and I tried in vain to locate Gonzalez's car and any witnesses who actually saw what had occurred. Then, about midnight on January 7th, we got a call from Sergeant Gerald Green, who informed Spear that the Metro-Dade Police Department had arrested three young women in Horacio Gonzalez's stolen car. The trio were taken to the Metro-Dade substation in the deep south end of the county, about an hour's drive from our own police department. Within a short time, Spear and I were heading south to interview those young women. During the long drive, Spear and I kicked around a few theories as to what could have happened. Why were three women found in the victim's car? Why was the vehicle found 15 to 20 miles from the murder scene? We also discussed what interrogative techniques we would use on the three suspects.

About 1:12 A.M., we reached the remote wooded area where the arrests had been made. We saw Gonzalez's car lying at the bottom of a small ditch on the side of the road. The locale was very heavily covered by brush, and it took us a few minutes to walk through the weeds and mosquitoes to get to the car. A Metro-Dade officer was guarding the car, awaiting our arrival. He informed us that the three female suspects had been taken to the substation and that the driver, who'd fled the scene, abandoning the car, had later been apprehended and he, too, was at the substation.

After verifying the vehicle tag and identification numbers, Detective Spear and I drove to the substation. We arrived there about 2:13 A.M. and spoke to the arresting officer, Greg Rivera, who told us how the incident had gone down.

Officer Rivera said he first spotted the car on U.S. 1 and Marlin Street. Seeing that the driver had committed a traffic infraction, Officer Rivera switched on his emergency equipment and attempted to stop the car. Instead of stopping, the car accelerated, and the officer gave chase. The car, occupied by four people, led Rivera on a high-speed pursuit that ended when the driver lost control and ran off the road into a ditch. After the car stopped, the driver jumped out and ran off through the brush, but his three female companions didn't get so far—they were quickly arrested by Officer Rivera.

Additional police units arrived and a perimeter was immediately set up. About 30 minutes later, officers caught up with the driver and arrested him, too. Meanwhile, when the driver had run from the car, he'd left the keys inside and the ignition on. When we heard this, Detective Spear and I looked at each other. Without exchanging a word, we realized we were both thinking the same thing: Where and how did the driver get Gonzalez's keys?

After all of the perps were in custody, Officer Rivera had run a computer check on the tag number and discovered that the car was reported stolen—taken in a homicide. The Metro-Dade police communications center called our homicide section, and that was how Sergeant Green was notified, and in turn called Detective Spear and me.

Having learned the details of the arrest, Detective Spear and I began to interview the three young women who'd been in the victim's car. All three were juveniles, and they all said that when the police started chasing the car, they'd told the driver to stop, but he'd refused. At one point he'd told them that he was going to drive the car into a canal and kill them all.

During our preliminary interviews of the three girls, only one of them was able to provide information relevant to the murder of Horacio Gonzalez. The other two girls had only gone along for a ride and had no knowledge of what had occurred earlier. The one girl who did know something gave us a good account of the night Gonzalez was killed. She said that she'd been with the driver, whom she identified as Alfonso Brown, on January 1st. Near dusk, she'd met Brown and he told her that he had rented a room at a local motel. Brown went there with this girl, who was a distant relative of his, and told her that she could stay there with her boyfriend if she wanted to do so. Her boyfriend arrived there about 11:30 P.M., by which time Brown had left.

About two or three hours later, she said, Brown returned and began kicking at the door. Brown showed the girl and her boyfriend a set of keys and said that he had gotten the car from his boyfriend. When Detective Spear showed her the keys that we recovered from inside Gonzalez's car, she identified them as the same set of keys that Brown showed her. The keys were on a very distinctive key ring, which the girl was able to positively identify. She said that Brown also showed her some money that he said he had gotten from a "trick."

After getting everything we thought we could from the three girls, it was time for us to interview Alfonso Brown. Detective Spear advised Brown of his Miranda rights, and the suspect agreed to speak to us without an attorney. At the time of our interview, Brown was wearing a woman's dress and actually looked very much like a woman. We explained to him who we were and told him about the case we were investigating.

Brown never denied being involved in the incident and gave us a lengthy statement as to what had occurred. Brown's statement contained some assertions that didn't match the evidence at the scene, and Detective Spear and I were able to disprove some of these self-serving claims. Meanwhile, Brown positively identified a photograph of Horacio Gonzalez and admitted to shooting him. Brown told us that he was dressed like a woman and was picked up by Gonzalez in the same area where the fatal shooting took place. Brown said he had been walking the street, posing as a prostitute, trying to make money. He told us that he was armed with a small .25-caliber pistol. Although we never recovered the murder weapon, the firearms experts were able to tell us that the projectiles taken from Gonzalez during the autopsy and a casing we found in the field had both been fired in a .25-caliber pistol. This type of evidence is not proof positive, but it weighs heavily on a jury when they are determining guilt or innocence.

Alfonso Brown told us that he and Gonzalez agreed on a price for Brown's sexual favors, but Gonzalez never suspected that Brown was really a man. After completing the agreed-upon acts, Brown said, Gonzalez refused to pay him. Gonzalez told Brown to get out of his car. Brown said he got out and ran around to the driver's side of the car. We knew that the electric windows on Gonzalez's car were not working and the only ventilation came through the two small vent windows on the front doors. As Gonzalez was trying to drive away, Brown pulled his gun, reached into the driver's-side vent window, and fired one shot at Gonzalez. At the same time, Brown said, he opened the driver's door with his other hand and pulled the wounded victim out of the car. As Gonzalez turned around, Brown said, he shot him again. Then Brown pushed the victim to the ground, removed Gonzalez's brown wallet from his back pants pocket, jumped into the victim's car, and drove away.

Brown told us that he parked the car several blocks away. Then he walked back past the area where Gonzalez was still lying mortally wounded in the street. From the same coin laundry where the manager who'd discovered the body worked, Brown gazed at the helpless victim lying in the middle of the street. For nearly half an hour, Gonzalez was stretched out in the street bleeding to death. We will never know if Gonzalez could have been saved had someone seen him and called 911.

Brown said he finally walked over to Gonzalez, who was probably now dead, and dragged the body into the overgrown field nearby. He covered up Gonzalez's body, walked back to the car, and drove to the motel where he had been staying. Before going into the motel, Brown said he threw Gonzalez's wallet into a truck yard across the street.

During our interrogation of Brown, he agreed to do a reenactment for us, to show us where he'd discarded the wallet, and which motel he'd been staying in. At 4:20 A.M., Detective Spear, Alfonso Brown, and I left the Metro-Dade substation with the suspect and returned to the crime scene. Crime scene technician Steve Evans met us there and took photographs while Detective Spear posed as Gonzalez and Alfonso Brown demonstrated exactly how and where the shooting had taken place. Brown showed us where he parked the car, which way he walked back to the body, how and where he dragged the body, and where the truck yard was in which he threw Gonzalez's wallet.

It took us until 6:00 A.M. to get done. Once we were back in the homicide office, we went over the whole story again, this time with the suspect speaking into a tape recorder. After taking a detailed confession from Alfonso Brown, who told us he was 18 years old (an adult under Florida law), we formally had him booked for the first-degree murder of Horacio Gonzalez.

Next, Detective Spear and I went to the truck yard, looking for the discarded wallet. It was more of a graveyard for old rusting trucks and truck parts. We dodged swarming bees, jagged pieces of protruding metal, and many other obstacles, until we found the wallet. Inside we found identification bearing the name Horacio Gonzalez. We called out a crime scene technician and had the crucial evidence photographed and collected.

That done, Detective Spear and I walked across the street to the motel where Alfonso Brown claimed he had been staying. We contacted the manager and showed him a photo of Brown. The manager positively identified the photo and remembered seeing Brown driving a car that matched the description of Gonzalez's car on January 2nd. By now, Spear and I had been working on the case for 30 hours, with only about three hours' sleep in between. We wrapped up everything else we had left to do and went home about 1:15 P.M.

It took us a couple of days to track down the boyfriend of the girl whom we'd interviewed on the night of

Brown's arrest. He verified that Brown was staying in that motel, dressed up as a woman, on January 1st. The youth told us that Brown came back a few hours later and told him that a "trick" had refused to pay him, so he killed him and took his wallet and car.

The next day, we got a call from the Dade County Jail, advising us that Alfonso Brown was not legally an adult. He had lied to us. He was not 18 years old. He was in fact only 16. Consequently, Brown was transferred from the county jail to a juvenile facility several miles away.

About a week later, Brown managed to escape from the facility, but he was later recaptured. Meanwhile, through our interviews of several relatives of his, it appeared that Alfonso Brown had a mental problem. He had been dressing up as a woman since an early age, and lately he'd been posing as a female prostitute to obtain money.

As we prepared the case for trial, it went through several prosecutors. The final prosecutor, Assistant State Attorney Rae Shearn, reached an agreement with Brown's defense attorney, and a plea was worked out. As part of the plea agreement, Brown was to receive psychiatric help during his prison stay.

During the last week of September 1993, Alfonso Brown pleaded guilty to the second-degree murder and armed robbery of Horacio Gonzalez. Judge Rudy Sorondo sentenced Brown to 27 years for the murder. The plea was agreed to by the victim's family to spare them the ordeal of a trial. Brown is currently serving his sentence.

"THEY BASHED KEN'S SKULL WITH A TIRE IRON!"

by Patty Shipp

The night was dark and calm, but that suddenly changed about 2:00 A.M., when Kenneth Reeves was awakened by a loud bang that sounded as though an automobile had crashed into something, perhaps another car. Then a dog started yelping.

"Perhaps someone ran over Major," Reeves said as he got out of bed. He was referring to a neighborhood dog.

"Don't go out there now," a family member suggested. "Call 911 first." But Reeves thought that if it was an emergency, maybe there was something he could do right away, before calling the authorities. He rummaged around his house for a moment, until he found a flashlight, and then he went out into the darkness to see what had caused the noise.

Reeves never returned to his home that night. In the morning, a 12-year-old member of the family went out to look for him. The boy walked down the road about a quarter of a mile. Abruptly, he spotted a figure lying in a grove of palmetto bushes near the road. He must be dead, the boy thought.

Detective Carlos Douglas, of Florida's Hernando

County Sheriff's Office, was the on-call detective for the week. He got the call on Sunday morning that a dead man was found in a stand of thick palmetto bushes alongside Griffin Road, in Hernando County, just a short way out of Brooksville. Douglas got into his dark-gray unmarked cruiser and headed east on State Road 50. He turned off on Griffin Road and followed the hummock-lined, winding pavement. Houses sat spaciously on large rolling lots and acreage. As he drove south on Griffin Road, he slowed the car. This was a beautiful, quiet area with a slightly rolling terrain. It was a very popular route for horseback riders.

Upon reaching the site where other deputies had started to gather, Detective Douglas pulled over to the side of the road and got out of his cruiser. Sergeant Lanny Corlew and Deputy Mike Nelson had already arrived. A man's body had been secured.

Douglas walked casually to the yellow body cover and pulled it back. From just looking at the injuries on the body, it was hard to tell what had happened. The man could have been struck by a vehicle, or he could have been murdered. Douglas called Captain Stevens at the sheriff's office and told him what was going on. "I'm not sure what happened here," Douglas said. "We've notified the highway patrol. They're on their way." In Florida, the highway patrol covers all traffic fatalities.

Douglas watched and asked questions while the deputies processed the scene. On the scene, and before authorities had arrived, family members and neighbors had already determined that the dead man was Kenneth Reeves, who had left his house in the wee morning hours to check out a noise. Now, his face looked like raw, chopped-up hamburger meat.

Douglas listened to what people who had appeared at the site and relatives of the victim had to say. Then the investigator walked to a nearby house and rang the doorbell. A woman came to the door. Douglas asked her if she had seen or heard anything unusual during the night. She said she had been sleeping and had been awakened by a loud noise sometime during the wee hours.

"I thought maybe a car hit a cow on the road," she drawled. "Or a horse. Horses and cows sometimes get loose from that field over there," she said, pointing to a nearby tract of land. The woman said she knew there was nothing she could do if a farm animal had been hit, so she went back to bed. Before she could doze off, though, she heard voices coming from the street out front. Then she heard a sudden rustling noise—a thumping noise—like a horse or a cow beating up against a tree.

She looked out the window. In the darkness, she saw a flashlight and several people. Then she saw the light fall to the ground. Again she heard a thumping noise, and thought she heard moaning, she said.

"Did you see anything unusual?" Douglas asked. "Perhaps a different vehicle in the area, or anything like that?"

"Well, there was a car pulled into the driveway over there," she said, indicating the next neighbor's yard.

Douglas listened to the woman talk. While the city was sleeping, something bad was happening to Kenneth Reeves. Douglas walked to the next neighbor's house. When asked if she had heard or seen anything unusual, the woman who answered the door said she had not.

"Did you have any visitors in the early morning hours?" Douglas asked.

"No."

"Your neighbor says someone was here."

"It might have been the paper man," she said. "The paper comes early out here."

After interviewing the neighbors, Douglas returned to the scene where the dead man lay. The body did not look as though it had been struck by a vehicle, Douglas thought, as he took another look.

Sergeant Corlew and Deputy Nelson thought it looked as if Reeves had been beaten to death. But who would do this to a man who had only gone from his house to check on a sudden noise and a yelping dog? Why would anyone beat Reeves to death? Unless, maybe, the killing had been planned. Someone could have started a loud racket outside, knowing Reeves would come out and investigate it. Maybe somebody had planned the whole thing.

But at this point, all the officers knew was that they had a death to investigate. That was all. No suspects. A vehicle which was no longer at the scene had definitely been involved. And Reeves had definitely gotten up to investigate the crash.

"We need to get somebody from a used-car dealership to come in to take a look at this," said Detective Scott Bierwiler, who had just arrived at the scene. Bierwiler pointed out bits of vehicle parts scattered about the area.

A crew from an auto-parts shop in Brooksville was called to the scene. The mechanics examined the broken automobile pieces. "They got to have come off a 1980 or 1981 Pontiac Phoenix," one of them said.

Investigators found fresh tire tracks on the east side of the road in dirt heading in a southerly direction near the spot where Reeves's body lay. Near the tire tracks, a rear taillight lens bracket and two license-plate light lenses were found.

The victim's body lay about 40 yards from a fallen tree. "Look at this tree," one of the cops said. The half-grown laurel oak, rooted close to a curve in the road, appeared to be battered. "Something must have slammed into this." Bierwiler stood near the tree, touching its damaged trunk. Some of its bark had been knocked clean off where a car could have hit it, deputies acknowledged. Not far from the first tree, a smaller tree had been struck and knocked down by a vehicle. "Look here." Bierwiler called another deputy over. On the fallen tree, there were traces of black rubber. "It looks like a car ran over this trunk."

About halfway between where the victim's body was found and the battered tree, detectives found a bloody shoe in the middle of Griffin Road.

Detectives added up what they had so far—the location of the battered tree, the location of the bloody shoe, and the location of the body. It seemed unlikely that Reeves could have been struck by a vehicle and then ended up in the palmetto bushes south of the shoe and tree. Another thing—if Reeves had been struck by a car, his body surely would have had signs of road burn. At this point, detectives couldn't see any indication of road burn. This body had a lot of trauma to the head. Officers felt they were looking at more than an accidental death.

The next day, in questioning the victim's family and friends, the sheriff's detectives learned that Reeves, a navy veteran, had no enemies. There was no one they could determine who would want to kill him. His friends at the American Legion Post recalled that Reeves had always been willing to help people, delivering Thanksgiving dinner to the needy, always being ready to help anyone in trouble.

While the detectives were securing and processing the scene on Griffin Road, other officers at the sheriff's office were following up on orders issued by the detectives. One directive was to go through the Field Interview Reports, which consisted of complaints that had come in during the week prior to the slaying. All reports that referred to the Griffin Road area were to be checked. One recent report turned up showing that within the last few days, a deputy had answered a complaint about an unfamiliar car parked on a side road just off Griffin Road. The identifications of the couple in the car showed that they did not live in the immediate area. The pair, who the officer thought had parked in the quiet place just to "make out," was asked to leave.

Deputies went to the home of the car owner. But the vehicle which had been seen on Griffin Road the night of the complaint had not been involved in an accident.

About noon on the day after the incident, Detective Douglas left the crime scene and went home to freshen up. Then, as he was leaving his house to resume the investigation, he heard over the police radio that a vehicle matching the one being sought had been located. Officers already at the scene where the brown 1980 Pontiac Phoenix had been found noted that parts broken and missing from the Pontiac Phoenix matched the broken pieces found near the laurel tree on Griffin Road.

An automobile matching the vehicle cops were looking for had been found, but there is nothing cut-and-dried when you are dealing with a homicide—Detective Douglas has said this time and time again. But once this investigation started rolling, it didn't stop.

Douglas drove straight to the location of the abandoned vehicle near the intersection of Olympia Road and Cortez Boulevard, behind Lebo's used-car lot. Already it had been a long day, and it was only 2:30 in the afternoon.

The Phoenix was brought to the Hernando County Sheriff's Office storage facility and crime lab, where it was completely processed by crime lab technicians. Numerous items were collected from inside the car, including clothes, fibers, bloodstains, a tire jack, and a bloody tire iron they believed was used by the killer who beat Reeves to death.

There was damage on the left rear quarter panel and bumper of the four-door sedan, with several particles of tree bark embedded in the dents. A tire had been removed from the vehicle. A taillight lens bracket was missing, and both license-plate light lenses were broken with pieces missing. The left rear tire had blown out and was completely sheared. The missing parts of the vehicle and the condition of the rear tires matched evidence found at the scene near the body, Detective Rick Kramer, who was assigned to work the case with Douglas, wrote in his report.

The car had also contained four cassette tapes, found on the dashboard, and a woman's dark brown purse.

Among the other items in the car was a car muffler. A speaker and stereo were found on the passenger floorboard, along with a pair of white high-top tennis shoes, a hair brush, two knives, perfume, and shorts.

Fingerprints were lifted from inside the Phoenix. The bloody tire iron was sent to the FBI lab in Washington, D.C.

The detectives thought that this was surely the car that had struck the tree on Griffin Road. And the appearance of the interior indicated that whoever had been inside could have been involved with Reeves's slaying. The seats were covered with watered-down blood.

A license check on the abandoned vehicle showed that the car was registered to Scott Russell, a resident of Sumter County, which is located just northeast of Hernando County. Detective Douglas went to the residence and a woman answered the door. "Hello ma'am," Douglas said, keeping a cool tone in his naturally calm voice to avoid alarming the woman. She already seemed quite nervous at his appearance.

"A car registered at this address was involved in an accident," Douglas said. "It might be related to a homicide we're investigating."

A boy, about 8 years old, in the room behind the woman, twitched. Douglas couldn't help noticing how strange the child was acting. While Douglas talked with the woman, the youngster left the room, and he and a man who had been in the next room left the house.

Douglas didn't know if the man was the boy's father or maybe an uncle, or some other relative or friend. "Where are they going, ma'am?" Douglas asked.

The woman told Douglas that the man who left driving the truck was Scott Russell, and that he was taking the child he had been baby-sitting home. The boy lived a few miles down the road.

Douglas suspected that Russell and the boy knew something, so he wasted no time hurrying to the address the woman had given him. En route, the lawman picked up his radio and requested a check on the truck Russell was driving.

Detective Douglas and Officer Mark Gongre quickly rendezvoused at the boy's address. A Sumter County deputy had already stopped the truck when Douglas arrived.

Upon checking the man's driver's license, which identified him as 18-year-old William Scott Russell, Gongre said, "Your car was involved in an accident. A person was killed." Gongre read the man his rights. "Do you know what happened last night?"

Gongre could see that the man was scared, and very upset. "Where's the kid who was riding with you?" the lawman asked.

Russell pointed to a child who was walking toward the truck with a woman.

Russell agreed to accompany the officer to the Hernando County Sheriff's Office to answer questions and willingly got into Detective Douglas's car. A woman relative leaned over and stuck her head inside the detective's car window. Russell started crying then. "I'm sorry about this," he told her.

"What's gonna happen to him?" the woman asked the lawman.

Detective Douglas knew the car that had been involved

in the accident was registered to this man. "He's gonna be charged," Douglas answered.

The boy who had been in the truck approached the police car window. Russell, still crying, removed his Florida State baseball hat and put it on the youngster's head.

"I'll go back with you. Yeah. I will," Russell said. "I didn't kill anybody. I'll help you find the one that did it."

Douglas watched Russell. It was obvious to the sleuth that Russell knew what had happened.

Russell said that a person riding in the car with him had killed Reeves. The man's name was James Howze, Russell said. "Well, I seen him hit him [Reeves] with a tire iron," Russell said. "Howze punched the man first. The guy [Reeves] sounded like he was snoring—making snoring noises."

Russell gave the detectives a layout of Howze's dwelling. A SWAT team went there to see if Howze was home, but they didn't find him there.

The SWAT team officers spent the rest of the evening with Russell, having him take them around to Howze's hangouts and houses where he often partied, while the detectives combed the Griffin Road area. Detectives went to a vacant house just off Griffin Road. A neighbor said he had seen a woman who was unfamiliar in that neighborhood come out of the vacant house earlier that morning. The detectives obtained a search warrant and went inside. It was obvious that someone had been holed up in the house. The detectives found traces of blood, as well as a bloody shirt. The house was processed by crime scene technicians, and the bloody shirt was sent to the FBI lab in Washington, D.C.

In voluntarily talking with the detectives, Russell said he had been driving the car on the morning of January 24th. Russell had been baby-sitting and ended up taking the child and other friends from Sumter County to a keg party in Hernando County. Many of the partygoers were drinking liquor and beer excessively, and some were even doing drugs. Russell, Howze, a girl, and the boy left the party to ride around.

Russell, the boy, Howze, and the girl went for a wild ride. They sped east on State Road 50, until they came to Griffin Road. "Turn here, turn here," someone said. Russell whipped the car southward from the highway onto the road, and whizzed along while everyone in the car laughed and cheered.

After a short way down the road, Russell turned around. The detectives were not sure if Russell switched seats with Howze to let Howze drive at this point or not. But whoever was driving, the car was traveling at an excessive speed, and as it whipped around a curve, it missed the roadway and slammed into the laurel oak tree alongside Griffin Road. The men got out of the car and saw that the left rear tire had blown out.

They took the tire iron and jack from the car trunk and started out to find a tire to steal. A little way down the road, they encountered a man, later identified as Reeves. The man started screaming and yelling, saying they should be more responsible. Howze got angry and hit Reeves several times in the face with his fist; the blows were so hard that he broke his hand. When Reeves was hurt pretty badly, Howze threw Reeves over his shoulder and carried him some 30 or so yards and threw him in the palmetto bushes. Before leaving him there, Howze struck Reeves several times with the tire iron.

Both Howze and Russell were covered with Reeves's blood at this point. They got back into the Phoenix and drove on the blown-out tire to an area on the north side of State Road 50 to look for someplace to clean up. Finally, they found a house with a waterhose hooked to a faucet. They got out of the car and hosed themselves off. After hosing their clothes to wash off the blood, the group split up. Russell and the boy got into the car and drove off, while Howze and the girl took off on foot to find a place to hole up for the night.

Russell and his young companion made it about four miles east on State Road 52, heading toward Sumter County, when Russell decided that the car could go no farther. He parked behind Lebo Auto Brokers, a used-car dealership, in hopes of finding a tire to steal. He didn't find anything that would fit his car, so he went across the street, to Blanche's, a type of convenience store, and called relatives of his to come there and pick him up.

A few days later, after James Howze learned that William Russell had fingered him as the person who had killed Reeves, and that sheriff's detectives and the SWAT team were hunting him, Howze contacted the Channel 10 television station, which covers the Tampa Bay Area. He said he wanted to be interviewed by TV reporters so he could tell his story prior to his being arrested. A camera crew arranged to meet Howze at an abandoned convenience store in Pasco County, just south of the Hernando County line.

But Howze's television debut did not go uninterrupted. A team of detectives pulled up at the convenience store right behind the TV crew. The detectives identified themselves and took Howze into custody.

A woman who had ridden with Howze to the location jumped out of his car, creating quite a commotion. She screamed and yelled something while officers handcuffed Howze and patted him down.

Sergeant Mark Rivenbark and Detective Phil Bishop flanked Howze and held each of his arms. They allowed him to say what he wanted to say to the TV cameras before they hauled him off to jail.

Although Howze said he could not remember whether he or Russell had killed Reeves, Howze said he found it hard to believe that he himself was the killer. "I just can't imagine me doing something like that," he declared.

In his statement to the media, Howze said that on Saturday night, he and Russell, who both resided in Sumter County, went to a pool hall along with another friend from Brooksville. While they were there, other friends invited the trio to a keg party. Soon they were standing in someone's front yard, drinking from two kegs of beer. Howze said he'd already taken the drug Prozac and had drunk almost a full bottle of vodka, and he later took some Valium.

Howze remembered riding around Brooksville. He remembered Russell waking him up, because Russell thought Howze might be sick in the car.

"The last thing I really remember good was that I was in the car, going too fast down the road. We hit a tree, but it didn't stop the car. We went on to the end of the road, looked at the damage, and saw we had a flat tire."

About two o'clock Sunday morning, Howze and Russell left the car to find a tire to borrow, Howze said.

"After that, I don't know. After that, I can't remember," Howze said.

The next thing Howze knew he was in the woods. Russell shook him awake and said, "Come on, we've got to go." He had no idea he might have killed a man, he said.

James Howze, 20, and William Scott Russell, 18, were indicted on February 11, 1993—Howze for first-degree murder and Russell for second-degree murder.

Along with the evidence found at the scene of the slaying and in the Phoenix, other evidence against the two also included scientific comparison of known samples of the suspects' hair, blood, and saliva. Physical evidence was recovered that would be necessary to confirm the defendants' presence at the scene and in the automobile, Detective Douglas wrote in his report.

Douglas, assigned as case agent in the Reeves slaying, had led the investigation, working with Detective Rich Kramer and other members of the sheriff's office. If the case went to trial, Douglas would assist Assistant State Attorney Don Scaglione and Jane Phifer, an investigator for the State Attorney's Office, who would prosecute the case before Judge Jack Springstead. Defense Attorneys Alan Fanter and Richard Howard were assigned to defend Russell and Howze.

Crime scene Investigator Gray Kimble was ready to testify as to how evidence was processed at the crime scene, and Dr. Janet Pillow, a medical examiner from Leesburg, would report on the cause of death. Other items, such as the car and photographs of the crime scene, would be included in the state's evidence against the defendants.

The detectives believed that it was actually Howze who struck Reeves repeatedly until he was dead, and if the case went to trial, that is what the prosecution would try to prove.

There was no trial, however. Both men ended up pleading to lesser charges. William Russell entered into a plea bargain that would require him to testify against Howze. Russell pled no contest to manslaughter and was sentenced to 10 years in the Florida Department of Corrections.

James Howze, too, entered into a plea bargain with the State Attorney's Office and avoided a trial by jury, which could have resulted in a death sentence upon conviction. As a result of his deal, Howze was sentenced to 25 years in prison for murder in the second degree.

Both men are currently serving their terms.

"ONE OF US HAS TO DIE!"

by Steve Hamilton

On Friday afternoon, July 2, 1993, a call came into Kansas's Pittsburg Police Department from a woman in Leawood, Kansas, an affluent residential suburb of Kansas City, Missouri. The woman, whose voice indicated she was trying to keep her emotions under control, said she was worried about her 19-year-old daughter, Stephanie Schmidt, a student at Pittsburg State University.

The woman had last talked to her daughter on Wednesday, when they discussed Stephanie's plans to be home for the July 4th weekend. During the conversation, Stephanie told her mother that she and two girlfriends were going to a bar that night in Frontenac, Kansas, a small community adjacent to Pittsburg, to celebrate Stephanie's upcoming 20th birthday. The bar was a popular hangout for college students.

When Stephanie didn't arrive at home by noon Friday, her mother became concerned. She called the apartment shared by Stephanie and another girl in Pittsburg. Despite repeated calls, there was no answer. Finally, the mother called a Pittsburg restaurant where until recently her daughter had worked part time. She talked with a girl who still worked there—she was one of the girls who'd joined Stephanie for the birthday party. The girl told Stephanie's mom that the group went to the bar in Frontenac as planned, but about midnight or a little later, Stephanie left because she wasn't feeling well. She'd gotten a ride home with a friend, and the other girls stayed at the bar a little longer.

The girl hadn't tried to call Stephanie since that night because she knew that Stephanie had planned to go home the next day. Stephanie wasn't really ill, but she had left the bar because she was developing a sore throat, the girl said.

Stephanie was very close to her family, her mother told the police. She would not have changed her mind about coming home without telling them. The officer on the line took down the information provided by the woman and assured her that the police would check on her daughter.

Pittsburg is a typical, clean Kansas college town with little crime or violence. The town's population was 18,000 and revolved, to a large degree, around the university and the 6,000 students enrolled there. In a community that size, missing-person reports were infrequent. When such a report was made, it usually involved students who'd simply been lax in writing home or in telling their parents where they'd spent a weekend.

Nonetheless, the investigators assigned to check into the missing-person report—Detectives Terry Presser and Kenneth Orender, a 16-year veteran with the Pittsburg PD—sensed from the very beginning that this case might not be routine. It was quite obvious that her mother was genuinely concerned about Stephanie's well-being, and from what the woman had told the sleuths, Stephanie was not the kind of girl who would deliberately cause her family to worry.

Her mom described Stephanie as being 5 feet 2 inches tall, weighing about 115 pounds, and having blond hair nd hazel eyes. The young woman was a graduate of Blue Valley High School near Leawood, and she had enrolled at Pittsburg State University in the fall along with several of her high school friends. The companions who last saw her told the investigators that Stephanie was wearing denim shorts and a blue-and-green plaid top.

The detectives' first order of business was to go to Stephanie's quarters in the apartment complex near the campus. They found the door locked and received no response to their knocking. The sleuths noticed several newspapers lying by the door, suggesting that no one had been in the apartment for two or three days.

The investigators contacted the apartment manager to have her unlock the door. The manager hadn't seen Stephanie or her roommate for several days, but she wasn't concerned because she knew that they were leaving town for the holiday weekend. After entering, the sleuths searched the apartment, but they didn't find anything out of the ordinary. There was, however, no indication that Stephanie had packed any clothes for a trip.

Detective Orender asked the manager if she'd noticed any unusual activity around the girls' apartment, loud parties, or suspicious-looking men hanging around. The manager shook her head. There had been no parties or boisterous activity during the last week or, for that matter, since the girls had started living there. Anytime they'd had company, the visits had been quiet and uneventful.

"They never caused a bit of trouble. They were just nice young college girls," the manager said.

The detectives obtained the name of Stephanie's roommate and called her. She told them that she'd left early for the weekend and didn't know that Stephanie was missing until now, when the officers told her.

Orender's next move was to contact Detectives Doug Sellars and Mike Swift at the Frontenac Police Department and brief them on the missing-person report. He asked them to check out the bar where the girls had partied on Wednesday night. Orender told Sellars and Swift that Stephanie apparently hadn't returned to her apartment—or, if she had, it had been only briefly—since leaving the bar.

After briefing Sellars and Swift, Orender interviewed Stephanie's friend at the restaurant. The girl said she'd talked to Stephanie's mother earlier, but hadn't been able to tell her much. She'd gone over the events of the evening and told the mother that the group had decided to celebrate Stephanie's upcoming birthday that Wednesday, because Stephanie was going home the next day.

Detective Orender asked her what had occurred while the girls were in the bar. Had there been any unusual incidents, anything that was out of the ordinary?

Nothing happened, the girl told him. They laughed and talked, danced some, and had some drinks. It was just like most evenings in the bar, she said.

"Did you leave at the same time?" the detective inquired.

The girls said that Stephanie left before the others did because she developed a sore throat and decided she'd better go home. A man, Donnie Gideon, who joined them during the evening, offered to drive Stephanie home so that the others wouldn't have to leave.

"Who's Donnie Gideon?" Orender asked.

The young woman identified Gideon as Donald Ray Gideon, about 30 or 31 years old, who worked at the same restaurant where the girls did. There were no romantic attachments between Gideon and the girls. "He was just a good friend," she explained. It wasn't unusual for Stephanie to ride home with him.

"So, the last time you saw her was when they left the bar?" Orender asked.

The friend said she hadn't seen Stephanie again, but she talked to Gideon the next day, Thursday, when he came to work at the restaurant. As they talked about the party, she asked Gideon what time he'd gotten Stephanie home.

Gideon told her that he didn't take Stephanie home, after all. While they were walking to his pickup truck, he said, Stephanie saw a young man she knew from college and went over to talk to him. A few minutes later, she returned and told Gideon that she was going to ride home with her old friend, instead.

"So I went one way and she went the other," Gideon told the young woman.

The girl said she had no idea who the man was whom Stephanie actually rode home with. Stephanie hadn't mentioned him earlier in the evening, so it must have been a chance encounter. Gideon had told her that he'd never seen that young man before. He said the man was about Stephanie's age, probably another student.

Now Orender asked why Gideon happened to be at the birthday party.

The young woman explained that earlier in the day, Wednesday, she'd mentioned to the other employees at the restaurant, including Gideon, that she, Stephanie, and another girl were going out to celebrate Stephanie's birthday. She invited anyone who wanted to participate to drop by the party. She recalled that at first Gideon said he wasn't in the mood to party. Later, though, he said he might drop by.

A little before midnight, Gideon came into the bar and sat down with the group. They talked, danced, and had another drink or two. Then, around 12:30 A.M., Stephanie said she had a sore throat and was going to leave.

One of the girls offered to drive Stephanie home, but Stephanie urged her to stay, saying that Gideon had volunteered to give her a lift.

"I said something like, 'Drive carefully,' as they left, and that was the last time I talked to her," the girl said.

The young woman described Gideon as a good friend "to all of us." They had worked together for six months, she said, and "he seemed like a nice guy, kind of quiet." Since he was by himself so much, the girls often invited him over to their apartment to watch television. He was quiet and pleasant around them, and he never made any suggestive remarks or a play for any of them. They liked him and felt sorry for him, the young woman continued, because he didn't seem to have many friends. None of the girls were attracted to him or wanted to date him. He was just "one of the gang."

The investigators' interest was piqued when they heard that Gideon had once told the girls that he'd been in jail when he was younger. He said he'd been in a bar fight in which he'd beaten up another man, and was sent to jail for it. The girls thought he was probably just bragging when he talked about fights he'd had while he was in jail.

The detectives were intrigued by Donald Gideon's admission that he'd been in jail. The restaurant owner said that Gideon had never mentioned a criminal record when he was hired. Later, the owner said, he heard something about Gideon once being in jail for a fight of some kind, but nothing more.

When Detective Orender checked out Gideon's record, he learned that the man's previous brush with the law was considerably more serious than a mere bar fight. He'd been released only eight months earlier, after serving 10 years of a 10-to-20-year term imposed in 1982 in Labette County, Kansas, on a rape conviction.

The victim in that incident was a 20-year-old female student at the Labette County Community College. The police records showed that Gideon, then 20 himself, met the girl through acquaintances, and they'd gone on a date. During the evening, Gideon attempted to have sex with the girl, and when she refused, he pressed a straight razor against her throat, threatened to kill her if she resisted, and then raped her.

When he was arrested, Gideon asserted that the sex had been consensual. He stood trial, a jury found him guilty, and he was sentenced to a prison term.

Detective Orender also learned that Gideon was turned down for parole five times during those 10 years, the last time just three weeks before receiving a mandated prison release. While in prison, Gideon was convicted of eight violations, three involving fights with other inmates. He nevertheless got full credit for good behavior toward his mandatory release date.

Orender was told by the Kansas Parole Board that there were grave concerns regarding Gideon's release, but because he'd served half the maximum sentence, he couldn't be kept behind bars any longer.

The disclosure of Donald Gideon's background rekindled the earlier concerns about Stephanie Schmidt's safety. However, the authorities were careful not to label him a suspect simply because of his previous rape conviction. As far as the sleuths had been able to determine, Gideon had no other problems with the law since he'd been back in Pittsburg.

Don Marshall, Pittsburg's assistant police chief, emphasized that there was absolutely nothing Gideon could be charged with. At most, he was regarded as nothing more than a material witness in Stephanie Schmidt's disappearance.

"We'd sure like to talk to him, though," Marshall commented. "We think he could clear up a lot of questions."

Getting to talk with Gideon was not going to be so easy, however. He hadn't been seen since he left the restaurant on Friday afternoon. He'd been given the holiday weekend off so he could go on a camping trip. He wasn't due back until Tuesday morning, July 6th. Moreover, no one seemed to know where he'd planned to camp.

Meanwhile, the Pittsburg authorities and the Crawford County Sheriff's Department, along with agents from the Kansas Bureau of Investigation (KBI), continued to search the area around Pittsburg and Frontenac, especially in the old abandoned strip mines that at one time had been a big part of the local economy. Detective-Sergeant Tim Hervey of the sheriff's department, who was well acquainted with the rugged terrain around the abandoned mines, directed the search. Airplanes and helicopters were also brought in, as well as teams of search dogs.

"We're not sure just what we're looking for," one deputy commented. "We're still hoping the young woman just decided to take off on her own and she'll show up at home."

Although they publicly expressed optimism that Stephanie Schmidt was alive and well, the officers were nevertheless aware of the grim possibilities in her disappearance—especially if she did indeed leave Frontenac with Donald Ray Gideon.

Gideon's relatives were confident that he wasn't involved in the girl's disappearance, that he would be back at his job on Tuesday morning, just as he was supposed to be. They thought it was just coincidence that he and the young woman had dropped out of sight about the same time. They contended that Gideon had changed his life-style and his past was now a closed book.

"He knows getting out of prison was his second chance, and that he's lucky to get a second chance at all, so he can't blow it," one relative declared. "He's working and being a good citizen. He really has turned his life around."

The law enforcement officers hoped that Gideon's kinfolk were right.

"We're not saying foul play was involved," Detective

Orender observed, "but that's always a worst-case scenario in a missing-persons investigation."

But on July 6th, when Gideon did not return to work and had not been heard from, the authorities could wait no longer. An arrest warrant was issued, accusing him of violating his parole by failing to stay in contact with his parole officer.

"We don't know where he is and therefore we've issued the warrant," explained Bill Miskell of the Kansas Department of Corrections. Miskell stressed that the warrant was only for the alleged parole violation, and no charges had been filed in Stephanie Schmidt's disappearance.

Wanted fliers bearing Gideon's picture and description were distributed in the region. They stated that he was last seen in the Frontenac bar where he'd offered Stephanie Schmidt a ride. Anyone with information about Gideon was urged to contact the Pittsburg Police Department. He was described as being 5 feet 7 inches tall, weighing 150 pounds, and having brown hair and eyes. He was 31 years old. He was believed to be driving a faded blue Ford pickup truck with Crawford County license plates.

As word of Gideon's criminal background became common knowledge in Pittsburg, concern for Stephanie's safety mounted, along with public indignation that Gideon had been living in the town with no one apparently aware of his past rape conviction.

When the owner of the restaurant where Gideon was employed learned that Gideon had served 10 years for raping a college student, he said he definitely would not have hired him had he known about it.

"I think everybody at work would like to have known about it," the owner said.

As it was, none of the people there knew. The new knowledge sent chills through the girls at the restaurant who had befriended Gideon, and their worry about their girlfriend was intensified.

Unfortunately, in Kansas, employers learn about a convict's background only if he volunteers the information, or if, for some reason, they call state authorities about a particular individual.

While many persons in the Pittsburg area were surprised to learn about Gideon's background, Police Chief Gary L. Baldwin of nearby Parsons, Kansas, was not one of them. As a young detective, Baldwin had investigated the 1982 rape for which Gideon was sent to prison, and he remembered him well.

"What I remember most about him was that he was cold. He had no remorse," Baldwin recalled. "He was more concerned about how getting caught would affect his life than about what he had done would affect the girl. And he got caught because after he did what he did to the girl down here, he brought her back to the college and left her."

Chief Baldwin had strongly opposed Gideon's release on parole. "I talked to the victim, and she was even more adamant. I've probably seen ten thousand cases since, but his case really left an impression on me," the chief said.

For Stephanie Schmidt's family, the anguish increased with every passing hour. The only thing that kept them going during this terrible ordeal was the support of their many friends and the hope, no matter how slim, that Stephanie was still alive and would somehow be safely returned to them. The family sent thousands of fliers with Stephanie's picture and description around the country in the hope that one of them might trigger a lead on their daughter's whereabouts.

Later that same night, there was a new development in the search for Donald Ray Gideon. His family received a collect call from him. He told them that he just wanted to get away from Pittsburg for a few weeks and was on the West Coast. He said he felt like he needed a change of scenery.

The police learned that a family member who talked to Gideon asked him directly about Stephanie Schmidt and where she was. Gideon replied that he hadn't seen Stephanie since the night at the Frontenac bar and didn't even know she was missing. The relative didn't mince words and asked him point-blank, "Donnie, did you kill that girl?"

"I didn't kill anyone," Gideon reportedly responded. The relative told the police that Gideon sounded genuinely surprised by the question and insisted he knew nothing about the situation.

"I know he's got a past, but I really believe him," the relative told the police.

The authorities weren't so sure, though. But it was a little surprising that, if he was indeed involved in Stephanie's disappearance, he'd made a telephone call that gave away his location.

The call was traced to a pay phone at a grocery store in Crescent City, California, near the Oregon border. That raised another concern for the authorities, who immediately notified border officials on the Canadian line to keep their eyes peeled for Gideon.

"It's a good sign he's heading toward the Canadian border," commented Leawood Police Sergeant Craig Hill, who was serving as a liaison between the Pittsburg police and Stephanie's family.

That call also brought the FBI into the investigation. With evidence that Gideon had left Kansas, a federal warrant was filed in Kansas City, Missouri, charging him with unlawful flight to avoid confinement for violating his parole. FBI Agent Max Geiman said that the warrant would enable bureau agents to take an active role in the search for Gideon, especially on the West Coast.

Geiman noted that Gideon was last seen on the afternoon of July 2nd at a service station in Crawford County, filling his pickup with gasoline. Earlier that day, Gideon had withdrawn $1,000 from his bank and had closed his savings account.

"He obviously was planning a trip—possibly a long trip," Geiman remarked.

In following up on Gideon's phone call, the investigators determined that Gideon's truck had apparently broken down, and he made the call while he was waiting for it to be repaired. However, he left before the work was finished, telling a mechanic that he was going on to Seattle and would be back later to pick up the truck.

Gideon was now officially a fugitive and the subject of a nationwide manhunt. Because of the widespread interest in the investigation and the mystery surrounding Stephanie's disappearance, the television show *America's Most Wanted* prepared a segment to be aired on Friday night, July 16th, focusing on the manhunt. It brought even more dramatic results than the authorities could have hoped for.

At 6:00 A.M. on Saturday, July 17th, the morning after the show was telecast—Donald Ray Gideon called Florida's Volusia County Sheriff's Department to say that he wanted to surrender. He told the officers that he was calling from a phone booth in nearby Ormond Beach and would wait there for them. When a team of deputies arrived, Gideon was standing by the phone booth. He admitted his identity and surrendered without incident. In response to the deputies' questions, Gideon said that Stephanie Schmidt had not accompanied him to Florida. He declined to say where they had parted company. Then he refused to answer any more questions. He said only that he decided to give himself up after seeing *America's Most Wanted* the night before and learning that he was being sought as a parole violator. He steadfastly refused to answer any other questions.

When the Pittsburg police and KBI agents were advised of Gideon's surrender, they were elated, but when they learned that Stephanie was not with him, they realized the chances that she was still alive were not good.

Sergeant Jeanie Absher of the Volusia County Sheriff's Department informed the Kansas authorities that Gideon was carrying a hard-bound book with a pink-flowered cover which he'd apparently been using as a journal or diary. The entries began on July 2nd and consisted for the most part of travel-related notations. No mention was made of Stephanie Schmidt.

Florida investigators determined that Gideon arrived by bus in Daytona Beach around July 10th. He paid for 10 days in advance for a room in a beachside motel in the middle of the tourist strip. He told sleuths that after seeing the television show, he gathered together some belongings and "just started walking." He ended up 12 miles away on the outskirts of Ormond Beach, where he decided to call the police.

When Gideon continued to refuse to answer questions about Stephanie Schmidt, the Florida deputies decided to postpone any further interrogation, pending the arrival of Kansas authorities. He was arraigned on the unlawful flight charge and ordered held without bail. He agreed to waive extradition and return to Kansas, where the parole violation charge was pending.

Pittsburg Police Chief Shanks sent Detective Orender and KBI Agent Scott Teeselink to Florida to take custody of Gideon and return him to Kansas for further proceedings.

"If he refuses to talk to law enforcement officers, we can't force him to talk," the chief noted.

On July 20th, Orender and Teeselink arrived in Florida and attempted to interrogate Gideon. He admitted that he'd been on the run, but he asserted that it was because of the parole violation. He maintained that it had nothing to do with Stephanie Schmidt. He flatly denied knowing anything about her and insisted that she did not get into his truck that Wednesday night. After about 30 minutes, Gideon declared that he would not answer any more questions.

Later that day, Detective Orender and Agent Teeselink started driving back to Topeka, Kansas, with Gideon in tow. He would be held there on the parole violation. During the drive, the lawmen attempt to establish a rapport with Gideon, hoping that he would voluntarily make a statement about the missing girl. But it was to no avail. They stayed overnight in Paducah, Kentucky, and arrived in Topeka late the following day, where they deposited Gideon in the Shawnee County Jail.

Gideon remained uncooperative until the evening of Monday, July 26th. That was when he abruptly admitted to KBI agents that he had murdered Stephanie Schmidt. Gideon related that he offered Stephanie a ride home from the bar. He said she didn't hesitate to get into the pickup truck with him because they had worked together for several months and were friends. When they neared her apartment in Pittsburg, however, he suddenly drove past it and prevented her from jumping out when she protested. He drove on to a secluded area outside of Pittsburg, where he stopped the truck and forced the young woman to have sex with him, Gideon told the agents.

After he raped Stephanie, he handed her a screwdriver and pointed it to his heart saying, "One of us has to die!" Stephanie dropped her hand, and then he choked her to death, Gideon said. Just before he killed her, Stephanie begged him, "Make sure my mom and dad know that I love them both."

After he strangled Stephanie with his bare hands, he tied her bra around her neck and dumped her body among some weeds. When the agents asked Gideon why he murdered the victim, he told them, "To hide the rape."

The following morning, with tears in his eyes, Kansas Attorney General Robert Stephan, a long-time friend of the victim's parents, called to tell them about Gideon's confession and inform them that Stephanie was dead. As difficult as it was for him, Stephan felt that the family should hear the tragic news from a friend.

After Gideon's admission, the agents wanted to know where he'd dumped her body. Gideon said it was near where the rape occurred, a few miles outside of Pittsburg. He gave the investigators general directions, but an initial search by about 40 officers failed to locate the body. After more than five hours of unsuccessful searching, the authorities decided to have Gideon flown from Topeka to Pittsburg by the KBI.

About four o'clock that afternoon, he led the officers to the wooded area in northern Cherokee County near Weir, Kansas, where they discovered the body hidden in the weeds and underbrush. The law enforcers had no doubt that the body was Stephanie Schmidt, though they couldn't make a positive identification until her dental records could be checked.

"We reasonably believe it's the lady who's been gone from Pittsburg," said Cherokee County Sheriff Pat Collins.

A mobile crime laboratory from the KBI in Topeka was sent to the scene, along with the dental records for positive identification.

When asked his reaction to the discovery of the body, Sheriff Collins replied tersely, "We're people, too. We're made out of the same stuff."

The site where the body was found was about 100 yards from a gravel road near Weir, just off U.S. Highway 69. It was less than 20 miles from the Frontenac bar where Stephanie was last seen alive.

The discovery of the body was the final, crushing blow for Stephanie's family. They had clung to the hope that somehow their daughter might still be alive. Now, that faint hope was dashed.

As word spread through the Leawood community that Stephanie's body had been found, friends converged on her family's home to offer what comfort they could.

"They never gave up hope," a family friend commented. "It's their daughter, and whatever comes into play there you hold onto that."

It was indeed a bitter end for the family and friends of the bright, lovely young college student who had no way of knowing that the man she'd trusted as a friend and coworker would turn out to be a vicious rapist and murderer.

An autopsy disclosed that Stephanie was sexually assaulted and strangled—probably within an hour after leaving the bar where she'd gone to celebrate her birthday.

On Wednesday, July 28, 1993, Gideon appeared in the Crawford County District Court, where he was formally charged with first-degree murder, aggravated kidnapping, and aggravated criminal sodomy in the slaying of Stephanie Schmidt.

Wearing handcuffs and shackles, Gideon showed no emotion as he was escorted into the courtroom by sheriff's deputies. During the brief hearing, the charges were read to him, and he said he understood them. Attorney Ed Dosh was appointed to represent him.

During a discussion on scheduling a preliminary hearing, Gideon interrupted to say, "Let's just get this over with!"

Following the hearing, a member of Gideon's family said that the defendant wanted to go back to prison for the rest of his life.

"If there was a death penalty, he would have wanted

it. He doesn't even want a lawyer. He does have a conscience," the relative declared.

Gideon had been in trouble with the law since he was 13 years old, when he and a friend were arrested for breaking into the local YMCA and stealing a car. Other problems followed, but he did manage to earn his high school diploma.

"Alcohol was a bad thing for him," the relative said, referring to occasions when Gideon would fly into rages when he was drinking.

When Gideon appeared for his preliminary hearing on October 6, 1993, he abruptly—and against his court-appointed lawyer's advice—entered guilty pleas to first-degree murder, aggravated kidnapping, aggravated criminal sodomy, and rape.

Judge David Brewster set November 18th for Gideon's sentencing.

Gideon faced a sentence of 92 to 204 months on the kidnapping charge and 69 to 154 months on the other charges. On the first-degree murder charge, Judge Brewster could impose Kansas's "Hard 40" sentence, which means that a defendant must serve at least 40 years before being considered for parole.

Following Gideon's guilty plea, John Bork, a deputy Kansas attorney general, said that he would ask the judge to run the sentences consecutively. "What we're interested in is that he never get out of prison," Bork said.

"The most relevant part of the plea is that neither the state nor the family will have to go through years of appeals, motions, and hearings. I think it will help end this phase of the issue for the family," Attorney General Stephan commented. "The pain will never stop, but at least this part of the episode is over."

The Schmidt murder triggered an avalanche of criticism about the Kansas parole system that made it possible for Gideon to return to society even though there were grave concerns about his future conduct and the fact that those around him were not aware he was a sex-offender. Stephan said he planned to seek a change in the law that would require all sex offenders to be registered and to make the information public.

"I'm of the mind that all sex offenders are going to be repeaters," Stephan said. "I think the law should apply to any first time offender. I think law enforcement officials should have the discretion to release that information publicly."

On Thursday, November 18, 1993, Judge Brewster sentenced Donald Gideon to 99 years and 8 months in prison, noting that he would have to serve 88 years before he could be considered eligible for parole. It was the maximum term the judge could impose.

"I'd like to say justice has been served, but until we have the death penalty, I don't think it can be. At least, it gets him off the streets and away from hurting people," one of the victim's relatives said following the sentencing.

"We should be protected from him," Deputy Attorney General Bork commented. "That's the maximum he could have gotten. He should die in prison unless he lives to be one hundred and nineteen."

Donald Gideon told the authorities he did not receive the proper counseling after his first rape conviction. Nevertheless, he took full responsibility for his actions.

"I knew I had a problem. I knew I could snap out of control," he told the court. "People ain't born rapists. People ain't born killers. All these people hate me. I know my fate, I accept it," Gideon declared.

Defense Attorney Dosh told the judge that Gideon had suffered from emotional disturbances and mental problems since he was a juvenile and often went into rages against women when he was drinking. He said that Gideon had expressed remorse for the murder, and after he surrendered, he'd cooperated fully with law enforcement officers in helping find the body and closing out the case.

On Wednesday, January 26, 1994, the victim's family testified before the Kansas House Judiciary Committee in support of stronger sex-offender legislation. The legislation would require probation officers to notify employers, in writing, about a sex-offender's first conviction and amend the habitual sex offender registration act to make it apply to all sex offenders, not just repeat offenders.

"The public is what we ought to be concerned with," Stephan said in pushing for the proposed changes in the law. "People do have a right to know."

"DESPERATE MANHUNT FOR THE KILL-CRAZY TEEN!"

by Bill G. Cox

If you saw the HBO television movie *Without Warning: The James Brady Story,* then you also saw the gun shop that was later the scene of one of Houston's most cold-blooded murders. The murder that happened there on Thursday morning, June 27, 1991, had its element of irony.

The owner of the Alamo Gun Shop located in Bellaire, Texas, was 47-year-old Walter J. Chmiel, a friendly man who frequently voiced his strong feelings in favor of gun ownership and adamantly against gun control. In view of his anti-gun control opinion, friends were surprised that Chmiel had allowed his gun shop to be used in a movie advocating gun control. In the TV movie, the shop was used to portray the one in Dallas where John Hinkley Jr. bought the gun he used to shoot former President Ronald Reagan and his press secretary, Jim Brady.

The "Without Warning" part of the movie title was all too appropriate to the violence that struck the Alamo Gun Shop that fateful June morning in 1991.

Chmiel was a man who practiced what he preached—he was carrying four pistols that morning—but none of them did him any good. Without warning, he was killed by a large-caliber slug in his forehead as he filled out a receipt for a gun sale.

When a customer walked into the popular gun store that morning, he came face to face with the merciless killer and the sight of owner Chmiel, bleeding and lying apparently dead on the floor. Without doubt the slaying had happened only a minute or two before the customer arrived.

A young man with a large gun in his hand whirled and leveled the gun, ordering the shocked customer to help him load at least two dozen pistols into a bag.

Then the grinning gun wielder toyed with the customer like a cat with a mouse, ordering him to beg for his life.

The terrified customer to this day does not know why he wasn't slain, but suddenly his sadistic tormentor unaccountably turned and fled from the shop, leaving the emotionally drained patron to report the robbery and murder.

First officers on the scene were from the Bellaire Police Department. Bellaire is the largest of six incorporated small cities within the city limits of sprawling Houston; Bellaire bills itself as "the biggest city in Houston."

Homicide detectives and technicians from the Houston PD also responded.

The gun store owner was obviously dead from the large bullet wound in his forehead. Four pistols were found on the victim, and friends later confirmed that Chmiel usually kept himself heavily armed to deal with trouble that might come through the door. Houston, one of the nation's most murder-wracked cities, never lacks trouble.

Since Chmiel apparently had made no attempt to draw any of his weapons, detectives theorized that he might have had a passing acquaintance with the killer and hadn't been suspicious when he came into the store.

From the still badly shaken customer, the detectives obtained a description of the violent armed robber.

He was described as a young black man in his late teens or early 20s. The customer hadn't seen him get into a car, but the investigators believed the killer probably had a vehicle parked nearby to make his escape. The surviving witness had seen no one else with the gunman, he told detectives.

A canvass of the neighborhood and interviews with other business people did not produce any tangible leads. No one had seen the killer enter or leave the store, no one saw him getting into or out of any motor vehicle nearby. After pulling the daylight robbery and murder, the brazen gunman had vanished like a wraith.

Police issued a bulletin for a young black man in an unknown vehicle in possession of a large number of automatic pistols, but no suspects were picked up in the concentrated police search that followed.

When an inventory was made of the gun shop, detectives learned that 26 guns were missing. Judging from the type of guns taken, said Detective-Sergeant John J. Silva, the killer "knew the difference between quality weapons and something that isn't a quality weapon.

"He went after high-capacity weapons, automatic and semiautomatic," the detective told reporters working the story. "He stayed away from revolvers and less deadly type weapons. He went for weapons with a high capacity to kill."

The list of stolen guns was printed and circulated to other law enforcement agencies and to local pawnshops.

But the types of guns indicated that they probably wouldn't be pawned or sold to a fence at cut-rate prices. Instead, they would likely be sold to buyers with unlawful needs for guns, or used by the killer or killers in subsequent armed robberies or other criminal adventures, the detectives feared.

One thing was certain in the minds of the investigators: The killer appeared to be a reckless psychopath who probably killed or tormented his victims for the fun of it. To say, in the usual police jargon, that he was heavily armed and extremely dangerous was putting it mildly.

The next day, with the gun shop murder a top priority within Bellaire's and Houston's law enforcement agencies, a police patrol unit in Bellaire spotted a burgundy colored Toyota Corolla with two men riding in it. The officers recognized the vehicle as one reported stolen from a young woman on the night of June 26th after she had been abducted as she walked to her car from her apartment.

A gunman had forced her into the car at gunpoint and driven the terrified woman to a motel on Houston's south side, where the kidnapper holding a gun to her head forced her to submit to anal sodomy. Later, he drove the rape victim from the motel and kicked her out, keeping her Toyota.

The patrol car officers switched on the emergency dome lights to stop the stolen vehicle.

Instead, the driver accelerated. With the police unit in hot pursuit, one officer radioed for backup units as the patrol car careened along the city streets at high speed.

Suddenly, the fleeing car braked to an abrupt stop, and one man jumped out and vanished into the darkness. While uniformed officers spread over the area in a search for the suspect, other officers handcuffed the other occupant of the stolen car and took him to headquarters for questioning.

When the Toyota was searched, the investigators found several automatic and semiautomatic weapons in the trunk, matching the descriptions of the guns taken from The Alamo Gun shop on June 27th. Other items discovered in the stolen car included several pieces of jewelry and a blue backpack bearing a woman's name and address in Burlington, North Carolina.

When interrogated, the suspect in custody denied any knowledge of either the guns or the jewelry. He told detectives from the homicide and sex crime units that he had only recently met the man who fled from the car. He said the fugitive's name was Randolph Greer, who had come to Houston recently from Greensboro, North Carolina. Greer had resided off and on in Texas, the detectives learned.

According to the suspect, Greer had asked him to find a storage place for the guns and jewelry but had not told him where the guns and jewelry came from. He denied knowing anything about Chmiel's killing or the abduction-rape of the woman who owned the Toyota.

Bellaire police held the suspect on a charge of evading arrest and for further investigation. Meanwhile, the murder probe and the kidnapping-rape case the night before the gun shop robbery-slaying centered on Greer.

The detectives obtained a driver's license photo of Greer, who they learned was 18 years old. When it was placed in a photo lineup, the terrorized witness who had come into the gun shop immediately after the murder identified the photo of Greer as the sadistic gunman.

The rape victim who owned the Toyota also identified the man in the picture as the same one who had kidnapped and sodomized her.

Detective Sergeant Robert Bomar of the Houston sex crimes unit, who was working the rape case, thought the suspect sounded familiar. Bomar recalled that the motel to which the rapist had taken the woman was the same one where another abducted woman had been taken by her kidnapper and repeatedly assaulted about six months earlier.

The 25-year-old woman, Bomar remembered, had been

abducted on January 3, 1991, while trying to use a bank's automated teller machine. Bomar recalled that the motel, which was located on South Main Street near the famous Astrodome, provided a perfect setup for the kidnapper. It had a walk-up registration window where the victim was probably forced to register at gunpoint while the kidnapper stood around the corner, out of sight of the motel clerk.

The rape victim, who was then subjected to an ordeal that lasted several hours and included anal sodomy, had told detectives of one particularly sadistic touch by the sex-crazed kidnapper: He had held his gun, from which he had secretly removed the clip, to the victim's temple and "dry-fired" the unloaded weapon several times. Each time he pulled the trigger, he laughed at the terror he caused his naked victim. This cat-and-mouse game of mental torture called to mind the sadism of the gun shop killer, Detective Bomar observed.

With the identification of Greer from his driver's license by the murder scene witness and the June 26th rape victim, and with the recovery from the stolen car of some of the guns taken from the gun shop, Houston authorities issued a warrant for Greer's arrest on a charge of capital murder. The suspect's extremely dangerous character was emphasized in the pickup bulletin broadcast on radio and sent via teletype to area and state law enforcement agencies.

With a full-scale manhunt on for the suspected robber-killer and rapist, Bellaire police began checking on other items recovered from the stolen car on the theory that the suspect was probably involved in other violent crimes. Detective-Sergeant Jim Harris of the Bellaire Police Department was especially interested in the woman's backpack bearing the owner's name and address in Burlington, North Carolina.

Was the backpack's owner another victim whose body was yet to turn up somewhere? the investigator wondered.

Harris placed a call to the Burlington Police Department and was switched to Detective-Sergeant Kevin Crowder. Harris told Crowder about the jewelry and backpack found in the car the suspect had stolen. When Harris told the Carolina sleuth the name and address on the backpack, Crowder recognized it immediately as that of a 23-year-old Burlington woman who had been abducted and raped on February 9, 1991. Her car and backpack had been taken by the rapists, Crowder said.

The jewelry found in the car in Texas also rang a bell with Crowder. He said that over $100,000 worth of jewelry, gold, and cash had been taken by two gunmen who shot three persons, fatally wounding one, in a daylight armed robbery of a jewelry store at nearby Greensboro, in June 1991—just over three weeks before the Bellaire robbery-murder.

In the Burlington rape case, the young woman had just returned to her apartment and was changing clothes when someone knocked on her door. She couldn't see anyone through the peephole, so she opened the door for a better look. Suddenly, she was shoved aside by two men who charged through the door.

The duo threw the terrified woman onto a bed, tearing off her clothes and sexually assaulting her. During the attack, she was also anally sodomized. When she cried out in pain, the rapist who was brandishing a gun slammed her on the head with the weapon. As she began reciting the Lord's Prayer, the gunman berated her with obscenities and told her to shut up.

The woman believed she would be killed, but after the vicious rapes, the intruders took the keys to the victim's automobile and left the apartment. They fled the scene in the car, which held the backpack recovered nearly four months later in Texas that was filled with a large quantity of jewelry.

While investigating that rape, Burlington detectives found a strong apparent link with the kidnapping one day before of a 68-year-old automotive engineer who had been robbed and abducted from his home in Greensboro, not far from Burlington. The engineer had managed to escape from the car's trunk as he was being forcibly taken to some unknown destination for some unknown purpose. His car turned up in a store's parking lot only 100 yards from where the Burlington rape victim lived.

The engineer's description of his kidnappers matched the description the Burlington rape victim gave of hers—two men: one large, and one small and thin.

The woman's car was found three days later on February 12th in Greensboro.

Crowder told Sergeant Harris he would pass along the information on the Texas gun shop robbery-murder to Greensboro police, since the Bellaire and Greensboro robbery-slayings sounded similar. He phoned Detective Jay F. Whitt at the Greensboro Police Department. Whitt is a 20-year veteran of the department and has been in homicide eight years.

"It looks like your jewelry store killers may have hit in Texas," Crowder said.

The Greensboro homicide and robbery case that happened a month before the Texas killing was on the minds of law enforcement officers throughout North Carolina, for it was a particularly brutal and senseless act of violence.

It happened shortly before 5:00 P.M. on Saturday, June 1, 1991, in the northeast part of the city of 190,000 residents. Susan Cole, a 34-year-old employee, was behind the front counter at Bryson's Jewelry Store when two young men, one large and heavy and the other smaller and thin, entered.

Almost immediately there were "popping" sounds. At first she thought it was firecrackers, someone celebrating the Fourth of July early.

Cole could hardly believe her eyes as she saw one customer, 32-year-old Tim Smith, slump to the floor. The next thing she knew, the gunman was behind the counter firing a volley of shots into Robert F. Parker, a salesman in the store. Cole tried to hide beneath the counter, but the small robber with the big gun and a deadly calm coldness found her and fired a shot into her arm.

Cole heard the badly wounded Parker protesting that he had not set off an alarm, but his defensive cries were drowned out by two more shots.

In the nightmarish events that followed, Susan Cole heard breaking glass as the men smashed the display counters and swept jewelry into a blue bag. Then she was being dragged from the front of the store toward the rear, and she heard the gunman muttering, apparently to himself, "She's not dead yet! She's just pretending! Put one in her head!"

The gunman then fired twice at her. One bullet drilled through the back of her head, lodging in her jaw. The other slug struck her in the back. Shortly thereafter, the wounded woman heard the bandits finish looting the smashed display counters and leave the store.

Miraculously, Susan Cole dragged herself 20 feet to a telephone and managed to dial 911. The first patrol car officers to reach the scene quickly summoned supervisors and homicide detectives.

The officers saw that Robert Parker was dead, his body riddled by four bullets. The other critically wounded victims were loaded into ambulances. Before they were rushed to the hospital, Cole was able to describe the bandits as two young black men, one large and the other thin. The smaller man, he said, had done the shooting.

Later, when able to talk to investigators further, Cole would recall that the pair had come to the store earlier, at about 2:20 P.M. They had looked at jewelry and chatted with Parker.

When they came back two hours later, they started shooting without saying a word, apparently intent on killing all of the people in the store.

Detective Dwight Rooker was the lead detective at the crime scene. He initiated a massive canvassing of the area by uniformed officers and detectives in search of witnesses who might have seen the gunmen or the vehicle they were driving. He also contacted Agent Ed Hunt of the State Bureau of Investigation (SBI) who was stationed in Greensboro, and requested that a team of crime scene technicians be dispatched from the state crime lab at Garner.

Upon their arrival, the evidence experts took numerous photographs and also made a video. They processed the store foot-by-foot for possible fingerprints or trace evidence such as fibers or hairs. The criminalists carefully collected the discharged shells found in the store. The shells had been fired from a .380-caliber semiautomatic, it was noted.

A blood spatter expert was also summoned. Later, the expert provided the detectives with a theory, based on the physics of blood spatters, about where the victims had been in the store when shot and from what angle the shooter had fired.

The intensive hunt for possible witnesses yielded the first tangible clues in the robbery slaying. The investigative teams found witnesses who had noticed a small to medium-size rose-colored car parked at the front of the jewelry store at the approximate time of the crime. The make was unknown, but one witness thought he had noticed a university sticker in the rear window. One witness recalled that the car might have had a New York license.

This information was quickly broadcast to all law enforcement units, with a partial description of the jewelry thought to have been taken in the robbery.

Now almost a month after the jewelry story robbery and murder, Whitt listened to Detective Harris recounting the details of the gun shop murder in Texas.

Whitt felt certain that the killer in Bellaire was one of the pair that pulled the Bryson Jewelry Store heist.

The Texas killer was described as a small, thin black man who had lived in Greensboro and had relatives both there and in Houston.

Not only that, the sleuth learned, but the gun shop owner in Bellaire had been slain with a .380-caliber semi-automatic. Whitt told Detective Harris that he would be in Houston as soon as he could get there. Detective Rooker, who had been the lead investigator, was starting a three-week vacation just before the information was received from Texas.

Whitt had taken over the jewelry store probe, intending to finish followup interviews and other continuing work on the murder probe.

But on July 2nd, Detectives Whitt and Crowder and SBI Agents Bob Padgett and Dave Hedgecock flew to Houston in an SBI plane. There they conferred with Sergeant Harris of the Bellaire PD and Detective Sergeant D. A. Ferguson of the Houston homicide section.

The North Carolina officers quizzed the suspect in custody. He reiterated his story that he knew nothing about how Greer came into possession of the guns and the jewelry. Later, when Detective Whitt was able to talk with the suspect one on one, the detective asked him if he knew of any associates of Greer's in Greensboro.

"Yeah, there's this great big guy he ran with," the suspect said. "This dude's his main man in Greensboro."

The suspect did not know his name, however. But he did recall Greer saying that his buddy in Greensboro had been shot in the leg with a 9mm pistol on the weekend that Greet left Greensboro to come to Houston.

The North Carolina Officers examined the jewelry recovered from the suspect's car and, after comparing it with exiting photos of the stolen gems, positively identified it as coming from Bryson's Jewelry Store. One of the bags in which the jewelry had been carried also contained some cards and papers bearing Greer's name, his former address in Greensboro, and the name of a girlfriend he had there.

Detective Whitt got on the phone to his office in Greensboro and asked detectives to look for a shooting incident involving a large man who had been treated at a local hospital after being shot with a 9mm pistol in early June.

Detective Gary Evers recalled such a case that he had investigated. The shooting victim had indeed been a large man named Donald Eugene Chambers, a 19-year-old thug who had a record of violent offenses. Chambers had been treated for a gunshot wound in the leg received during a brawl at a local nightclub. And the weapon had been a 9mm handgun.

The detectives believed Chambers might have been the cohort with Greer in the Bryson Jewelry robbery and shootings.

The North Carolina officers returned to Greensboro on July 3, 1991, bringing back some of the jewelry recovered by the Texas officers, along with the backpack and other evidence. The store's owner identified the jewelry as coming from Bryson's.

On that same day, Greensboro detectives received word that Randolph Greer had been taken into custody in Bellaire. The murder suspect was arrested without incident at a southwest Houston motel about 8:00 P.M. on July 3rd.

Sergeant Harris received a tip from an informant that led to Greer's capture.

Thinking that Greer and Chambers might be the "small and large" suspects who had pulled other robberies and rapes in North Carolina in past months, Greensboro detectives called a multiagency meeting on July 5th to discuss the cases and the evidence that had been gathered.

Attending the meeting in Greensboro were investigators of the Greensboro Police Department, the Guilford County Sheriff's Department, the State Bureau of Investigation, the Burlington Police Department, North Carolina's High Point Police Department, and Virginia's Danville Police Department.

The Greensboro detectives had identified the burgundy-colored car seen in front of the jewelry store at the time of the heist-slaying.

As it turned out, the car had been stolen during the rape of a Greensboro woman on May 31st, the day before the jewelry store holdup. She had been abducted from an apartment complex by a black man and driven to the southern part of the city, where she was sexually assaulted. She had managed to escape from the attacker, but he stole her Oldsmobile Cutlass Calais. After the vehicle was recovered two weeks later in Charlotte, it had apparently been used the next day in the jewelry store job.

As witnesses had said, the Cutlass had a university sticker in the rear window.

Other cases in which Greer and Chambers were suspected included the rape of the Burlington woman on February 9th; the robbery of a Pizza Hut in Danville, Virginia, on February 11th in which the victims, including members of the Greensboro College basketball team, were held up with a .380 semiautomatic; the robbery of an elderly Greensboro man of $200 and credit cards at a supper club parking lot on U.S. Highway 29 north of

Greensboro on February 13th; and a restaurant robbery in High Point, North Carolina, on April 27, 1991.

After obtaining a mugshot of Greer from the Bellaire police, the Greensboro sleuths held photo lineups, mixing the suspect's picture with other offender photos. Greer was identified as the Bryson Jewelry Store killer, as one of the men involved in the Burlington rape, as one of the men who robbed the High Point restaurant, and as one of the men who kidnapped and raped the Greensboro woman and stole her car on May 31st.

At this point, Greensboro detectives received lab reports on the fingerprint processing of several of the stolen automobiles. Prints on the Burlington rape victim's car were identified as those of Donald Chambers. His prints, which police already had on file from previous arrests, were also found on the car of the Greensboro engineer kidnapped on February 8th.

Since Detective Evers had investigated the shooting in which Chambers was wounded at a nightclub, he was assigned to bring in the suspect. Evers spent about 45 minutes in routine discussion with Chambers, then introduced Detective Whitt.

Whitt told Chambers that he had become a suspect in the North Carolina crimes and that Greer was in custody in Texas. He advised Chambers of his legal rights, stressing that he did not have to answer questions.

Chambers gave a statement, allegedly admitting his part in the jewelry store robbery; in the February 9th abduction-rape of the Burlington woman; in another abduction-rape on March 11, 1991, at a Greensboro apartment house; and in the restaurant robberies in High Point and Danville. Greer had been with Chambers in those crimes, the suspect told police.

The investigators learned that after the jewelry store shootings, the two suspects had driven the car to Charlotte, where they parked it and took a bus to Ohio. They stayed about a week, pawning some of the stolen jewelry and having false identification papers made.

The weekend after they came back to Greensboro, Chambers was wounded in the nightclub brawl. Greer, who witnessed the shooting, then headed for Houston.

After obtaining the statement from Chambers, the sleuths obtained a search warrant for an apartment on Utah Street in Greensboro where the suspects had lived for a time and which was still Chambers's residence. A 14-page affidavit attached to the warrant listed at least 27 items found in the apartment, including the license plate from the stolen getaway car used in the jewelry robbery (another license had been put on the car); some personal property belonging to the Burlington rape victim; some jewelry, including a watch, thought to belong to the May 31st Greensboro rape victim; a blue calendar book bearing murder victim Parker's name; a cartridge case for .380-caliber ammunition; and personal papers of Greer's.

The license plate from the February 8th kidnap victim's car was found outside the apartment, police said.

The warrant affidavit tied the recovered items to the various crimes in which the pair was suspected.

Following up the Ohio angle, Detectives Rooker and Whitt went to Parma, Ohio, where they were assisted by Detective John Bomba in locating the motel where the suspects stayed. They recovered some jewelry that had been pawned in that town.

Both Greer and Chambers were facing other charges at the time of their arrests in the multistate crime rampage. They were free on bond, awaiting trial on crimes in Guilford County. Greer was charged with communicating threats and assault. He also was wanted in Texas for illegal use of a credit card.

Chambers faced charges of second-degree rape and second-degree sexual offense involving a mentally retarded 13-year-old girl in High Point on September 2, 1990.

In Houston, Greer was indicted for capital murder in the gun shop robbery and murder, in which he apparently had acted alone. Police determined that the man nabbed when Greer jumped from the car being chased on July 3rd was not involved in the case.

Greer was also indicted later in North Carolina in the Bryson Jewelry Store murder and several other of the crimes in which he and Chambers had been linked.

Chambers was indicted for first-degree murder in the jewelry store case as well as for other rapes, kidnappings, and robberies in which he and Greer were allegedly involved. Both suspects were held in custody with bond denied.

Sergeant Bomar of the Houston sex crimes unit, who investigated the rape cases attributed to Greer, said about the suspect, "He has absolutely none of the normal human feelings we associate with tenderness and compassion towards another human. He uses humans, and then he disposes of them."

Greer, now 19, went on trial for the gun shop murder in mid-June 1992 in state district court in Houston. The man who had walked into The Alamo Gun Shop while the accused killer stood over the body of owner Walter Chmiel told the jury the gunman held him at gunpoint, forced him to help fill a bag with 26 new pistols, and was then forced by the gunman to beg for his life. Police witnesses outlined the case that their murder investigation had built against Greer.

The jury convicted Randolph Greer of capital murder on June 25th. The worst testimony was still to come in the punishment phase of the trial when it would be decided whether the teenager should be sentenced to life in prison or to death by lethal injection.

Four women from Texas and North Carolina testified

that they had been raped at gunpoint by Greer during his violent forays in the two states.

One Texas victim who told of Greer subjecting her to anal sodomy sobbed, "I didn't want to die. I kept thinking I ought to do something [to resist]. But when you've got a loaded gun pointed at you . . . I was terrified."

The rape victim from Burlington, North Carolina, testified that when she cried out in pain while being anally sodomized, Greer struck her on the head with his gun. And when she started reciting the Lord's Prayer, he called her an obscene name and ordered her to shut up. A third victim told of Greer holding the gun to her head and pulling the trigger even though, unknown to her, he had unloaded it.

Susan Cole, the employee of Bryson's Jewelry Store who survived after being shot three times by a man she identified as Greer, broke into tears as she testified.

"I heard a popping sound that I originally thought was firecrackers," she said. Then, she told of watching in stark terror as Greer gunned down a customer, Tim Smith, and store salesman Robert Parker. Parker later died from his wounds.

The gunman turned his gun on her after shooting the others, Susan Cole said.

"He was very cool-looking, like he's sitting here right now," the woman said, sobbing. "He looked like he enjoyed every minute of it, like he enjoyed having that power over people."

During the woman's testimony, Greer yawned, looked at his fingernails, and turned around to look at relatives.

The defense, seeking to save the youthful offender from the death penalty, called witnesses who testified that Greer as a student made grades below average, but never ran with youth gangs, never smoked, drank, or used dope. According to defense witnesses, he never got into trouble until 1990.

A psychiatrist told the jury that what sent Greer over the edge into a sort of mania may have happened in 1990, when he got a 15-year-old Greensboro girl pregnant and had to drop out of school. The psychiatrist said that Greer suffers from a genetic predisposition toward a manic-depressive condition.

In seeking the death penalty for the defendant, Prosecutor Luci Davidson of the Harris County Criminal District Attorney's office described Greer as a gun fancier with a sort of devotion to controlling victims.

"He was what the legislature intended when they drafted the laws on these issues [the death penalty]," she said.

The jury deliberated four hours and returned a verdict mandating the death penalty for Greer. The verdict will be automatically appealed to the Texas Court of Criminal Appeals. Greer is on Texas's death row at this writing.

Meanwhile, North Carolina authorities decided not to try Greer immediately on the jewelry store murder in Greensboro, since he received the death penalty in Texas. Should legal technicalities bring about a reversal of the verdict, he would be brought to Greensboro for trial on the first-degree murder charge, prosecutors said.

On November 17, 1992, Donald Eugene Chambers was convicted of breaking and entering, armed robbery, and conspiracy in connection with a break-in and robbery of a North Carolina couple in their apartment. He received 57 years for the crime. He is still awaiting trial for his part in the Greensboro jewelry store caper and must be presumed innocent of the charges until and unless proved otherwise by due process in a court of law.

"THE LOVE THEM & LEAVE THEM KILLER"

by Charles W. Sasser

Thursday, July 8, 1993, was well on its way to becoming another scorcher. By 8:30 A.M., the sun over Tulsa, Oklahoma, was already undulating in a white sky. Todd Hinds sweated profusely as he peddled his bicycle to work at a nearby manufacturing plant in the 6100 block of North Yale Avenue just outside the city limits.

Hinds suddenly braked his bike, stared, then took off like a scared deer to find the nearest telephone. Stammering, he told the Oklahoma Highway Patrol that he had found a dead woman lying in a ditch; she appeared to have been struck by a hit-and-run driver.

Jurisdiction for the case fell to Sheriff Stanley Glanz, Tulsa County Sheriff's Department, who in his short tenure as top lawman had turned the 300-man department into a modern law enforcement agency. A young stocky deputy, Detective Matt Palmer, found himself assigned to investigate his first homicide. In the heat of that summer morning, he also initially assumed the woman had been struck by a car.

The body lay facedown in the roadside ditch, almost hidden from view by thick, two-foot-high weeds. She appeared young and was clad in blue shorts, a white T-shirt, and white sneakers and socks. Dried blood matted her long dark hair. Rigor mortis creeping into the limbs indicated that death had occurred 12 hours or so earlier.

It was only when authorities turned the body over for a more careful examination that they received two surprises: First, the victim was obviously pregnant, in her fifth month; second, she was no hit-and-run victim. Someone had fired a bullet point-blank into the victim's face. The victim had also been shot three times in the back of the head with a large-caliber weapon, and displayed a gunshot wound in the left leg and in her left arm.

"Shot five times in all, six wounds," mused Detective Palmer.

He speculated that the victim had been shot in the leg first. That's what brought her down. As she lay begging in the grass, her assailant most likely shot her through the arm and into her face. The last three shots to the back of her head had probably been for good measure.

"To make sure she was good and dead," Palmer said.

It was definitely overkill.

In roping off the scene and searching the area foot by foot for evidence, detectives recovered a .38-caliber bullet that had gone completely through the victim's skull and into the ground beneath her head. That and the way blood had soaked into the soil assured lawmen that the pregnant girl had not been killed elsewhere and dumped here; she had been shot where she lay, in this North Tulsa County bar ditch.

Just to the left of the body, near the right hip, Detective Palmer found the second piece of significant evidence—a cover from a trailer hitch with the brand name Draw-Tite on it. Apparently, the killer had lost it from his, or her, car.

The victim's only possession was a black cigarette case containing $30 in cash, plus an Oklahoma driver's license and a Tulsa Junior College student ID card, both in the name of Vaughnie Marie Bradley, age 24.

"The thirty dollars in the case probably means the motive for murder wasn't robbery," Palmer decided.

The state medical examiner soon eliminated a possible second motive for homicide: the victim hadn't been raped. But if she wasn't murdered for sex or money, then for what?

The address on the deceased's driver's license led Detective Palmer to the modest home of Vaughnie Bradley's father and stepmother in the 5600 block of North Gillette Avenue in Tulsa. After the shock wore off, the parents said their daughter had been living with them in recent months. They filled in detectives on the victim's recent activities.

According to the parents' statements, Vaughnie was the pregnant unwed mother of three young children, the oldest of whom was seven. She enjoyed camping, and her daily routine consisted of watching TV, studying, or staying with the kids. "She was a beautiful girl," the family members said.

Recently, Vaughnie began attending classes at Tulsa Junior College and became engaged to a man named Bob Sand, the father of her unborn child. Sand lived in Oklahoma City, the state's capital about 100 miles to the southwest.

"She spent almost every weekend in Oklahoma City," Vaughnie's father said. "One of the last conversations I had with her was about how high the phone bill was from her calling Bob."

"Have you seen Bob here in Tulsa this week?" detectives inquired.

"I don't think I've ever seen him up here."

It was only natural—and good police work—for detectives to look at boyfriends, husbands, and exes whenever a woman turned up murdered.

The victim's father then detailed his daughter's last night on earth, beginning with his picking her up from college at about 5:00 P.M. on Wednesday. At home, Vaughnie prepared spaghetti for dinner. Afterward, she took her books outside to study in the shade of trees on the lawn.

She received a telephone call shortly after 7:00 P.M.

"She seemed upset over the call," the father recalled. "I was suspicious . . . [but] she refused to let me know who it was. Why didn't she tell me who it was? She didn't have to make excuses."

Shortly after receiving the phone call, Vaughnie said she was going for a walk. "Will you take the kids for a little while?" she asked her stepmother. "The doctor told me I needed the exercise."

Darkness neared. Vaughnie did not return. Her father drove around the neighborhood looking for her.

"I was worried," he said, "but I really didn't think anything was wrong. I figured she must have met somebody for a ride and didn't want the family to know who she was out with."

Had Vaughnie met someone she knew for what was to become her last ride? Or had she been abducted off the neighborhood streets?

If authorities were initially suspicious of boyfriend Bob Sand, their suspicions quickly proved groundless. Sand had the perfect alibi. He was a convict who was serving time behind bars in an institution of the Oklahoma State Prison system in Oklahoma City.

What other men had Vaughnie been romantically involved with? police wanted to know.

Lawmen learned that before Sand, Vaughnie had lived common-law for almost three years with a man named Gaylon. Before the couple split up in 1992, they had a son, who was now three. The ex-lovers were scheduled to appear in court on July 12th for a hearing about Gaylon paying child support. Instead, Vaughnie ended up dead in a ditch on the night of July 7th.

"Vaughnie didn't want anything else to do with Gaylon, except child support for their baby," the victim's father informed police. "But he was giving her all kinds of trouble. He kept threatening her. . . . He had been calling her a lot and hanging up on her."

Police discovered that Gaylon Franklin was a former convicted felon. His record also sketched an unflattering portrait of a man whom police described as a "woman user, woman abuser." From California to Oklahoma, Franklin had left a trail of ex-wives and ex-lovers and young children for whose welfare he refused to accept responsibility. He owed a California ex-wife $10,000 in back child support, and a Bartlesville, Oklahoma, ex-wife another $10,000 in back support. California court documents revealed that Franklin had been convicted there for spousal battery.

Apparently, Franklin had also abused the Bartlesville ex-wife. Cindy Peters told police that on one occasion Franklin had beaten her so severely she was hospitalized. After their divorce, a tall skinny man wearing a ski mask broke into her home one night. He beat her with his fists and then raped her. Peters had not notified police.

"I was afraid he'd kill me," she explained. "I know it was Gaylon in the ski mask, but I was afraid to tell on him."

The woman then reportedly demanded, "How am I going to get my money for child support if he's in jail?"

But Gaylon Franklin wasn't in jail—not yet. In fact, detectives didn't know if he had anything to do with Vaughnie Bradley's homicide.

On Thursday afternoon, as the case grew more complicated, Detective Palmer telephoned homicide Investigator Gary Ross at home and asked for help in investigating the whodunit. "Since this was my first homicide," Palmer would later explain, "I felt I could use Gary's knowledge."

Ross, a 13-year veteran of law enforcement, had earned a reputation for cracking difficult crimes. He had been at the gun range for periodic qualification that day. He arrived at the downtown Tulsa County Sheriff's Office at about 5:00 P.M. to join forces with his younger colleague.

In the meantime, deputies were on Gaylon Franklin's trail, looking to question him about the slaying and his relationship with Vaughnie Bradley. The trail led Deputies Tom Fike and Joe Morgan to a South Tulsa fast-food Mexican restaurant where Franklin worked. Officers questioned Taco Bell employee Connie Crystal, who insisted she had been to Franklin's house the previous night at about the same time Vaughnie was disappearing from North Tulsa.

Franklin lived near South Lewis Avenue and 55th Place, officers learned, some dozen miles across the city from the victim's home and perhaps 15 miles from the site of her death. Franklin could not have murdered Vaughnie in North Tulsa if Crystal saw him at the same time in South Tulsa.

Obtaining Franklin's home address, Fike and Morgan left the Taco Bell to confront him. They learned later that as soon as they left the restaurant, Crystal ran to Franklin's house to warn him that police were on their way. Franklin, therefore, seemed to expect the deputies when they arrived. He readily agreed to accompany them downtown to give a statement, cheerfully declaring that he had nothing to hide.

His new wife of only a few months—his fourth or fifth by some counts—remained at the residence to wait. Annelle was a tall blonde who was some 10 years older than her husband.

It was about 6:00 P.M. when the detective team of Palmer and Ross braced Franklin in an interrogation room at the sheriff's substation on East Admiral. The detectives observed that the tall dark man with the bad complexion seemed surprisingly unperturbed.

According to accounts of the interrogation, Franklin said he returned home at about 1:00 P.M. on Wednesday and spent the afternoon cooking a stew, watching TV, and taking a nap. His wife Annelle came home at 6:00 P.M. They had dinner, then worked on their checkbook until eight o'clock. Franklin left home for a short time after that, he said, to return a defective attic fan to the nearby Target department store. He was home again by 9:00 P.M. His coworker at Taco Bell, Connie Crystal, could verify that; she came by about that time to deliver some business mail to him. He stayed home the rest of the night. His wife Annelle would verify that.

It sounded airtight, it sounded good, detectives admitted. If it were all true, sleuths would have to cast elsewhere for a suspect. Yet, police also knew that alibis could be manufactured.

Detective Ross continued to question Franklin.

"Have you ever been violent toward your wives and other women?" Ross asked the suspect.

"Of course not," Franklin responded. "I'm a nonviolent person."

Ross slapped down a fax copy of Franklin's California conviction, proving that he had beaten at least that wife. Franklin stared at it. "It's not as bad as it seems," he said.

Ross then pointed out that on at least two occasions, Vaughnie Bradley had sought refuge at a battered women's shelter when she was living with Franklin.

"She was the one who attacked me," Franklin retorted. "She was a doper and strung out a lot of the time. That's why we broke up. She was always involved with dope and spending our money on dope. Then if I said something, she'd jump on me. I had to defend myself."

"If you ask me," Franklin concluded, "it was probably one of her doper friends who killed her."

Police had no evidence to justify Franklin's arrest. It seemed he could prove his innocence. Nonetheless, detectives obtained a signed search waiver from Franklin giving them permission to search his house and vehicle.

Franklin shrugged. "I have nothing to hide," he reiterated. He remained at the sheriff's office while Detectives Palmer and Ross drove to his house to execute the search warrant and to question his wife.

They arrived around 8:00 P.M., almost exactly 24 hours after Bradley's death. Detective Palmer had been pounding the streets, questioning potential witnesses since early that morning. It was going to be a long night.

Ross recalled that as soon as he and Palmer stepped from their unmarked car at the Franklin house, his eyes were drawn to a shiny new black Camaro that was parked in the driveway. Attached to the rear bumper was a trailer hitch whose newness glinted in the last of the day's sunshine.

Ross examined the hitch. Its brand name was Draw-Tite, the same as that on the black trailer hitch cover recovered near the victim's bullet-riddled body. The hitch cover fit the trailer hitch "like a glove."

Further searches of the car and the house, however, failed to turn up additional clues. A .380-caliber semiautomatic pistol that Annelle turned over to the detective partners—the only weapon in the house, she said—could not have been the murder weapon. Bradley was killed with a .38-caliber, apparently a revolver since no ejected shell casings were found at the crime scene.

Annelle then supported her husband's statement by claiming that he had been with her throughout the evening of July 7th, except for that short period of time when he went to the Target store. If police were to believe her and Connie Crystal, Franklin simply could not have murdered his former lover.

Yet, certain clues could not be ignored. There was the Draw-Tite trailer hitch and cover. There was the matter of motive, with the child support hearing coming up in four days. There was Franklin's history of violence toward women. And there was the continuing bad blood between the victim and Franklin and his having threatened her.

"Something just doesn't feel right," Detective Ross said as the two detectives left Annelle at home. "She's wanting to tell us something else. She provided her husband an alibi, but her body language says she's lying."

The partners pounded the nighttime Tulsa streets, crisscrossing trails that lawmen had already traversed during the day, rechecking and chipping away at their suspect's alibi.

Connie Crystal left the first big chink in Franklin's armor when she reneged on her story. No, she now stated upon requestioning, she had not delivered mail to Franklin's house on Wednesday night after all. She had agreed to say so only because Franklin had asked her to—but that was before she knew he might be mixed up in murder.

A relative of the victim's knocked out the next chink in Franklin's defenses. She related to police a conversation she'd had with Vaughnie Bradley two weekends before, while they were driving together to Oklahoma City to visit Bradley's fiancé in prison.

According to the statement, Bradley said she had recently spoken to Franklin—and he wanted her to return to his hearth and bed. She said he promised to leave his new wife Annelle and take Bradley and her children out of state, where presumably they would live happily ever after. He had plenty of money for the move, he told her, because Annelle had recently received a $10,000 cash settlement from her own ex-husband. Franklin had persuaded Annelle to hide the money in their house rather than put it in a bank. If Bradley would just say yes and come back to him, he would steal the $10,000 and run away with her.

"Vaughnie told him no," the relative informed detectives. "She told him she didn't want anything else to do with him except for child support."

Detectives shook their heads in astonishment.

"Maybe when Vaughnie turned him down," said Detective Ross, "he decided he'd rather kill her than pay her child support."

Armed with this information about the $10,000, a possible key to the mystery, the fast-working deputies once again confronted Annelle. When Ross sprang the news on her, her jaw reportedly dropped, and she actually started trembling. The look on her face spoke louder than a shout as to her sudden understanding of how her husband had undoubtedly betrayed her.

"No one was supposed to know about that money," Annelle murmured. Certainly Vaughnie Bradley and her relative would not have known unless Franklin told them—and he surely wouldn't have told Bradley unless he actually intended to run away with her and take Annelle's $10,000 to sweeten the pot.

Reportedly stunned but nonetheless enlightened as to her husband's true nature, Annelle gave up all her defenses, and her double-dealing husband as well. She had lied the first time, she now said, in order to protect him. She wouldn't lie anymore.

Franklin had not gone to the Target either alone or with her on Wednesday night, Annelle declared in her statement. He had gone elsewhere, alone, in the black Camaro, leaving around 7:30 P.M. He told Annelle he was going to a pay telephone and call Bradley "to talk about child support."

When he returned home around 9:30 P.M., he supposedly strode into the house and announced, "Well, I did it. . . ."

"Did what?" Annelle asked him.

"I shot Vaughnie and left her in a ditch in North Tulsa. I don't know if she's dead or alive."

Annelle said Franklin had always appeared so kind and nonviolent. But now, after all this, she was "scared to death."

"Would he have killed me instead of Vaughnie if she had taken him up on his offer to run away with him?"

Detectives Ross and Palmer said they thought Franklin might have.

Now that Gaylon Franklin no longer had alibi witnesses, the tide of the investigation turned against him. It was about midnight when the investigators arrested Franklin for shooting his ex-lover. According to them, the accused killer revealed no emotion, especially no remorse.

"No, Mr. Ross," he said politely, "I didn't do it."

Franklin spoke of the murder, detectives said, as though his former lover, the mother of his child, was nothing more than another possum road kill.

"By the way," he said as deputies escorted him to jail, "who won the Drillers baseball game tonight?"

The tide, once it turned, turned completely.

Both Annelle and Connie Crystal apparently felt used by Franklin. Around 2:00 A.M., after Franklin's arrest, the two women met at the Franklin residence with one thing in common on their minds. Annelle later said she and Connie were determined to find any evidence of murder that Franklin might have left in the house.

At 10:30 A.M., Detective Ross received a telephone call. It was Annelle.

"I just found a gun," she blurted out.

Ross and Palmer hurried to South Tulsa. The Franklin home was in disarray, as though a burglar had struck.

The house had been turned inside out by two women on a common mission.

A Smith & Wesson .38-caliber revolver lay on the floor next to the recliner chair that Franklin always used. The women had found it, they said, when it dropped out of the chair's springs where it had apparently been hidden. Annelle also found pornographic photos of her husband having sex with other women.

It didn't take firearms experts long to determine that the bullets from Vaughnie Bradley's skull had been fired from this gun.

On Monday, July 13, 1993, Tulsa County District Attorney David Moss filed first-degree murder charges against Gaylon Ronald Franklin Jr. But although he remained in jail without bond awaiting trial, the accused killer continued to scheme against the women in his life.

According to a cellmate who later testified at Franklin's trial, Franklin admitted to him that he killed Bradley. Franklin met Bradley and drove her to northern Tulsa County, where they argued. Franklin then shoved the pregnant Bradley out of his Camaro and was going to leave her on foot by the side of the road. But then, in her anger, Bradley kicked Franklin's car. That was when he jumped out and shot her to death.

It was Bradley's kicking the car, police surmised, that had dislodged the Draw-Tite trailer hitch cover that provided a vital link between Franklin and the crime scene.

After confessing to one murder, Franklin then offered his cellmate $5,000 if he would kill Annelle when he was released from jail. However, instead of accepting the kill-for-hire contract, the cellmate turned police informant.

On Friday, June 18, 1994, Gaylon Ronald Franklin Jr. stood convicted of first-degree murder in the slaying of Vaughnie Marie Bradley. Tulsa District Judge Jay Dalton sentenced the convicted killer to serve life behind bars with no possibility of parole.

"D-DAY FOR THE CHEERLEADER'S SEX-KILLER"

by John Griggs

The Roanoke River careens wildly out of the mountains of southwest Virginia, snakes across North Carolina's sprawling coastal plain, then empties into the Atlantic Ocean by way of Albemarle Sound. In the spring, striped bass swim out of the sound and upriver, against current, to a point near Roanoke Rapids, North Carolina, where they spawn. Veteran lawman William C. "Bill" Bailey, a lifelong resident of the area, remembers a time in his youth when you could net a pickup truck's worth of striped bass—or rockfish, as the locals call them.

Whelette Collins, who died naked and shivering in the darkness near the river, was a stranger to this world.

As sheriff of Halifax County, Bill Bailey began working the Whelette Collins case with the discovery of her body on December 4, 1980. Bailey had been sheriff for ten years when the case broke. When an end to the case finally seemed possible in January 1995, Bailey had been officially retired for almost a decade. In those first days of 1995, Bailey thought back over one of the biggest cases of his career.

In December 1980, Whelette Collins was a 20-year-old

freshman honors student at North Carolina Wesleyan College, a Methodist school in Rocky Mount, about 40 miles southwest of Roanoke Rapids. A cheerleader for the junior varsity basketball team, Whelette was a promising artist, actress, and designer. Although she didn't have a steady boyfriend, she had already designed her wedding dress.

A city girl from New York, Whelette might have passed her whole college career without ever going anywhere near the river, and her career would probably have carried her far from northeastern North Carolina. But a stranger came out of the shadows, snuffing out Whelette's life in the river bottom and plunging two of her friends into a nightmare that would forever change them.

At about 7:30 on the night of Wednesday, December 3, 1980, Whelette, Teresa Barkely, and Charlotte Weaver had just finished cheering their team on to a home-court victory against Methodist College and were headed to a nearby store for sodas. The three women were still in their cheerleading outfits and were sitting in Teresa's car in the lighted gym parking lot when a small, dark-haired man walked up, knocked on one of the car's windows, and pointed a handgun at them.

The stranger ordered the women to let him in. Afraid for their lives, they complied. The man ordered Teresa to drive to the end of the football field. There, he ordered the women out of their car and into his vehicle. He forced Charlotte and Teresa into his car trunk; Whelette he dragged into his front seat.

The man drove off with his captives, leaving behind the sprawl of Rocky Mount for the fields of tobacco and cotton, bordered by lush woods, in the surrounding countryside.

About 45 minutes after leaving the college, the kidnapper turned the car off the main road and onto a dirt path. The old vehicle lurched through a potholed path that ran into a deep stand of woods. Finally, the stranger stopped the car and cut the engine. He got out, releasing Charlotte and Teresa from the trunk. For a few minutes, as he lurked a few feet away from his car, the kidnapper let Charlotte and Teresa talk to Whelette. In the darkness, the women could barely make out piles of gravel and a pond nearby. They figured they must be in some kind of gravel pit. A large hill loomed in front of them.

The women shivered in their skimpy cheerleader uniforms. The temperature was below freezing. Teresa told Whelette that she had found a lug wrench in the trunk, and that they'd have to attack the stranger. Whelette told Teresa that she didn't think violence would be necessary; the man would let them go. Teresa pressed Whelette, but Whelette felt they could talk their way out of the situation.

The abductor abruptly ended the discussion when he forced Charlotte and Teresa back into the car trunk. Charlotte and Teresa huddled together, terrified. In the cramped, oppressive darkness of the car boot, their thoughts ran wild as to Whelette's fate: They figured the stranger had dragged her off, but they didn't know what he'd do to her. As Charlotte and Teresa worried about their friend, they began to focus on their own survival.

"We've got to think about things," Teresa told Charlotte. "If Whelette doesn't come back, we are not to separate. If we're going to die, we might as well die together and die fighting."

Teresa took bobby pins from her hair and a safety pin from her cheerleader's uniform and straightened them out into what she hoped would be effective weapons. Teresa hid the lug wrench she'd found in the trunk in Charlotte's uniform. Minutes later, the girls heard voices. Charlotte and Teresa could hear Whelette crying and begging her kidnapper for a blanket. They heard the man snicker and say, "I can put you out of your misery." Charlotte and Teresa heard what sounded like someone running. The kidnapper banged on the trunk and said he'd be right back.

"Whelette has run away," Teresa whispered. "She's either going to get away or he's going to kill her."

Several minutes later, the kidnapper returned to the car. He unlocked the trunk and let Teresa and Charlotte out. He told them to choose among themselves who was going to go with him to look for Whelette. When the captives refused to make that choice, the man asked them to yell for Whelette.

"Who do you think you're fooling?" Teresa asked the stranger. "She's either gotten away or you've done something with her."

The abductor forced Teresa and Charlotte into the backseat of his car and began to drive slowly down the path. Charlotte passed the lug wrench to Teresa. When the kidnapper stopped the car, Teresa began hitting him in the back of the head with the wrench.

Teresa and the man got out of the car, continuing to struggle. Teresa kept hitting the man until he pulled his handgun, grabbed the wrench, and threw it into the woods. The abductor then marched Teresa back to his car. As he leaned into the vehicle to say something to Charlotte, Teresa took out one of her pins and stabbed the kidnapper in the neck. The man screamed and fell over on Teresa. She and the stranger wrestled for his gun. Charlotte got out and bit the kidnapper. Teresa kicked him in the stomach. He lost his grip on the gun. Teresa seized it, pointed it at the stranger, and pulled the trigger.

Instead of a gunshot, however, the gun emitted a hollow click. Teresa examined the weapon and realized for the first time that they'd been kidnapped and put through hell by a scrawny man who had been armed with nothing but a starter pistol.

Teresa dropped the gun, and she and Charlotte began running through the brush, not taking the time to see what the stranger was doing. After running a few hundred feet, they came to what they realized was a river. They could hear heavy motor traffic in the distance and figured it was from Interstate 95. They began following the river, working their way to the sound of the traffic. Charlotte and Teresa didn't know it, but the river they were following was the Roanoke, the banks of which were lined with dense briars that cut their bare legs and impeded their progress. But finally, as Thursday's dawn broke, Teresa and Charlotte climbed a steep hill, reached the interstate, and began walking north along the highway.

A passing motorist spotted the shivering cheerleaders, their uniforms torn and their legs scratched and bleeding from the brush. The motorist spotted a state trooper and flagged him down. Minutes later, the trooper found the women still walking beside the interstate.

Charlotte and Teresa were too nervous to talk, but the trooper knew something bad had happened to them. The trooper transported the women to a nearby gas station. From what little he could gather, the trooper figured that whatever happened to the women occurred in Halifax County, where Bill Bailey was sheriff. The trooper radioed the Halifax County Sheriff's Department, headquartered in the county seat of Roanoke Rapids, and relayed what he had.

Sheriff Bailey, attired in his traditional garb of sports coat, tie, and dress pants and driving to work in his unmarked car, heard the radio traffic. Though he headed about 27 deputies, Bailey was a hands-on manager. He picked up his microphone and told the dispatcher that he'd take the call himself.

About 7:30 A.M. on Thursday at the service station, Sheriff Bailey talked to Teresa Barkely and Charlotte Weaver. The women were seated in the trooper's car, still shivering and nearly hysterical. Bailey escorted Teresa to his car. He put his heater on full blast and told Teresa to try to calm down and not say anything until she was ready.

Soon Teresa had collected herself enough to tell Bailey that she and her friend had been kidnapped the previous night and had gotten away, but that a third woman, Whelette Collins, had not escaped.

Bailey knew he had to find the third cheerleader as soon as possible. As the car warmed up, Teresa started to talk. She said she didn't have any idea how to get to the area they'd run from, the area where she believed Whelette still was. She could only say that she believed they'd been at some type of gravel pit.

Sheriff Bailey knew of a couple of gravel pits in the area. He decided to try one that was only a few miles away. He relayed his plans to the state trooper, then, with Teresa in his car and Charlotte with the trooper, the lawmen drove to the spot.

On the way, Bailey elicited from Teresa descriptions of the kidnapper, the car, and Whelette Collins. He broadcast the descriptions over his radio, advising deputies to be on the lookout for all three. Bailey also commanded several deputies to respond to the gravel pit.

The sheriff eased his car off the blacktop and onto a dirt path, heading to the gravel pit near the small Halifax County town of Weldon.

"If you see anything familiar, just let me know," Bailey told Teresa.

The car approached a large man-made hill several hundred feet from a pond.

"There's the mountain we were on last night!" Teresa exclaimed. "We were right there last night!"

Bailey stopped his car and got out. He spotted what appeared to be blood at the hill's base. Teresa had told Bailey that she and Charlotte fought the kidnapper, and the sheriff figured that the struggle had occurred at the foot of the hill. From what Teresa said, that had to be the kidnapper's blood.

Bailey got back into the car and continued down the path. He had gone about two or three hundred yards when he met a car coming from the opposite direction. Teresa studied the car's black-haired driver, who appeared to be alone in the vehicle.

"That's him, that's him!" Teresa yelled.

Sheriff Bailey picked up his mike and said, "I got him up here."

Bailey dropped his mike, parked the car, and jumped out. He pulled his Smith & Wesson .38 and pointed it at the man in the other car, which had stopped about 100 feet away. Bailey heard the driver rev the car's engine. The vehicle started toward him, but the driver stopped after going just 50 feet. Bailey ordered the man out of the car, and the man complied. As he frisked the slightly built suspect and handcuffed him, Bailey noted that the man's hair, pants, and shoes were wet, but his thick, insulated coat was dry.

Minutes later, Bailey's deputies pulled up to the scene, braking their cruisers in the dirt path. As the deputies watched the suspect, Bailey walked over to the small shallow pond that was created when the gravel pit was dug. The water in the pond appeared murky around the edges. Realizing that the pond's water was usually clear around the edges, Bailey suspected that something must have recently disturbed the water. Bailey walked back over to the suspect.

"She's in this gravel pit, isn't she?" Bailey asked the suspect.

"Talk to my lawyer," the suspect replied.

"I will," Bailey said.

A deputy walked up to Bailey.

"Let me have him," the deputy said to Bailey.

"No," Bailey answered.

"I'm not going to hurt him," the deputy said. "I know him."

It turned out that the deputy had once dealt with the suspect when someone complained that he'd been wearing women's clothing in the restroom of an area truck stop. The deputy knew the suspect as 23-year-old Kermit Smith Jr. of Roanoke Rapids.

Bailey allowed the deputy to walk Smith a few feet away for a private talk. Meanwhile, Bailey followed his intuition and radioed for the Roanoke Rapids Rescue Squad, an agency that could help search the pond. Bailey had helped start that agency. Minutes after Bailey radioed his request, the deputy told Bailey that Smith had confirmed that a woman was in the pond.

As the rescue squad workers arrived, Bailey directed them to start in the areas where the water was murkiest. The squad members worked from a boat, dragging the pond with long hooks. The pond was just a few hundred feet away from the Roanoke River.

Sheriff Bailey's breath showed white in the cold air as he barked orders to his men in his cigarette-roughened voice. If other circumstances had brought him to the river, Bailey might well have enjoyed watching the morning mist float off the river and listening to the songs of birds. As it was, Bailey was not a happy man. The natural order of things had been ruined. The most lethal predator, the only one that kills for no reason, had struck. Bailey had a homicide on his hands.

Working in water about 18-feet deep, the rescue squad workers snagged what they believed to be an arm, but it slid loose of the hook and splashed back into the water. The squad members hooked a leg and pulled until the nude body of a woman broke the water's surface. The workers pulled the body to shore. The body's legs were stuffed into the openings of a cinder block, which had weighted down the corpse.

Years before, Sheriff Bailey had pulled double-duty, filling in as coroner in addition to being sheriff. Bailey gave up the coroner's duties, feeling he wasn't qualified to pass judgment in medically complex cases. But he felt comfortable about assuming the cause of death of the body just pulled from the pond: The woman's head felt like a marshmallow; evidently she'd been bludgeoned to death.

Teresa Barkely and Charlotte Weaver identified the victim as Whelette Collins. Deputies transported Teresa and Charlotte back to headquarters in Roanoke Rapids so they could give statements about the incident. In a separate car, officers brought Kermit Smith to headquarters as well. Other deputies, officers with the Roanoke Rapids and Weldon police departments, and State Bureau of Investigation agents remained at the crime scene, gathering evidence. They sent Collins's body to the state medical examiner's office for autopsy.

At headquarters, a calm Kermit Smith confessed to Chief Investigator E.C. Warren of the Halifax County Sheriff's Department that he had kidnapped the women and raped Collins, and that he was responsible for Collins's death. He had weighted down Collins's body by forcing her arms through a cinder block and then thrown it into the pond. Smith said that he had lost his car keys while struggling with Teresa and Charlotte and had walked home. When a relative had returned him to the gravel pit that morning to get his car, Smith found that the body had surfaced. The cinder block had broken loose. It was then, Smith said, that he wedged the legs through a cinder block and let it sink again. That sequence of events explained the suspect's wet hair and shoes. Smith had been leaving the crime scene in his car when he met the sheriff's vehicle.

Smith gave no motive for his actions. Sheriff Bailey felt the suspect was just plain mean.

Detectives charged Smith with the first-degree murder

of Collins and with kidnapping Collins, Barkely, and Weaver. Smith was placed in the Roanoke Rapids jail without benefit of bond.

The investigators interviewed the relative of Smith who drove him to the gravel pit. The relative said that Smith had come home early that morning with a busted head, explaining that he'd been beaten and robbed at the gravel pit and had lost his car keys there. Before driving Smith to the gravel pit with his extra set of car keys, the relative said, she took him to Halifax Memorial Hospital, where doctors sewed up the head wound.

Hospital records confirmed the story. Based on those records and what the two cheerleaders had said, Smith got his wound when Teresa whacked him with the lug wrench.

As Thursday wore on, officers continued to work the crime scene. By the pond, they gathered two cement blocks with blood and hair on them. Investigators believed Smith had crushed the victim's skull between two blocks by placing her head on one block, then slamming the other onto her head.

Lab specialists would later match the blood and hair found on the cinder blocks with samples of Collins's blood and hair. They would also compare the blood found at the bottom of the hill at the crime scene with Smith's blood and determine that the blood belonged to the suspect.

Meanwhile, the sleuths catalogued other important pieces of evidence they found at the crime scene. A deputy found Collins's blue cheerleading skirt hanging on a limb down by the river. Deputies also found the starter pistol that Smith had used to kidnap the women in the grass near the dirt path.

On Friday, pathologists had a preliminary autopsy report: Whelette Collins had in fact been bludgeoned to death. Her skull was broken in several places. She had also sustained a fractured rib and bruising all over her body. There were scrapes on her hands that suggested she had tried to fight off Smith. Pathologists also determined that she had been raped.

Sheriff Bailey figured that Smith meant to rape and kill Charlotte Weaver and Teresa Barkely as well, but their tenacity had saved them. Checking with an old friend, Detective Horace Winstead of the Rocky Mount Police Department, Bailey learned that in recent weeks, there had been several reports of a Peeping Tom in the area around the North Carolina Wesleyan campus. Those reports ended with Smith's arrest, though Smith was never charged in any of those incidents.

In the meantime, Collins's death sent waves of shock and disbelief across the Wesleyan campus. "You wouldn't expect it to happen here," one student told a reporter.

"It's an awful thing, just a senseless thing," a school official said. Officials tightened security on campus. "The general reaction is, it could have been me," the school official said. "I think [students will] be more cautious."

Collins had been a promising student who had taken advantage of as many chances as her killer had blown. A loner, Smith had spent one year at North Carolina State University in Raleigh on a scholarship. For unknown reasons, Smith had dropped out and returned home and was soon doing time for a burglary conviction. The day Collins died, Smith had been out of prison just six weeks.

In April 1981, a Halifax County Superior Court jury convicted Smith of first-degree murder and kidnapping and recommended that he receive the death penalty for the murder conviction. The trial judge affirmed the sentence and tacked on an additional 65 years for the rape and kidnapping convictions. For the next 14 years, lawyers filed the inevitable appeals as Smith sat on death row.

Sheriff Bailey retired in 1986, but from time to time,

he continued to appear at hearings on Smith's fate. Finally, the only real outlet left to Smith's lawyers was a pardon from Governor Jim Hunt. Death penalty opponents the world over rained letters on Governor Hunt, asking him to commute Smith's sentence to life in prison. Hunt held a hearing on the issue. During that hearing, Governor Hunt watched a videotape that Smith's lawyers had prepared.

On the tape, a doctor who examined Smith said that he suffered from sexual disorders, manifested by a long history of compulsive voyeurism, cross-dressing, and sexual sadism. "Although intellectually gifted, it is now clear that Kermit Smith was afflicted at birth with a debilitating psychiatric disorder," the doctor said. "He received no medical or psychiatric intervention, and indeed suffered a series of traumatic life experiences which exacerbated his psychiatric condition. We seek not absolution, but the exercise of mercy and the recognition of human frailty."

Governor Hunt issued his decision in a press release.

"It is outrageous that Whelette's friends and family had to suffer for fourteen years to see justice served," Hunt said in the release. "It is wrong to allow such a case to drag on for so long after conviction, bringing new agony to the victim's friends and family at every turn. It is a wrong that should be righted."

Officials set an execution date of 2:00 A.M. on Tuesday, January 24, 1995, at Central Prison. Smith, faced with the option of the gas chamber or lethal injection, chose lethal injection. In a press conference, Smith joked to reporters that he chose lethal injection because he'd tried to kill himself with carbon monoxide in 1977, and it hadn't worked. But Smith was dead serious when he claimed that he was a victim.

"My death sentence has been unlawfully imposed," Smith contended. "The only thing I'm going to say is what the judge imposed on me: 'Lord have mercy on your souls.' "

Smith claimed that he was looking for work and had stopped to stretch his legs when he ran into his three victims. Smith contended that he asked them directions, and one of the women refused him, using a sarcastic voice.

"That was something that simply pushed me over the edge," Smith said.

As his last meal, Smith chose four pieces of Kentucky Fried Chicken—all white meat—a Pepsi and a Mountain Dew. At 12:00 A.M. on January 24th, Smith requested and was given a drug to calm his nerves. At 1:50 A.M., prison workers wheeled Smith, strapped to a gurney, into the execution chamber. A blue sheet covered him from head to feet. He nodded to several people who were watching the proceedings through the chamber windows.

At 1:57 A.M., Smith looked at a relative of Collins and appeared to mouth something, perhaps, "I'm sorry." At 2:00 A.M., Smith told one of his relatives, "I'm okay. Don't worry about me."

The shot was administered. Smith's eyes began to close. Officials pronounced Smith dead at 2:12 A.M. He was the seventh person executed in North Carolina since the death penalty was reinstated in 1977.

Charlotte Weaver witnessed the execution, as did relatives of Collins and Smith and a few selected reporters. One of Smith's relatives said that Smith was remorseful, although he hadn't shown it. She said that his last words to her were, "I'll see you on the dark side of the moon."

Sheriff Bailey didn't attend the execution, but he followed it from his home.

"I think he got what he deserved," the 72-year-old Bailey said of Smith in a recent interview. "I'm not glad to see anybody get the death penalty or get murdered. But when you kill somebody else for no reason at all. . . ."

The Roanoke River still flows wild out of Virginia and into Carolina, and every year the striped bass repeat their spawning mission. The river continues to flow past the gravel pit where Whelette Collins died on that icy night 14 years ago. Collins is gone, and so is Smith.

APPENDIX

"SEX-CRAZED CABBIE CRUSHED KATHY WITH HIS WHEELS!" *Front Page Detective*, December, 1994

"THEY WHACKED WALTER FOR HIS WHEELS!" *Front Page Detective*, January, 1994

"BEAST OF THE BRONX!" *Inside Detective*, February, 1993

"DERANGED DRIFTER'S BUS STOP BLOODBATH!" *Front Page Detective*, February, 1993

"GUN-TOTING, WHEELCHAIR-BOUND KILLER" *Official Detective*, June, 1995

"PRETTY CABBIE'S ONE-WAY RIDE TO TERROR!" *Inside Detective*, April, 1995

"CROSS-COUNTRY FUGITIVE'S LAST VICTIM WAS A COP!" *Inside Detective*, April, 1995

"BEAUTY QUEEN WAS KILLED FOR HER RED CADDY" *True Detective*, December, 1992

"SLOW DEATH WITH A 4000-POUND WEAPON!" *True Detective*, December, 1992

"2 MOMS HITCHHIKED TO RAPE-MURDER!" *True Detective*, August, 1994

"MIAMI PERVERT BUTCHERED, THEN DEFILED A WOMAN AND A MAN!" *True Detective*, March, 1995

"VICIOUS CAREER CRIMINAL ESCAPED TO CARJACK & KILL!" *True Detective*, April, 1995

"ARIZONA'S REST STOP KILLERS SNUFFED THE IVY LEAGUE LOVERS" *Master Detective*, February, 1994

"STRIPPED AND STRANGLED IN A LIMO!" *Inside Detective*, November, 1994

"HOMICIDAL TRUCKER!" *Inside Detective*, April, 1994

"HITCHHIKING TEEN HOOKER'S HORROR ORDEAL!" *Front Page Detective*, February, 1993

"WHY DID THE BUDDIES BEHEAD THEIR RED-HEADED FRIEND?" *Master Detective*, November, 1993

"HANGING IN A CLOSET!" *Official Detective*, April, 1994

"TRIO BLAZED A 3-STATE TRAIL OF BLOOD!" *Master Detective*, April, 1993

"SADISTIC HANDYMAN DEFILED & STRANGLED THE PRETTY HOUSEWIFE!" *Official Detective*, August, 1993

"THE DESPERATE TEEN CROSS-DRESSED TO KILL!"
Inside Detective, May, 1994

"THEY BASHED KEN'S SKULL WITH A TIRE IRON!"
Inside Detective, February, 1995

"ONE OF US HAS TO DIE!" *Front Page Detective,* August,
1994

"DESPERATE MANHUNT FOR THE KILL-CRAZY
TEEN!" *Official Detective,* April, 1993

"THE LOVE THEM & LEAVE THEM KILLER" *Official
Detective,* January, 1995

"D-DAY FOR THE CHEERLEADER'S SEX-KILLER" *Official Detective,* August, 1995

TRUE CRIME AT ITS BEST
FROM PINNACLE BOOKS